MODERN AMERICA
POPULAR RELIGIO

MODERN AMERICAN POPULAR RELIGION

A Critical Assessment and
Annotated Bibliography

CHARLES H. LIPPY

Bibliographies and Indexes in Religious Studies,
Number 37
G. E. Gorman, Advisory Editor

GREENWOOD PRESS
Westport, Connecticut • London

Library of Congress Cataloging-in-Publication Data

Lippy, Charles H.
    Modern American popular religion : a critical assessment and
annotated bibliography / Charles H. Lippy.
       p. cm.—(Bibliographies and indexes in religious studies,
ISSN 0742-6836 ; no. 37)
    Includes bibliographical references and index.
    ISBN 0-313-27786-9 (alk. paper)
    1. United States—Religion—1960- —Abstracts. 2. United States—
Religious life and customs—Abstracts. 3. United States—
Religion—1960- —Indexes. 4. United States—Religious life and
customs—Indexes. I. Title. II. Series.
BL2525.L566 1996
200'.973—dc20   95-46009

British Library Cataloguing in Publication Data is available.

Library of Congress Catalog Card Number: 95-46009
ISBN: 0-313-27786-9
ISSN: 0742-6836

First published in 1996

Greenwood Press, 88 Post Road West, Westport, CT 06881
An imprint of Greenwood Publishing Group, Inc.

Printed in the United States of America

The paper used in this book complies with the
Permanent Paper Standard issued by the National
Information Standards Organization (Z39.48–1984).

10 9 8 7 6 5 4 3 2 1

Contents

Contents

Series Foreword

...It was in 1966 that John Lennon commented that the Beatles were "more popular than Jesus."...The juxtaposition of the central figure of the Christian faith with those of the popular musicians aroused the nation and focused attention on their interrelationship between religion and the popular arts. Rock musicals with biblical themes such as Godspell and Jesus Christ Superstar, led some to suggest their compatibility, while others saw popular music, literature and movies as the mythic expression of an alternative belief system described as everything form secular to satanic.

- Jeffrey Mahan in *Explor* (Fall 1984)

Popular religion is a manifestation of popular culture, conferring the coherence of an overall vision on the whole gamut of social practices. It is also a cultural system of communication, using symbolic practices and interpretation. Just as every spoken language develops historically, imposing changing speech patterns (popular) on grammatical conventions (official), so too the religion experienced by the people is modelled by a creative force originating in the orchestration of their conditions and contradictions with their historical consciousness forged in their struggle for life.

- Paulo Suess in *Concilium* (1986)

These statements by Jeffrey Mahan and Paulo Suess exemplify what in recent years seem to have been the two main themes in the study of understanding of popular religion. On the one hand we have popular religion viewed as a function of mass culture, a culture in which Tim Rice and Andrew Lloyd Weber (now clearly a part of the Establishment as Sir Andrew) can use the key biblical theme as a vehicle for a series of popular entertainments. On the other hand we have a religion "of the people," an idea most clearly articulated by Peter Williams: "...the religion that is 'of the people' lies outside organized eccelsiastical structures; it is the religion of nonspecialists contrasted with that of an elite."[1]

The tendency in our largely ahistorical era in which popular culture internationally is dominated by American mass culture pumped ruthlessly through the media is to view both constructs of popular religion as uniquely modern and particularly America. The reality, of course, is hardly further from the truth.   For example, Richard Pervo convincingly argues that the New Testament writings were shaped by popular story forms of the time, concluding that "there is heroism, virtue, villainy, sex, violence, tension and suspense, feminist inspiration, and noble sentiment. Such hagiography was the soap of Christians for more than a millennium."[2]   What Pervo perhaps unfortunately terms "hagiography" was manifest not only in the biblical record but also in Christian belief and practice from the beginning. Thus the cult of saints, the Rosary and Novenas contributed significantly to devotion in the Early Church, in the Middle Ages and down to our own time in many countries. True, "in the wake of Vatican II...there has been a fundamental shift in Catholic life, at least in Western Europe and North America. There has been a marked disaffection, among educated Catholics, from forms of piety that once dominated Catholic life."[3]

One consequence of this repudiation of traditional forms of devotion by what Kieckhefer terms "the more self-consciously sophisticated elements in the Church" has been the redefining of such devotion as distinctly "popular," that is, "...one can now speak of a specifically popular form of Catholicism in distinction from the more theologically inclined version that has repudiated the

---

[1] See Peter W. Williams, *Popular Religion in America: Symbolic Change and the Modernization Process in Historical Perspective* (Englewood Cliffs, NJ: Prentice-Hall, 1980); Catherine L. Albanese, "The Study of Popular Religion: Retrospect and Prospect," *Explor* 7 (1984): 9.

[2] Richard I. Pervo, "Entertainment and Early Christian Literature," *Explor* 7 (1984): 32.

[3] Richard Kieckhefer, "The Cult of Saints as Popular Religion," *Explor* 7 (1984): 41.

devotional forms."[4] And wherever one goes, from Hanoi to Andalusia, from Liverpool to Melbourne, one finds popular religion practised in one form or another -- for me, nowhere more movingly than in a darkened St Francis Xavier Cathedral in Hanoi, hearing the Rosary sung in Vietnamese by a congregation of hundreds and afterwards meeting an aged French-trained Vietnamese priest who explained the enduring value of the Rosary as incorporating both traditional cultural values of the Vietnamese people and popular Buddhist concepts.

Whether we view popular religion as a function of mass culture or as a religion "of the people," or indeed as a hybrid of these two poles, the consequences remain powerfully influential in all cultures. First, it incorporates a reaction against socio- and politico-religious elitism -- an idea most fully grasped by Latin American churchmen, who see popular religion as specifically the religious expression of the poor and the disenfranchised that allows them to develop an alternative means of socio-political mobilization.[5] Here a strong focus is on the destruction of elites wherever they may exist -- whether in society, politics, or religion -- but always with somewhat "revolutionary" overtones born of the Marxist paradigm which many modern developing country theologians and churchmen find so helpful. Second, it expresses a pastoral concern that the Church always be faithful to its inclusive origins by appealing to all people and not just to what Maldonado characterizes as the aesthetically-inclined, bourgeois middle classes.[6] Popular religion is where the majority of the population in most countries is to be found, and it is also a "...colossal example of a by no means negative syncretism between the Gospel and peoples' own cultures, their own creations, heritages...."[7]

It is this "anti-negative" theme that Charles Lippy takes up in *Being Religious, American Style*, and which he repeats in the opening chapter of the present work. That is, many scholars have first defined religion in terms of institutional beliefs and practices moderated by religious professionals, and confined popular religion as what remains after the institutions and the professional have taken their share. In Lippy's words, "often scholars have seen this conglomeration of "left overs" as somehow less authentic than the religion of the organized traditions and therefore as something that need not be taken as seriously" (p. 5). Quite clearly Professor Lippy is not of this ilk, but rather in

---

[4] *Ibid.*, 42.

[5] Paulo Suess, "The Creative and Normative Role of Popular Religion in the Church," *Concilium* 186 (1986): 124.

[6] Luis Maldonado, "Popular Religion: Its Dimensions, Levels and Types," *Concilium* 186 (1986): 3.

[7] *Ibid.*, p. 4.

the tradition of such scholars as Robert Bellah and Peter Williams, who see positive symbiosis in the relationship between popular religion (or popular religiosity, to use Lippy's preferred term) and popular culture, and between popular and institutional religion.

Today it is beyond question that popular religion is, and always has been, a significant force in human history, whether one considers this in strictly religious terms or extends it to the social and political as well. In recent years it may have been our African and Latin American co-religionists who have awakened us to this reality, but it is in the US that the reality has been studied most thoroughly, arguably because American popular religion or popular religiosity (as distinct from popular religion in other countries) has been most clearly visible through the pervasiveness of the American media. And of course the media have an impact on all of us -- whether we live in the Australian outback, the Canadian Northwest or the Outer Hebrides, we know perhaps more than we care to admit about popular religious movements in the US.

This worldwide awareness of American popular religion is matched by an almost exponentially growing body of literature on the subject. One of the great difficulties for students and scholars alike is that this literature lies embedded within numerous academic disciplines; thus one finds popular religion studied and commented upon by historians and sociologists, psychologists and political scientists, theologians and scholars of religion. To help give shape to this ever-expanding and spreading corpus of documentation we have been fortunate in securing the agreement of Professor Charles Lippy of the Department of Philosophy and Religion at the University of Tennessee, and an oft-published Greenwood author, to prepare a volume devoted to the bibliography of American popular religion. With this compilation Charles Lippy confirms his place as a leading scholar of popular religion in America. In the introductory essay he places the subsequent bibliography in context and summarizes key concepts and practices. This goes beyond introducing readers to the volume, serving also as a basic overview of the topic for students new to the field. In the classified bibliography of nearly 600 entries Dr Lippy thoroughly covers the key literature on the several facets of popular religion in the US; while many readers (myself included) will bemoan the fact that only seminal or essential works have been included, this is in fact the volume's strength. That is, one will turn to this compilation as a starting point, and to find what a respected scholar thinks is "the best" (my words, not his) literature on the topic. In his careful annotations the author clearly draws out the essence of the cited works, placing them in perspective and comparative context.

The overall result is a work that satisfies the needs of both scholars and students of popular religion in America. Consequently, *Modern American Popular Religion: A Critical Assessment and Annotated Bibliography* is a welcome addition to Bibliographies and Indexes in Religious Studies, and one which we hope might inspire other scholars to offer related projects on popular religion in other countries, or on specific components of popular religion. To this end, we would be pleased to consider proposals for works related to Professor Lippy's impressive bibliographic survey. As Catherine Albanese reminds us. "it is worth remembering that our place as scholars is only one place to stand -- even as scholars -- and that our norms, like those of the people we study, are culture-bound. We do well, therefore, to identify the continuities between the people we study and ourselves. If we do this, we will find ways to counter the myth of triviality and to introduce a depth dimension to our work.[8]

The Revd. Dr G. E. Gorman
Advisory Editor
Charles Sturt University - Riverina
August 1995

---

[8] Albanese, *op. cit.*, p. 14.

Preface

Over the last two or three decades, scholars of American religion have become ever more attuned to the ways in which the religiosity of ordinary people is by no means restricted to formal religious institutions and their doctrines and practices. Rather, the religiosity or spirituality is much more amorphous and expressed in diverse ways. Association with an organized religion or even acceptance of specific beliefs coming from a particular religious tradition may be only a part of the religion of the people themselves.

As I discuss in the introduction, many scholars have identified this increasing individualization or privatization of religion as a concomitant of the greater complexity that has come to industrial, urban societies over the last century or so. Hence it is appropriate to look at the interpretive work that has enriched our understanding of modern American popular religion.

The titles annotated in this bibliography include articles, essays, books, theses, and dissertations that cover a wide range of individual topics. The citation format allows users to locate each title readily, for it includes all the standard bibliographical information.

Of particular value to those wishing to pursue further inquiry are the three indexes. The first identifies the authors of every title annotated. Since many individuals have written on different facets of modern American popular religion, this index enables one to identify all the titles included by a particular author. The second index lists every title annotated by title.

Perhaps most important is the third index that offers a listing by subject. Many works touch on more than one aspect of modern American popular religion, but each is annotated under only one classification. Hence the subject index serves as a cross-reference tool in two different ways. First it brings together all entries that treat a specific aspect of a larger subject. Second, it enables the user to find entries annotated in one chapter that also deal with subject matter grouped in another chapter.

When I agreed to undertake preparing this bibliography and critical assessment, I was engaged in two other projects for Greenwood Press. One was a monograph, *Being Religious, American Style: A History of Popular Religiosity in the United States*, that appeared in 1994. The other, edited with P. Mark Fackler, was published in 1995 as *Popular Religious Magazines of the United States*. Work on both of those meant repeated delays in completing this bibliography.

For their patience as delays occurred as well as for their encouragement and helpful suggestions, I am grateful to the editor of this series, Gary Gorman, and also first to Marilyn Brownstein and then especially to Alicia Merritt at Greenwood Press. Many librarians at the University of Tennessee at Chattanooga, Emory University, and Clemson University offered gracious assistance as I was trying to track down citations.

What has been overwhelming is the extent of work that has been done on modern American popular religion, although many writers do not use that designation to describe what they are analyzing. As I conclude the preparation of this volume, I am keenly aware that I have references to more than twice as many titles as I have been able to include. The sheer amount of literature that deals with some dimension of modern American popular religion reinforces my conviction that however amorphous popular religion may be and however difficult it may be to define precisely what popular religion really is, this elusive phenomenon is truly the core of religiosity in America today.

C.H.L.

MODERN AMERICAN
POPULAR RELIGION

1

The Literature of Modern American Popular Religion

The designation "modern American popular religion" immediately presents two problems: (1) determining what constitutes modern America, and (2) defining popular religion. Both are subject to lively debate among scholars.

For purposes of this bibliography, I shall limit my understanding of "America" to the United States. This restriction is, of course, increasingly difficult. Many of the movements that have shaped religious life in the United States have by no means been restricted to this nation alone. Fundamentalism, for example, has had as profound an impact on Canadian religious developments in some areas as it has had in the United States. As well, the increasing use of radio and then television by religious figures in the twentieth century meant that geographical and national boundaries could be ignored altogether.

In the later nineteenth century during the last major wave of immigration, those coming especially from southern, central, and eastern Europe brought with them dimensions of a popular religiosity rooted in the cultural styles of their places of origin. Even when adapted to the American social climate, many of these practices retained a distinctive "old world" flavor that stretches the definition of what is American. In recent decades, Catholic religiosity in many communities and regions of the United States reflects the growing impact of a range of Hispanic influences, thanks to the presence of ever greater numbers of persons of Mexican, Cuban, and Puerto Rican heritage.

One should not forget as well immigrants from Asia who made their way to the western areas of the United States in the later nineteenth century, transplanting the religious styles indigenous to their homelands and amalgamating them with what was found in the new land. In the last third of the twentieth century, immigration from Asia has become a more prominent feature of the social landscape of the United States.

Fixing chronological limits also raises many issues. Religious currents rarely fit neatly into the decades or centuries that would make for easy categorization. Restricting "modern" simply to the twentieth century would require omission of many social and religious dynamics whose consequences remain vital to understanding popular religion today, but whose roots are clearly in the closing decades of the nineteenth century. The rapid industrialization that came to the United States in the decades between the close of the Civil War and the outbreak of the First World War brought far-reaching changes to the American economy that endured for a century or more.

Concomitant with industrialization came the growth of the nation's cities, as thousands left familiar farmland and villages in hopes of economic gain that might come through working in a factory in a city. Immigrants, too, swelled the population of the nation's urban centers, where they were often willing to work for long hours at low wages in order to secure a niche for themselves and their families in this strange land. In time, prevailing religious currents took new forms as, for example, in the revivalism of Dwight L. Moody and his peers and successors that sought to bring to the people directly the evangelical Protestant gospel.

In varying ways, urbanization and industrialization joined with other less readily definable impulses of the nineteenth century to yield what has long been called the Victorian Age. City and factory helped etch into popular consciousness the sense that there were appropriate spheres of influence for women and for men. The home became ever more the domain of women, while the factory and business became the realm of men (and the "working girl" for whom employment might be a temporary arrangement prior to marriage). Although religious nurture had long been an arena thought particularly appropriate for women, it became a more vital part of the cultural role given to women in the Victorian era as the home more than supplemented the religious institutions as the locus of vital piety and religion. The domestication of religion and the assumptions about religiosity and gender that marked the Victorian Age still form an important substratum of American religious life at the close of the twentieth century.

Hence, for this book "modern" will encompass the period from around 1870 to the present, for virtually all of the trends and currents discussed above that still remain important to understanding the contours of contemporary American life have come to the fore in that span of approximately 130 years. Many, of course, stretch back farther in the American experience, and many did not become significant until well into the twentieth century. But fixing the scope of this book to "from 1870 to the present" will allow a reasonable range and exclude relatively little.

Determining what constitutes "popular religion" presents a greater challenge, for there is no consensus among scholars when it comes to defining that term.   In the first chapter of *Being Religious, American Style* (008), I surveyed much of the theoretical and definitional literature dealing with popular religion.   To a large extent, scholars have tended to arrive at an understanding of popular religion in a negative fashion.   That is, they have presumed that religion should be understood and delineated by religious institutions and professionals.   When the beliefs, practices, and other apparatus fixed by the institutions and professionals are taken into account, it is clear that not all that could be classified as religion or religious has been included.   There remains a dimension that belongs to ordinary people themselves, apart from whatever formal doctrines and practices might be described.   Often scholars have seen this conglomeration of "left overs" as somehow less authentic than the religion of the organized traditions and therefore as something that need not be taken as seriously.

Hence some have called these religious expressions "folk religion" and often linked them to superstition, magic, and other dimensions of human life that defy easy rational analysis.   The implication is that what is "folk" is somehow less worthy than what is not, perhaps the vestiges of an earlier epoch in the evolution of religion that managed to escape the refinement of Enlightenment rationalism.   One example of this approach is the work of Gustav Mensching (011).   Less condescending are those who link folk or popular religion to the common values that emerge within a culture.   Some may be based on the formal beliefs and practices of established religious traditions; others may come from the folkways of the people.   But this mix is fundamental to all cultures, though the specific content will vary.   Here, the work of Wilbur Bock is illustrative (002).   It is a small step from this understanding of popular religion to the idea of civil religion, or some sort of interplay between dimensions of religion and nationalism, that has received much scholarly attention in the last three decades.   Indeed, one might construe certain manifestations of civil religion as popular religion.

Economic nuances have also often been connected with the idea of popular religion as folk religion.   Much of the stimulus for pursuing the study of popular religion has come particularly from anthropologists studying non-Western cultures where disparities between the formal religious traditions and the religious life of ordinary people have long been apparent.   The economic elite develops a vested interest in the institutions of religion, while those who are on the margins of economic and political power gain a positive social identity through nurturing a folk religion as an alternative.   Such is the perspective of Vittorio Lanternari (007).   Here, however, popular religion and official religion may not be polar opposites, but variants drawing on a single, larger tradition.

Connecting popular religion with folk religion has taken other anthropologists in a different direction.   Another common approach has been to see popular religion as reflecting the residue of beliefs and practices that go back to more simple, preliterate cultures that have managed to endure among ordinary people as society became more complex. There is still an economic nuance to this approach, for the stratum of society where this residue is more pronounced is generally thought to be the peasantry or the lower economic clusters within a more complex culture. Robert Redfield's classic distinction between the "great tradition" and the "little tradition" in peasant societies is an obvious example (012).

Yet others have despaired of finding a viable definition of popular religion because it seems so inchoate and therefore somewhat elusive. Robert Towler, for example, rejects the designation of popular religion and prefers to speak of "common religion" to identify whatever religious beliefs and practices prevail within a society that are not under the control of religious institutions (019). One advantage of Towler's understanding is its casting a wider net than other approaches. It emphasizes what Towler (p. 148) has called "a base-line of religiousness" that is not tied to coherent belief systems and therefore looks as much to expressions of popular religiosity as to organized movements and structured practices that exist alongside those of religious institutions.

In the American context, few have emphasized more than Peter Williams the symbiotic relationship of popular religion and institutional religion (021). For Williams (p. 228), popular religion is most obviously seen in movements that exist "outside the formal structures provided by most societies" for symbolic activity. Such movements tend to emphasize the ways the Divine intervenes or otherwise makes itself known in the routines of daily life and to transmit their beliefs, ritual practices, and the like from person to person and generation to generation without relying on the institutions established by formal religious traditions. Williams also asserts that popular religious movements are more likely to assert their influence during times of social change when long-held values and ways of making sense out of life no longer seem to work. What is most helpful about Williams's approach is the way it forces us to look at larger social currents for some of the stimulus for popular religion and the way it reinforces the practical side of popular religion. However one ultimately defines popular religion, it must enable ordinary men and women to endow their personal experience with meaning.

One of the earliest efforts to look at popular religion in American culture moved in a parallel, but different direction. In the late 1950s, Louis Schneider and Sanford Dornbusch examined one body of popular religious materials, namely books that were designed to inspire the masses. They concluded that one primary feature of popular religion was its emphasis on sentiment or feeling (014). Inspirational literature had as its intended result providing ordinary men and women with techniques that gave them a way to confront the problems of daily life and thereby achieve a modicum of personal happiness. Although there may well be more to popular religion than sentiment, Schneider and Dornbusch made a valuable contribution in again highlighting this practical dimension.

Among sociologists, who have generated a considerable body of literature on popular religion in recent years, the increasing privatization of religion looms as a major concern. As industrialization and urbanization brought greater complexity to social organization, meaning systems became ever more diffuse. No longer did religious institutions alone offer ways of endowing life with meaning. The vast array of value structures and meaning systems created something of a supermarket atmosphere in which persons could pick and choose from among them to create private, idiosyncratic ways of looking at life, but ones that made sense to them as individuals. Thomas Luckmann is well-known for calling this style of popular religion an "invisible religion" because it cannot be easily located or confined to any one organized system of belief (009).

Sociologists who have focused on the apparent weakening of traditional commitment to religious institutions, often overwhelmed by the presumed decline in membership and participation in the oldline Protestant denominations, have also argued that the real pulse of religion is to be found in the personal sphere of private life or in what Robert Wuthnow has called a "religious populism" (022) where individuals fashion personal belief systems that draw not only on the doctrines and creeds of established religions, but on a variety of alternative ways of being religious. Perhaps the epitome of this privatization of religion is the informant sketched by Robert Bellah and his associates whose religion was so personal and so private that she could label it only by her own name and therefore called her religion "Sheilaism."[1] What lurks behind all of these approaches is an appreciation of the multi-faceted nature of the pluralism that characterizes the religious life of the United States.

Studies of the religion(s) of the baby boomer generation have continued this appreciation of the privatization of religion and the eclectic character of the religiosity that results. One study of Presbyterian confirmands of the early baby boom years (091) found that by middle age roughly half were either active Presbyterians or uninvolved in organized religion, but personally religious. What is remarkable is that both groups shared common characteristics in terms of having little interest in formal systems of theology, a strong sense of individualism in matters of belief, and a propensity to construct personal beliefs by drawing on a range of religious options. A concern for spirituality over organized religion, for the sacrality of privately constructed religious world views over dogma and doctrine, was also a recurring theme in Wade Clark Roof's broader analysis of the religious journeys of baby boomers (109).

But if popular religion belongs to the private sphere, it may well be so inchoate and unorganized as to defy simple definition. In *Being Religious,*

---

[1] Robert Bellah, Richard Madsen, William M. Sullivan, Ann Swidler, and Steven M. Tipton, *Habits of the Heart: Individualism and Commitment in American Life* (New York: Harper and Row, 1985), p. 221.

American Style, I argued that it may be more fruitful to speak of popular religiosity rather than popular religion, particularly if the word religion conjures up notions of traditions, institutions, and organized belief systems. Religiosity captures the personal element, but avoids the saccharine sentimentality often associated with piety. Religiosity allows for the syncretistic character that others see as a hallmark of popular religion and also appreciates the symbiotic relationship many expressions of popular religiosity have with formal religious traditions. They may inform what individuals actually believe, but personal belief is rarely confined to fixed creeds and doctrines.

Most of the sociological studies that emphasize the privatization of religion claim that this relegation of "real" religion to the arena of private life is a recent phenomenon. If so, then popular religion must also be a relatively recent phenomenon. Neither is necessarily the case. Students of the western religious traditions outside the United States have devoted more and more attention to strands of popular religion and the kind of idiosyncratic world views that mark privatization which have flourished since the inception of Christianity two thousand years ago.[2] David Hall and Jon Butler have taken rather different approaches to uncovering the pervasiveness of strands of popular religion in North America during the colonial period.[3] As well, the burden of my *Being Religious, American Style* was to demonstrate how popular religiosity has been a constant feature of the American religious landscape when one becomes sensitive to the manifold ways ordinary men and women have sought to make sense out of their lives through an abiding belief in the presence of supernatural power.

What may be the case is that scholars have simply become more aware of the presence of popular religion, however one chooses to define the term, and that increasing awareness may have indeed been propelled by the media explosion of the twentieth century. Radio and television especially have made popular culture a national culture of sorts by bringing into the home, the heart of the private sphere, a plethora of values, ways of thinking about the world, and opportunities to appreciate alternative ways of understanding human experience. As many of the titles in the bibliography that follows will demonstrate, for numerous commentators what makes up popular religion is what is found on radio and television. So numerous are the television preachers who seek a following (and financial support) by proclaiming their own message

---

[2] One example is James Obelkevich, ed., *Religion and the People, 800-1700* (Chapel Hill: University of North Carolina Press, 1979).

[3] See David D. Hall, *Worlds of Wonder, Days of Judgment: Popular Religious Belief in Early New England* (New York: Knopf, 1989); and Jon Butler, *Awash in a Sea of Faith: Christianizing the American People* (Cambridge, Mass.: Harvard University Press, 1990).

without overt institutional ties and obvious commitment to a particular denominational tradition and without an identifiable doctrinal heritage that the phenomenon has earned its own designation: televangelism.

But the casual browser in any large book store will quickly notice other manifestations of a popular religiosity that has benefitted from the explosion of print materials in recent years. Often adjacent to or at least near those shelves that house books on religion are those that carry titles dealing with self-help and inspiration. So vast a literature has been generated in this genre that there are now bibliographies, noted below, that deal exclusively with them. But the very idea of self-help comes to the heart of popular religiosity as an individual phenomenon. One can improve one's own status in this life, one can give new meaning to one's existence, in an individual way, though usually through some personally fashioned reliance on a "higher power."

Many titles on these shelves bear the influence of a resurgent evangelical style in American Protestant circles. Once consigned to the fringes of religious life and seen as anachronistic by the intellectual elite, evangelicalism is a dominant feature of contemporary American religion. Its presence seems pervasive. Historians have become increasingly aware that the evangelical spirit, with its emphasis on a profound, often dramatic personal religious experience of God, never vanished, but continued to represent one constellation of beliefs and practices to which Americans turned for sources of meaning and power in life. One thinks especially of the work of Joel Carpenter in this context (138-140). The emergence of evangelically oriented contemporary Christian music, the publication of numerous magazines of a non-denominational nature that trumpet the evangelical world view, and the increased willingness to use the gains of technology to promote evangelicalism led Erling Jorstad astutely to conclude that the evangelical voice constituted the core of American popular religion in the late twentieth century (165).

Religious currents other than evangelicalism are also part of the contemporary picture. For nearly four decades; Americans have shown a growing interest in forms of Asian spirituality, more often by combining selected Asian views and practices with others to create an eclectic religiosity than by becoming formal devotees of a particular Asian religion. One thinks immediately of Transcendental Meditation, the International Society for Krishna Consciousness (Hare Krishna), the Unification Church (Moonies), and a host of other groups and movements whose influence has been more indirect than in gaining large numbers of converts and practitioners. The feminist movement has sparked fresh interest in exploring spiritual expression and a religious consciousness that emerges from the unique experience of being female. These efforts have also often moved in an eclectic direction. One result has been greater cultural appreciation of a variety of religious phenomena, ranging from wicca to goddess worship. As well, the renewed sensitivity to ethnicity that was one by-product of the civil rights movement of mid-century has brought more into public view the popular religiosity rooted in ethnic traditions rather than in formal religious institutions. Those still fascinated by connections between popular religion and folk religion rooted in forms of magic call attention to the ongoing intrigue with astrology, the pursuit of holistic and herbal-based medicine, and the like, to find evidence that this stratum of popular religiosity remains alive and well.

What then is popular religion or popular religiosity? There has been an effort to include representative titles in the listing that follows that will take into account all of the various understandings and approaches discussed above. There is, however, a conscious intention to avoid restricting coverage to organized groups and formal movements on the assumption that once beliefs and practices take on that degree of structure they cease to be individually based or popular. Hence the orientation is more to dimensions of popular religiosity than to formal religion in any of its manifold manifestations.

Determining what titles to include in a bibliography such as this is always highly selective and therefore instantly open to criticism. Another bibliographer would have made other choices. Not every work that touches on popular religiosity could be included. Given the number of titles of inspirational books currently in print, it would have been possible to devote the entire book just to them. I have chosen to focus primarily, but not exclusively, on secondary works that develop an interpretation of dimensions of popular religiosity rather than to discuss those that are themselves intended to nurture the personal spirituality of ordinary folk. Where I have included titles in the latter category, I have done so primarily because they have addressed topics that were formerly neglected.

The titles annotated fall into ten categories. I shall begin in chapter two with studies of a theoretical and contextual nature as well as reference works that deal with dimensions of popular religion. Here particularly books and articles that address the problem of how to define popular religion and the connections, for example, between popular religion and what some scholars have called folk religion will be noted. In this chapter, I also treat titles that provide some historical context for examining modern American popular religion. When Martin Marty completes his multivolume survey of modern American religion, that series will undoubtedly provide the most complete historical context. To date, however, just two volumes have appeared (043, 044). In addition, I include listings for several reference works, not all of which relate exclusively to popular religion or aspects of popular religiosity. Those that do not, such as the *Dictionary of Pentecostal and Charismatic Movements* (053), contain entries on particular topics that are indeed pertinent to the study of popular religion.

In the third chapter are listed those works that provide overviews of popular religion in the United States or that treat broad themes, usually in a historical vein. One such theme revolves around the idea of civil religion. Many of those who connect civil religion with popular religion do so because they assume that the constellation of symbols and values emerging from the political realm provide a common or popular identity for all the nation's inhabitants. Such an approach clearly underlies Robert Bellah's classical exposition in "Civil Religion in America" (067). Others have been more cautious, suggesting that there may be religious dimensions to public life, but intertwined in a much more complex fashion (for example, the work of John F. Wilson [123]), or variants that take account of distinctive regional cultures (as in the work of Charles Reagan Wilson concerning Southern civil religion [121, 122]).

Given the more strident evangelical presence in American society over the last few decades and the concomitant resurgent fundamentalism, many analysts have been quick to attach the label of popular religion to this matrix of beliefs and practices. Because statistics suggest that evangelical and fundamentalist religious groups are growing numerically as oldline groups decline in membership or struggle to hold their own, the perception prevails that the evangelical-fundamentalist cluster must be the core of popular religion. I have already called attention to the work of Joel Carpenter in setting out the historical framework for the present evangelical renascence. Also especially insightful are the writings of Nancy Ammerman on the internal dynamics of fundamentalism (129) and of James Davison Hunter (159, 160) on the paradoxes that prevail within evangelical circles. Parallel with the presumed popularity of the evangelical style has been the surge of political involvement that has led to a vital alliance between religious and political conservatives. Studies that look at the so-called religious-political Right are also included in chapter four.

Much of the public awareness of evangelicalism has resulted from the use of popular media, particularly radio and television, to carry this particular version of religiosity directly to the people. Indeed, several writers regard televangelism as the heart of American popular religion because of this connection. Although sociologists have led the way in looking at connections between the media and popular religiosity, others have also sought to interpret its power. Studies looking at the religious use of radio and television from many different perspectives are annotated in chapter five.

Other vehicles for reaching ordinary men and women with religious signals that help shape personal religiosity and world views come from the arts--popular music, mass circulation periodicals, television and film, cartoons, best sellers, and a range of other forms of expression. Chapter six probes this diverse field. It includes listings for works that examine the evangelical appropriation of popular music forms to create the genre of contemporary Christian music (239, 240, 259) as well as those that identify religious themes and motifs in best-selling fiction (260, 275, 302, 328). Popular religious periodicals such as *Commonweal* (244, 327), *Christian Century* (253), and *Christianity Today* (280) are included, along with studies of popular religious art.

Religiously oriented self-help programs, especially those emerging from the twelve-step approach developed by Alcoholics Anonymous, remain central to many strands of popular religiosity in modern America. Although there are already a spate of bibliographies identifying both primary and secondary materials classified as self-help, several more recent studies are annotated in chapter seven. As well, there is a growing body of literature that challenges the effectiveness of self-help approaches and is particularly wary of the religious dimensions of twelve-step programs. Such critical works are also evaluated in this chapter.

Another angle through which to explore modern American popular religion comes through the lives of individuals who have become celebrities or whose charismatic personalities have given them a large popular following. One thinks immediately of contemporary figures such as Billy Graham, Pat Robertson, Jerry Falwell, and the like. But there are many others, such as Charles E. Fuller, one of the first evangelicals to make heavy use of radio when it first became a popular medium, or the controversial Catholic priest Charles E. Coughlin, who fused religious and political commentary in his radio broadcasts during the era of the New Deal. For many such persons, balanced biographies have yet to be written. Many are hagiographic in tone; others are wildly negative. Among the best are those written by David E. Harrell, Jr., about Oral Roberts (391) and Pat Robertson (392). A sampling of biographical studies--balanced, hagiographic, and negative--forms the focus of chapter eight.

In constructing personal world views, many individuals look within themselves or turn to unconventional or alternative approaches to the supernatural, some but not all of which are identified with established religious traditions and long-practiced devotional exercises. Studies that treat these approaches are annotated in chapter nine. The range of materials here is extraordinary, including titles that deal with magic, witchcraft, and goddess worship, to those that look at Christian devotional materials designed to be used by individuals however they see it.

The ethnic dimension of popular religion provides the theme bringing together a diverse number of studies in the tenth chapter, extending from religious currents among Native Americans (such as the Ghost Dance and peyotism) and African Americans (such as the introduction of the holiday of Kwanzaa) to the expressions of popular religiosity among American Roman Catholics and Jews that have a base in ethnic identity and the immigrant experience. Several of the studies included in this chapter are models for scrutinizing the contours of popular religiosity. One thinks, for example, of Robert Orsi's brilliant appraisal of the *festa* of the Madonna of Mount Carmel central to Italian-American immigrant religiosity in what was once New York City's Italian Harlem (506).

The final chapter includes a smattering of titles that are relevant to understanding popular religion in modern America that simply did not fit into any of the other categories. Several look at the way sport in American culture has taken on a religious dimension; others treat topics as wide-ranging as clowns and religious theme-parks. All, however, are suggestive of diverse phenomena that illuminate ways countless individuals may construct their own personal religious world views and belief systems. All are therefore integral to an understanding of modern American popular religion.

Although more than 550 studies are annotated here, they but scratch the surface of secondary materials that probe aspects of popular religiosity in modern America. But they do provide a beginning for further study, and where works annotated themselves contain helpful bibliographies to stimulate ongoing reflection and research, I have mentioned them. As long as Americans engage in the human quest to make sense out of their own experience and as long as they look beyond themselves to a supernatural realm that will assist them in ordering their lives, popular religiosity will remain a vital dynamic of American religious life.

2

Theoretical, Contextual, and Reference Materials

THEORETICAL STUDIES

001 Albanese, Catherine L. "The Study of Popular Religion: Retrospect and Prospect." *Explor* 7 (Fall 1984): 9-15.

Albanese notes the problem in defining popular religion, arguing that a viable definition must include both the elite and the masses to avoid dividing the "people" into "us" versus "them." Albanese believes that an authentic popular religion must include only what all the people hold as sacred. While she avoids use of the term "civil religion" to denote this sacred, it is clear that she sees the civil sphere as offering a more workable basis for popular religion. Such, however, ignores whether all those who make up any collectivity, civil or religious, could ever fully share the same understanding of the sacred at any given time.

002 Bock, E. Wilbur. "Symbols in Conflict: Official versus Folk Religion. *Journal for the Scientific Study of Religion* 6 (1966): 204-212.

Bock believes every society blends aspects of folk religiosity with the more formal religion of established institutions to develop commonly held symbols systems. Individual clusters within the culture may draw on either or both in different ways to find meaningful rationale and support for common cultural values. An example for American culture is the celebration of Christmas. From the realm of folk culture and religion come the myths surrounding Santa Claus, the festive decoration of homes and Christmas trees, as well as the custom of exchanging gifts; from the arena of official religion comes the emphasis on the birth of Jesus. Bock argues that for ordinary people the meaning of most holidays represent is found in a fusion of such elements.

003 Doeve, J. W. "Official and Popular Religion in Judaism." In *Official and Popular Religion: Analysis of a Theme for Religious Studies*, ed. by Pieter Hendrik Vrijhof and Jacques Waardenburg, 325-39. The Hague: Mouton, 1979.

Doeve claims that official religion has predominated over popular religion in Judaism since the first century of the common era because the formal tradition has maintained an emphasis on corporate religious expression rather than individual religious expression. Doeve does believe that mysticism and Zionism have both demonstrated dimensions of popular religion, even if they have often been part of official religion. Doeve ignores, however, the interplay of ethnic and cultural factors with specifically religious ones in the history of Diaspora Judaism that has led other scholars to find a rich heritage of popular religiosity existing alongside the formal tradition.

004 Donders, C. J. M. "Some Psychological Remarks on Official and Popular Religion." In *Official and Popular Religion: Analysis of a Theme for Religious Studies*, ed. by Pieter Hendrik Vrijhof and Jacques Waardenburg, 294-322. The Hague: Mouton, 1979.

In this heavily theoretical piece, Donders explores the possibility of seeing popular religion as a dimension of personality structures that permeate behavior. This possibility, Donders claims, is complicated by most people regarding religion as a formal affiliation or an internalized, private belief rather than as an aspect of personality.

005 Elizondo, Virgil. "Popular Religion As Support of Identity: A Pastoral-Psychological Case-Study Based on the Mexican American Experience in the U.S.A." In *Popular Religion*, ed. by Norbert Greinacher and Norbert Mette, 36-43. Concilium, 186. Edinburgh: T. and T. Clark, 1986.

Elizondo uses the symbolic prominence of Our Lady of Guadalupe and festival celebrations to show differences in the function of popular religion based on social-cultural status. For persons who are in a dominant class, such symbols become part of a culture religion; for those who are dominated, they form a basis for resistance to oppression. Elizondo believes that popular religion is that which is common to the people of such particular social classes, not the private religiosity of individuals.

006 Henau, Ernest. "Popular Religiosity and Christian Faith." In *Popular Religion*, ed. by Norbert Greinacher and Norbert Mette, 71-81. Edinburgh: T. and T. Clark, 1986.

Henau defines popular religiosity as a universal religiosity as such that is not tradition specific and that may incorporate pagan practices and habits along with those drawn from a particular tradition. He claims it emphasizes holy places; a view of the world as totally interconnected; meeting needs of the moment through practices such as privatized prayer; mediations through phenomena such as blessings, relics, rosaries, and candles; a collection of rites designed to give popular belief plausibility; and feeling over rationality.

007 Lanternari, Vittorio. "La Religion populaire: Perspective historique et anthropologique." *Archives de sciences sociales des religions* 53 (1982): 121-43.

Lanternari assumes that popular religion and official (institutional) religion represent polar dichotomies rooted in social class distinctions. Popular religion emerges when the dominant classes develop a priestly stratum and religious institutions that wield economic and political power. In turn popular religion becomes the way the lower classes respond to the dominant classes, although Lanternari allows for the possibility that popular religion may take in an entire society if it is attempting to discard a religion imposed by an oppressive, external force.

008 Lippy, Charles H. *Being Religious, American Style: A History of Popular Religiosity in the United States.* Westport, Conn.: Greenwood, 1994.

The opening chapter of this book reviews the literature attempting to define or describe popular religion. Lippy concludes that the inability of scholars to agree makes use of the term problematic. As an alternative, he proposes talking about popular religiosity to denote what ordinary people think and do when they are trying to understand and interpret their everyday experience. Lippy believes that this endeavor has been a constant in human history and in American culture nearly always involves an inchoate belief in the supernatural. The final four chapters discuss themes in popular religiosity for the period covered in this bibliography.

009 Luckmann, Thomas. *The Invisible Religion.* New York: Macmillan, 1967.

As western societies, especially that of the United States, became more industrial and urban, the people in them developed an increasing array of secondary and tertiary relationships with other people and with institutions, according to Luckmann. From them ordinary people draw constructs that enable them to make sense out of their personal and common experience, a task that Luckmann sees as essentially religious in nature. As a result, individuals fashion idiosyncratic and highly personal religious world views, so much so that religion should be more identified with this very private (and hence invisible) realm than with organized religious institutions.

010 Meldonado, Luis. "Popular Religion: Its Dimensions, Levels, and Types." In *Popular Religion*, ed. by Norbert Greinacher and Norbert Mette, 3-11. Concilium, 186. Edinburgh: T. and T. Clark, 1986.

Popular religion for Meldonado represents a quest for more simple, more direct, and more profitable relations with the divine than formal religious institutions offer.   Hence it is a substratum, if not aberration of institutional religion characterized by its reliance on the intuitive, symbolic, imaginative, mystical, festive, theatrical, communal, and political.

011 Mensching, Gustav. "The Masses, Folk Belief, and Universal Religion." In *Religion, Culture, and Society*, ed. by Louis Schneider, 269-73. New York: Wiley, 1964.

Mensching talks about folk religion rather than popular religion, finding is roots in the magic that marked preliterate cultures. Such magic brought the power to manipulate and control supernatural powers for personal and social benefit. In this view, folk beliefs are common to a culture, although they may be culture-specific; they are not the privatized beliefs of individuals that others have identified as the locus of popular religion. Because the masses are credulous and moved more by subconscious feelings and motives, Mensching tends to have a negative view of folk religion. He also argues that mass or folk belief exhibits a sameness across cultures because of its base in magic and the vividness of the supernatural.

012 Redfield, Robert. *Peasant Society and Culture*. Chicago: University of Chicago Press, 1953.

An anthropologist, Redfield studied peasant societies and found in them a distinction between what he called the "great tradition" of religion that was transmitted through sacred texts (oral or written) and the labors of a priestly class, for example, and the "little tradition" of popular and often syncretistic beliefs, myths, rituals, and related practices that flourished among common people apart from the trappings of the more formalized "great tradition" and not controlled by its officials. Many other scholars whom Redfield influenced have seen the "little tradition" as basic to popular religion.

013   Roebroeck, E. J. M. G.   "A Problem for Sociology: Contemporary Developments in the Roman Catholic Church." In *Official and Popular Religion: Analysis of a Theme for Religious Studies*, ed. by Pieter Hendrik Vrijhof and Jacques Waardenburg, 166-99. The Hague: Mouton, 1979.

Roebroeck contrasts official religion and popular religion.   The former is comprised of the whole of the interrelated norms and teachings prescribed and controlled by religious institutions, while the latter represents all those attitudes and actions that are religious in nature but not prescribed and controlled by religious institutions.   The two, Roebroeck believes, exist in a dynamic relationship. He supports his argument with examples drawn from the European context.

014   Schneider, Louis, and Sanford M. Dornbusch.   *Popular Religion: Inspirational Books in America*.   Chicago: University of Chicago Press, 1958.

In this pioneering study of devotional literature, Schneider and Dornbusch look at popular religion from a functional perspective.   Identified less with formal doctrine and practice than with inner feeling, popular religion in their view is a practical matter; it is the religiosity that enables ordinary people to deal with the basic problems that they confront in daily life and put them into a framework of meaning.   Schneider and Dornbusch examined the content of forty-six best sellers published between 1875 and 1955.   They note that the audience targeted by these works was basically middle-class and that the readership was predominantly female. All were "technique-laden." That is, all had a practical orientation intended to inspire through sentiment the possibility of salvation and its attainment while at the same time addressing the problems of ordinary people.   Schneider and Dornbusch found that inspirational books regarded the function of religion as giving meaning to life, articulated in nonintellectual terms an idea of an immanent God, claimed that the self could be transformed but not through psychological and psychiatric means alone apart from religion, developed an understanding of salvation that was more this-worldly, shifted over the years from seeing religion as a means to material wealth to regarding it as a way to achieve mental health, placed primary emphasis on God's love, and, consistent with their antidogmatic strain, stressed the importance of subjective religious experience and participation in a religious community.

015 Seguy, Jean. "Images et 'Religion Populaire': Reflexions sur un Colloque."

Archives des sciences sociales des religions 44 (July-September 1977): 25-43.

Seguy calls attention to the tendency to reduce popular religion to an underground and hence marginal phenomenon because of the dominance of official religion. There is a concomitant need, therefore, to recognize that popular piety and devotion retain their own place within institutionalized religions even if they are nothing more than non-clerical expressions of personal religiosity or the personal devotion of clergy apart from their formal, liturgical role.

016   Shils, Edward.   "Centre and Periphery."   In *The Logic of Personal Knowledge: Essays Presented to Michael Polyani*, ed. by Paul Ignotos *et al.*, 117-30.   London: Routledge and Kegan Paul, 1961.

Shils does not here address the phenomenon of popular religion directly, but offers an understanding of the dynamics of culture with important ramifications for such. Shils argues that eery culture has a center or a central zone of values, beliefs, and symbols that govern the society. Within the culture, the elite organize and affirm this central zone and therefore make it a kind of official religion. But other members of the culture also share in this center, even as they move to the periphery. It is this more individualized appropriation of a central zone of values, beliefs, and symbols that form the basis for popular religion.

017 Staples, P. "Official and Popular Religion in Ecumenical Perspective." In *Official and Popular Religion: Analysis of a Theme for Religious Studies*, ed. by Pieter Hendrik Vrijhof and Jacques Waardenburg, 244-93. The Hague: Mouton, 1979.

Staples argues that in complex western societies the proliferation of formal religious options has brought a rupture of the commonly-held values and beliefs that once provided cohesion and integration and collapsed the distinction between what was once a common center of religious values and what was regarded as on the periphery. That means, says Staples, that historians can no longer interpret developments adequately only by examining documentation generated by religious officials and elites.

018 Suess, Paulo. "The Creative and Normative Role of Popular Religion in the Church." In *Popular Religion*, ed. by Norbert Greinacher and Norbert Mette, 122-31. Concilium, 186. Edinburgh: T. and T. Clark, 1986.

This essay makes the case that the popularity between popular religion and official or institutional religion is inextricably tied to the context of a classist society with its "hierarchical mediations of monotheism." But Suess also notes that popular religion can itself become an agent of oppression if it is appropriated by the ruling classes to further their dominance over the masses.

019 Towler, Robert. *Homo Religiosus: Sociological Problems in the Study of Religion*. New York: St. Martin's, 1974.

Relevant for the study of modern American popular religion are chapters seven and eight of Towler's work. There he discusses what he terms common religion, understood as beliefs and practices that are overtly religious but "not under the domination of a prevailing religious institution" (p. 148). Towler rejects the term "popular religion" as too vague. His common religion, diffuse and unorganized in the midst of highly developed official religion, forms "something of a base-line religiousness" (p. 152) transmitted by the whole of culture through the socialization process.

020 Vrijhof, Pieter. "Official and Popular Religion in Twentieth-Century Western Christianity." In *Official and Popular Religion: Analysis of a Theme for Religious Studies*, ed. by Pieter Hendrik Vrijhof and Jacques Waardenburg, 217-43. The Hague: Mouton, 1979.

As many others, Vrijhof regards popular religion as religiosity in general. As such, it is a constant in human culture, often syncretistic in nature and historically emerging prior to official religion. More the domain of laity than clergy or religious professionals, popular religion according to Vrijhof is less cognitive and lacking the dogmatic aspects of official religion. Vrijhof also argues that popular religion becomes discernible only when official religion has become a differentiated sphere within a given culture.

021 Williams, Peter W. *Popular Religion in America: Symbolic Change and the Modernization Process in Historical Perspective*. Englewood Cliffs, N.J.: Prentice-Hall, 1980.

Williams understands popular religion to encompass extra-ecclesiastical symbolic activity that occurs outside formal religious structures and becomes most prominent during times of social change and transition. For him, popular religion is best expressed in movements that exist separate from, but in tension with, established religious institutions, that transmit their beliefs and practices through unofficial channels, and that tend to see supernatural involvement in everyday life. Williams is thus more interested in movements that parallel formal religion than in the personal religiosity of individuals.

022   Wuthnow, Robert. *Experimentation in American Religion: The New Mysticisms and Their Implications for the Churches.* Berkeley: University of California Press, 1978.

A sociologist interested in the changing dynamics of religion in contemporary American culture, Wuthnow offers a chapter in this book entitled "The Coming of Religious Populism." For him, religious populism is akin to what others have labelled popular religion or common religion. It encompasses the personal value systems or beliefs systems that individuals create for themselves by drawing on the beliefs and values of mainstream religions and combining them with alternative beliefs and values. Fluid and constantly changing, religious populism has no need of internal consistency as do the doctrine and practice of formal religious bodies. Wuthnow thinks that this religious populism has resulted in part from the cultural and religious pluralism that have prevailed in the United States.

CONTEXTUAL STUDIES

023 Bigsby, C. W. E., ed. *Approaches to Popular Culture.* London: Edward Arnold, 1976.

This collection of essays does not deal directly with popular religion; most pieces have a literary orientation. However, the contribution by editor Bigsby, "The Politics of Popular Culture," suggests that what is now defined as popular culture has resulted from the processes of urbanization and industrialization. Intriguing as well is Philip Melling's "American Popular Culture in the Thirties: Ideology, Myth, Genre," which makes a case that Marxism had a religious function in the Depression decade by holding out a vision of an ideal future. When that apocalyptic hope failed, Americans, Melling claims, began to look to self-help phenomena to gain a secure identity.

024   Browne, Ray B., ed. *Rituals and Ceremonies in Popular Culture.* Bowling Green, Ohio: Bowling Green University Popular Press, 1980.

This collection of essays primarily treats secular rituals rather than those more obviously identified with religion. Those that are concerned explicitly with religion will be entered separately. Two others, however, are suggestive of the interconnections between popular religion and the larger culture. F. W. Westley, "Purification and Healing Rituals in New Religious Movements" (pp. 36-47) and Joseph W. Bastien and David G. Bromley, "Metaphor in the Rituals and Restorative and Transformative Groups" (pp. 48-60).

025 Caplow, Theodore, et al. *All Faithful People: Change and Continuity in Middletown's Religion.* Minneapolis: University of Minnesota Press. 1983.

Returning to Muncie, Indiana, in the late 1970s to see whether the speculation of Robert and Helen Lynd concerning the expected decline of religion had occurred, Caplow and his associates found that religion was still a vital component of life in this community. Besides the presence of strong religious institutions, this follow-up study discerned the emergence of a "common creed" among the people of Muncie that bears all the hallmarks of popular religiosity: a conviction of the efficaciousness of prayer as a means of harnessing supernatural power, a belief that God (however defined) provides all of life's meaning, and an assumption that personal religious experience requires no formal proofs or arguments to sustain its validity. Hence alongside traditional religion there was a vital popular religiosity that cut across denominational lines.

026   Caughey, John L.   "Fantasy Worlds and Self-Maintenance in Contemporary American Life." *Zygon* 23 (June 1988): 129-38.

Caughey examines the creation of fantasy worlds of both a religious and secular nature, claiming that they provide a positive sense of self-identity despite their lack of empirical reality. Although fantasy worlds of meaning may develop through social interaction, they are so individualized as to lack group context. Although Caughey does not so state, his thesis provides an important backdrop for popular religion because the world views that emerge from popular religion are themselves dimensions of the realm of fantasy that he discusses.

027 Chalfant, H. Paul, Robert E. Beckley, and C. Eddie Palmer. *Religion in Contemporary Society.* Sherman Oaks, Calif.: Alfred, 1981.

This sociology of religion textbook contains chapters on a wide range of religious and social movements, ranging from fundamentalism to Krishna Consciousness to Synanon. What is important for understanding the scope of popular religion is the concluding section of the book where the authors develop their argument that in recent years, religion has become ever more privatized and individualistic in its base. They believe this privatization, not such other forces as secularization and/or humanism, have brought about the perceived decline of influence of religion in contemporary American life.

028 Cochran, Clarke E. *Religion in Public and Private Life*. New York: Routledge, 1990.

Although the primary focus of this book is the connection between religion and politics, Cochran does highlight the ways in which religion cultivates "private life" and hence the values and virtues to which ordinary people subscribe. The more authentic religion becomes a matter of the private sphere, according to Cochran, the more there are abiding consequences for public policy, particularly in areas such as an understanding of justice, where issues of values come into play.

029 Fishwick, Marshall. *Common Culture and the Great Tradition: The Case for Renewal*. Westport, Conn.: Greenwood, 1982.

Fishwick, one of the leading student of popular culture, suggests here that every age lives by a mythology that is essentially religious in nature and usually expressed in a popular iconography. Hence he argues that greater attention needs to be paid to the artifacts of contemporary material culture. A chapter on sports is particularly provocative in arguing that in contemporary American culture professional athletics have taken on the trappings of religion and provide cohesion for American society.

030 Fishwick, Marshall. *Parameters of Popular Culture*. Bowling Green, Ohio: Bowling Green University Popular Press, 1974.

Two chapters of this book provide context for appraising modern American popular religion, one treating theology and one discussing mythology. Fishwick develops arguments that he has amplified elsewhere, namely that the pulse of popular religion and theology is not to be found in formal theology, but in broader cultural currents as old mythologies disappear. But the details of Fishwick's analysis in this study will appear dated, for the multisensory mythology that he believed marked the popular culture of the early 1970s has itself now vanished.

031 Fishwick, Marshall W. *Seven Pillars of Popular Culture*. Contributions to the Study of Popular Culture, No. 10. Westport, Conn.: Greenwood, 1985.

In the introduction to this book, Fishwick explores the ongoing dilemma of the lack of method and the impossibility of finding a single method to analyze popular culture. A chapter entitled "Theos" (pp. 81-101) provides a rapid, if somewhat simplistic historical overview of popular religion shaped by American Protestantism in the nineteenth century, built on the premise that what evokes a deep emotional response from large numbers of people, like revivalism then, should be classified as popular. Remaining constant in American popular religion, therefore, are notions of a personal God with parental attributes and the conviction that the United States is a divinely chosen nation with a God-given mission in the world.

032 Fishwick, Marshall, and Ray B. Browne, eds. *Icons of Popular Culture*. Bowling Green, Ohio: Bowling Green University Popular Press, 1970.

Of particular interest in this anthology is an essay by Spencer C. Bennett entitled "Christ, Icons, and Mass Media" (pp. 91-102). Bennett proposes that the understanding of the icon rooted in Eastern Christianity is relevant to the contemporary understanding of space and time. Film, for example, transforms the eternal into the immediate via technology much as the icon seeks to mediate the eternal within the confines of time.

033 Garvin, Philip, and Julia Welch. *Religious America*. New York: McGraw-Hill, 1974.

This work had its genesis as a photographic essay supported by the Rockefeller Foundation that sought to document the religious experience of ordinary Americans. It later became a series aired by the Public Broadcasting Company. The photographs, taken in 1971, are the work of Garvin; the essays on the many individuals were written by Welch. The personal vignettes touch on the religiosity of Episcopalians, Pentecostals, Hasidic Jews, Hutterites, Lutherans, Missionary Baptists, to followers of the Guru Ram Das and members of the Penitentes of New Mexico.

034 Geist, Christopher D., and Jack Nachbar, eds. *The Popular Culture Reader*. 3rd ed. Bowling Green, Ohio: Bowling Green University Popular Press, 1983.

Designed as a textbook for classroom use, the essays in this anthology also include questions for discussion. Several touch on popular religion or features of common culture that have religions dimensions, including family reunions, funerals, sports, and rituals associated with demolition derbies.

035   Gleason, Philip.   "Americans All: World War II and the Shaping of American Identity." *Review of Politics* 43 (1981): 483-518.

Gleason provides provocative background for understanding some of the cultural currents that nurture popular religion.   He looks especially at the role of ethnicity as a factor in determining personal identity in the period from 1920 to 1960.   While the importance of ethnicity declined during those decades, according to Gleason, World War II was critical in encouraging Americans to celebrate cultural pluralism.   Because the exigencies of war required national unity, social forces stimulated the growth of tolerance and the decline of ethnic prejudice.   Such enabled cultural pluralism to replace ethnocentrism as a fundamental characteristic of American life.   It may be, however, that ethnic particularity remains and receives manifestation in the popular religious practices forged from the unique experience of individual ethnic communities.

036   Goethals, Gregor.   "Sacred-Secular Icons."   In *Icons of America*, ed. by Ray B. Browne and Marshall Fishwick, 24-34.   Bowling Green, Ohio: Popular Press of Bowling Green State University, 1978.

Goethals examines the religious use of symbols in popular culture in contemporary America.   He looks, for example, at advertisements that portray concrete models of heroic human experience as one way popular culture gives a religious function to symbols of order.   He notes that the most common religious use of symbols deals with the family, science and technology, and nature.

037   Hammond, Phillip E.   "In Search of a Protestant Twentieth Century: American Religion and Power Since 1900." *Review of Religious Research* 24 (1983): 281-94.

Hammond addresses the resurgence of the conservative strand of American Protestantism, looking closely at the period from 1880 to 1920 and the very recent past.   He argues that although the media attributed much of the growth of conservative Protestantism to fears of secular humanism, the real reason for growth has been a political activism inspired by the decline of political power and influence of religion more generally, but especially the erosion of the political clout of the mainstream denominations.

038   Handy, Robert T.   "The American Religious Depression." *Church History* 29 (1960): 3-16.

Handy claims that a religious depression paralleled the Great Depression of the 1930s in terms of the status of traditional religious institutions, participation in them, and their influence on the fabric of American common life. Handy does not, however, discuss whether this religious depression was accompanied by shifts in personal religiosity, the arena of popular religion, but directs his concern exclusively to religious institutions.

039 Handy, Robert T. *A Christian America: Protestant Hopes and Historical Realities*. 2nd ed. New York: Oxford University Press, 1984.

Handy provides a penetrating overview of Protestant influence on American culture. He looks first at the nineteenth century, when evangelical Protestantism and the denominations associated with it, exercised a near hegemony in shaping cultural style. But the growth of non-Protestant bodies, the failure of evangelical Protestantism to deal adequately with social change resulting from urbanization and industrialization, and the challenges of such phenomena as the civil rights movement in the twentieth century offered challenges that undercut the hope for fixing a Protestant stamp on American common life. Here, too, Handy is primarily concerned with traditional religious institutions and does not give the same in depth attention to matters of personal devotion and the like, the heart of popular religion. But the book provides valuable background information for understanding the religious dynamics that have long been at work in the United States.

040 Klapp, Orrin. *The Collective Search for Identity*. New York: Holt, Rinehart, and Winston, 1969.

This book is valuable more for providing a sense of the ambience of modern American culture than of the dynamics of popular religion. Klapp argues that modern society forces exaggerated expectations on ordinary folk. The inability of most to live up to such expectations, according to Klapp, helps account for the interest in "cultic movements" ranging from astrology to Zen Buddhism to the Jehovah's Witnesses. These alternatives, along with such phenomena as hero worship, attempts to intensify personal experience (through drugs or sexual activity, for example), and crusades such as the Vietnam War, are all responses to a sense of failure and often attempts to regain some semblance of control.

041 Lundin, Roger, and Mark A. Noll, eds. *Voices from the Heart: Four Centuries of American Piety*. Grand Rapids: Eerdmans, 1987.

This anthology of excerpts from diaries, letters, and public works spans the period from the European settlement of North America to the late twentieth century. All are Christian; most come from the Protestant wing of Christianity. Some from the twentieth century offer glimpses of the personal piety that is basic to popular religiosity, especially excerpts from Dorothy Day, Catherine Marshall, Elisabeth Elliott, and the like. Ordinary people are represented along with the clergy and other religious professionals.

042 Lynd, Robert S., and Helen M. Lynd. *Middletown: A Study in American Culture*. New York: Harcourt and Brace, 1929; Idem. *Middletown in Transition: A Study in Cultural Conflicts*. New York: Harcourt and Brace, 1937.

In these classical sociological studies, the Lynds dissect the society and culture of Muncie, Indiana. They give some treatment to religion, centering primarily in the religious denominations and institutions that served the people of Muncie at the time they did their field work. The Lynds also hypothesized about the future influence of religion in the lives of the people of Muncie, claiming that trends they observed suggested a decline. However, the Lynds focussed on organized religion (which Robert T. Handy argued was experiencing its own "depression" in the 1930s). They did not look at personal or popular religion; hence they did not appreciate the dynamics of popular religiosity that continued to flourish during a period when organized religion was encountering numerous challenges.

043 Marty, Martin E. *The Irony of It All, 1893-1919*. *Modern American Religion* 1. Chicago: University of Chicago Press, 1986.

In this first of five projected volumes surveying developments in American religion from 1880 to the present, noted historian Martin Marty covers the period that ends with World War I. While Marty is primarily concerned with organized religion, he is careful not to restrict his analysis to religious institutions. Hence he examines such cultural phenomena as initial contemporary concerns over biblical inerrancy, the birth of the modern Pentecostal movement, and the powerful role of ethnicity, particularly among immigrant communities. All these are part of the larger picture of popular religion in that they are linked to the formal religious structures of American life, but not identified with any one religious tradition or institution. This study is most helpful in providing a sense of context for early twentieth century American religious life.

044 Marty, Martin E. *The Noise of Conflict, 1919-1941*. *Modern American*

Religion 2. Chicago: University of Chicago Press, 1991.

As in the first volume, Marty directs primary attention to the story of religious traditions. But for the period between the two world wars, he also scrutinizes dimensions of popular religion (although without using that designation). For example, he looks at the religious dimensions of the Ku Klux Klan as a movement originating among the people. He also examines the impact on ordinary people of figures like Fr. Charles Coughlin, who was among the first to make powerful use of the then new medium of radio to reach the masses. But the greatest value of this book is the way it delves into the religious texture of American life for the period it covers.

045 Marty, Martin E. "Where the Energies Go." In *Religion in the Nineties*, ed. by Wade Clark Roof, 11-26. *Annals of the American Academy of Political and Social Sciences* 527. Newbury Park, Calif.: Sage Periodicals, 1993.

In this essay, Marty identifies several characteristics that he feels distinguish American religion in the 1990s. His concern is not with popular religion as such, yet the qualities he discerns are all fundamental to nurturing popular religiosity. For example, he highlights the emphasis on personal religious experience, as opposed to corporate religious experience, along with a prevailing conviction that the individual is the final authority in matters of religion, not the religious group or its leadership. As well, Marty insists that the most important expectation that ordinary people have about religion is that it will give them a framework of meaning for their personal lives.

046 Mouw, Richard J. *Consulting the Faithful: What Christian Intellectuals Can Learn from Popular Religion.* Grand Rapids, Mich.: Eerdmans, 1994.

Writings from a personal commitment to a Protestant evangelical perspective, Mouw, who is president of Fuller Theological Seminary in California, makes a case that theological conservatives should cease casual condemnation of expressions of popular religion. His purview includes such diverse phenomena as the fascination with certain forms to magic to the lure of Las Vegas as a place of pilgrimage. His arguments is simply that critics of popular culture need to understand why it has appeal and what needs it meets in the lives of ordinary men and women, based on the assumption that people are drawn to what enables them resolves crises of faith and endow their lives with meaning.

047 Myers, Kenneth A. *All God's Children and Blue Suede Shoes: Christians and Popular Culture.* Westchester, Ill.: Crossway Books, 1989.

This monograph provides a fundamentalist critique of popular culture, defined primarily as the world views thought to be promulgated by the mass media (especially television and various forms of rock music). Myers is wary of these world views because he believes they exalt instant gratification for the individual, they emphasize violence and prurience, and they assume that all belief is relative.   Authentic religion for Myers teaches patience, puts the common good ahead of individual need, and insists on absolute standards. He does argue that formal religious traditions need to develop a comprehensive theology of leisure if they hope to provide a viable alternative. At the same time, Myers shows little appreciation for what attracts ordinary folk to manifestations of popular culture and the way they blends signals drawn from that arena with other beliefs and values to formulate workable ways of understanding and interpreting their personal experience.

048   Nelson, John Wiley.   "The Apocalyptic Vision in American Popular Culture." In *The Apocalyptic Vision in America: Interdisciplinary Essays on Myth and Culture*, ed. by Lois P. Zamora, 154-82. Bowling Green, Ohio: Bowling Green University Popular Press, 1982.

Nelson devotes primary attention to a critical analysis of Hal Lindsey's *The Late, Great Planet Earth*, but also looks at eschatological motifs in films such as the *Star Trek* series, *Star Wars*, and *Battlestar Gallactica*, the science fiction of Isaac Asimov, television series such as *The Six Million Dollar Man* and *The Bionic Woman*. He also argues that films of the "anti-Western" genre such as *Bad Day at Black Rock* and *McCabe and Mrs. Miller* illustrate a contemporary apocalyptic eschatology. Nelson attributes the attractiveness of such popular representations of apocalyptic themes to a widespread sense that humanity has lost control of its destiny. Popular apocalyptic speaks not only of the end of an age when control is gone, but it also offers hope for a future when supernatural intervention will again bring order and coherence to life.

049 Noll, Mark A. *A History of Christianity in the United States and Canada*. Grand Rapids, Mich.: Eerdmans, 1992.

Noll structures this survey in an idiosyncratic fashion, combining chapters that are chronologically oriented with others that are look at particular topics. It is valuable in providing an overview of the dominant religious tradition in the United States, and the biographical sketches of influential figures in the modern period are especially helpful. Several, such as Aimee Semple McPherson, Fulton J. Sheen, Billy Graham, and Catherine Marshall had large popular followings as evangelists, media personalities, and/or writers. As well, Noll gives some attention to popular literature and visual media, such as the novel

Ben Hur and the film based on it, that had an impact on the religiosity of ordinary folk.

050 Schlesinger, Arthur, Sr. *The Rise of the City, 1878-1898*. History of America Library 10. New York: Macmillan, 1933.

Chapter 10 of Schlesinger's study, "The Changing Church" (pp. 320-48), offers considerable insight into the forces that allowed popular religiosity to flourish in the last two decades of the nineteenth century, although the focus is not popular religion per se. Schlesinger notes several consequences of the increasing urbanization of American society: the gradual popular division of life into sacred and secular spheres, the ideological conflicts over theories of evolution and over the application if higher literary criticism to sacred texts, the emergence of new religions such as Theosophy and Ethical Culture, and the surge in immigration that accompanied the rise of the city. In different ways, all encouraged the relegation of religion to the arena of private life where many strands of popular religiosity are nurtured.

051 Sherrill, Rowland A. "Recovering American Religious Sensibility: An Introduction." In *Religion and the Life of the Nation: American Recoveries*, ed. by Rowland A. Sherrill, 1-22. Urbana and Chicago: University of Illinois Press, 1990.

Relying heavily on sociological constructs advanced by Thomas Luckmann, Sherrill argues for the increasing relegation of religion to the private sphere in late twentieth century America. Religion can no longer be limited to formal institutions, according to Sherrill, for individuals more and more develop a personal religious world view that draws on many sources. Organized religions and their belief systems are only one such source. This diffusion of religion allows countless idiosyncratic expressions of religiosity to emerge and thereby gives credence to the mushrooming of popular religiosity in the contemporary period.

REFERENCE MATERIALS

052 Branson, Mark Lau. *Reader's Guide to the Best Evangelical Books*. San Francisco: Harper and Row, 1982.

Presuming that the Protestant evangelical style reflects the religiosity of many, Branson offers this reference work to enable persons to find books that will reinforce their world views. Branson focuses largely on traditional religious categories such as biblical interpretation and doctrine, the church and ministry, and Christianity and culture. He includes few titles of the "self-help" sort that have mushroomed in recent years.

053 Burgess, Stanley M., and Gary B. McGee, eds. *Dictionary of Pentecostal and Charismatic Movements.* Grand Rapids, Mich.: Zondervan, 1988.

This very helpful reference work includes entries on persons, groups, beliefs, practices, and other phenomena identified with the pentecostal and charismatic strains within Christianity. The primary focus is the United States. While longer entries are clearly sympathetic to their subject, each treats context and influence and concludes with a brief bibliography of titles for further study.

054 Chase, Elise. *Healing Faith: An Annotated Bibliography of Christian Self-Help Books.* Bibliographies and Indexes in Religious Studies, No. 4. Westport, Conn.: Greenwood, 1985.

This standard reference work, now somewhat dated, begins with a helpful preface that discusses the recent growing interest in religiously-oriented self-help. Chase notes the built-in contradiction that marks self-help: individuals seek inward healing by drawing on an outer, supernatural source of strength. The more than 700 entries include books published for a mass audience between 1970 and 1984. Titles are topically organized into three major divisions: spiritual psychodynamics (conversion, success, prayer, inner life, and the like), family and developmental issues (teens, gender identity, marriage, parenting, intimacy, divorce, aging, death), and the wider community (discipling, evangelism, Christian social action, support networks). Author, title, and subject indexes make for easy use.

055 Choquette, Diane. *New Religious Movements in the United States and Canada: A Critical Assessment and Annotated Bibliography.* Bibliographies and Indexes in Religious Studies, No. 5. Westport, Conn.: Greenwood, 1985.

Now somewhat dated, given the proliferation of literature in the past decade, Choquette's bibliography remains a solid overview of materials on newer religious movements of especial use to those who regard such movements as manifestations of popular religion. Choquette includes titles on various groups as well as studies analyzing the attractiveness and plausibility of alternative religions as well as the controversy that frequently surrounds them.

056 Gentry, Linnell. *A History and Encyclopedia of Country, Western, and Gospel Music.* Reprint, St. Clair Shores, Mich.: Scholarly Press, 1972.

This reference work, first published in 1961, contains reprints of articles, many of which were originally published in the first half of the twentieth century. Hence there is little material here that illuminates the more recent explosion of interest in gospel music, particularly "gospel rock" and other current manifestations. But essays on the gospel hymn and favorite hymns of the 1950s provide historical context for understanding the spectacular growth in the later twentieth century of various genres of religious music intended to have mass appeal. Biographies of singers and musicians are also helpful.

057 Katz, Bill, and Linda Sternberg Katz. *Self-Help: 1400 Best Books on Personal Growth.* New York: R. R. Bowker, 1985.

This bibliography claims to exclude specifically religious titles, and the number of titles included alone suggest the import of self-help for the American experience in the last half of the twentieth century. However, it is not clear how the compilers define religion; many of the self-help works listed clearly have religious dimensions, as does virtually all of the genre, if one presumes that one function of religion (as of self-help) is to provide a sense of wholeness and well-being for individuals.

058 Klein, Christa Ressmeyer. "Literature for America's Roman Catholic Children (1865-1895): An Annotated Bibliography." *American Literary Realism, 1870-1910* 6 (1973): 137-52.

Literature designed for children often provides keen insight into the beliefs, practices, and values religious traditions see as most important; hence the effort to implant them into children. In this survey, Klein demonstrates that Catholic children's literature of the late nineteenth century fostered a Catholic identity as a distinct subculture. How formal religious teaching merges into popular religiosity can be seen in titles offering guidelines for social behavior and works of fiction.

059 Melton, J. Gordon. *Biographical Dictionary of American Cult and Sect Leaders.* Library of Social Sciences. New York: Garland, 1986.

Melton opens this reference work with an historical essay looking at the recurring presence of sects and cults in American religion and the role of the leader or founder in forming these kinds of religious groups. The table of contents provides an alphabetical listing of the individuals profiled; subjects span the sweep of American history. Leaders of contemporary alternative religious movements are represented, but in relatively small numbers.

060 Melton, J. Gordon. *Encyclopedic Handbook of Cults in America*. Rev. ed. Religious Information Systems Series, 7. New York: Garland, 1992.

Melton considers cults to include virtually all unconventional religious groups. In this book, he divides the groups he will discuss into four categories: established cults, New Age cults, newer cults, and counter-cult groups. Established cults include such well-known religious organizations as the Mormons, Christian Science, Unity, and the Jehovah's Witnesses. Newer cults span the gamut from Scientology to the International Society for Krishna Consciousness to The Way, International. All essays offer overviews of history and beliefs. Melton concludes the book with an essay on the history of violence in the social response to cults.

061 Melton, J. Gordon and Isotta Poggi. *Magic, Witchcraft, and Paganism in America: A Bibliography*. 2nd ed. Religious Information Systems Series, 3. New York: Garland, 1992.

The title indicates the scope of this helpful resource. Melton is sensitive to the long history of these three religious phenomena in American life; hence the titles included are not restricted to contemporary manifestations, but provide a good historical foundation for understanding current interest in all three. For the contemporary period, the bibliographic essay in Margot Adler's *Drawing Down the Moon* is a useful complement.

062 Melton, J. Gordon, Jerome Clark, and Aidan A. Kelly. *New Age Encyclopedia: A Guide to the Beliefs, Concepts, Terms, People, and Organizations That Make Up the New Global Movement toward Spiritual Development, Health and Healing, Higher Consciousness, and Related Subjects*. Detroit: Gale Research, 1990.

The detailed subtitle reveals the intended scope of this reference tool. The volume opens with an introductory essay that attempts to delimit what constitutes New Age phenomena, placing emphasis on the way New Age claims to provide transformative experience that brings wholeness and spiritual power to adherents. There is a good bibliography that follows. The hundreds of entries cover both contemporary New Age manifestations as well as those that have long histories, especially in western culture. Some of the groups are also discussed in Melton's *Encyclopedia Handbook of Cults in America*.   Users will appreciate the comprehensive indexes that enable easy location of material.

063 Osterreich, Shelley Anne. *The American Indian Ghost Dance, 1870 and 1890: An Annotated Bibliography*. Westport, Conn.: Greenwood Press, 1991.

The Ghost Dance was a popular movement originating among the Paiute and rapidly spreading to other Plains tribes in the closing decades of the nineteenth century that caused great consternation among United States government officials because of the revitalized spirit it brought to subjugated peoples. Osterreich provides perceptive comments on materials, some well-known and readily accessible and others less so, that both describe and analyze this popular religious phenomenon.

3

Overviews and Studies of Broad Themes

064 Albanese, Catherine L. *Nature Religion in America from the Algonkian Indians to the New Age*. Chicago: University of Chicago Press, 1990.

Albanese develops the thesis that one substratum of American religiosity has focused on nature and the power that is inherent in the natural realm. The chapters that treat the continuing fascination with nature in the twentieth century are particularly relevant for understanding the dynamics of popular religiosity. New Age expressions, for example, are extraordinarily eclectic in their content, exhibiting the syncretism that is fundamental to virtually all popular religiosity. For adherents, establishing a sense of harmony with the natural forces of the cosmos brings a feeling of order and control to life and thereby allows individuals to develop world views that make their own experience coherent and meaningful.

065 Avallone, Susan. "Receptivity to Religion." *Library Journal* 10 (15 October 1984): 1891-93.

Avallone discusses the increased demand among readers and library users for specifically Christian materials in the early 1980s. The greatest interest was in those that were not theologically sophisticated or academic in focus, but more simple and addressed to a mass audience. What is important is the implication of this trend: individuals were seeking literature from which they might extract elements of meaning in the construction of personal belief systems. Such an endeavor is central to the continuing power of popular religiosity with its roots in personal, private religious experience and belief.

066 Belk, Russell W. "A Child's Christmas in America: Santa Claus as Deity, Consumption as Religion." *Journal of Popular Culture* 10 (Spring 1987): 87-100.

This elaborately documented article claims that the popular image of Santa Claus, based primarily on the poetry of Clement Moore and drawing first released by Thomas Nast, is that of a god of consumption. By emphasizing the role of Santa Claus as a gift giver, American culture is actually socializing children into their later role as consumer. This religion of consumption, according to Belk, perpetuates the myth that people deserve what they get and get what they deserve in other arenas of life.

067 Bellah, Robert. "Civil Religion in America." In *American Civil Religion*, ed. by Russell Richey and Donald G. Jones, 21-44. New York: Harper and Row, 1974.

Bellah's classic essay first appeared in 1967 and has been reprinted many times. Propelled by a desire to see if there were religious forces that provided a basis for social cohesion in American culture, Bellah concluded that there was a civil religion that affirmed an ambiguous belief in a providential God who acted in American history, especially in wars and battles, to create a special nation. He finds corroboration in references to God in presidential inaugural addresses, in the pilgrimages to battlefields and other places basic to American history made by tourists, and in the elevation of figures who embody the American ideal (such as George Washington and Abraham Lincoln) to near divine status. While Bellah insists that there is a theology or ideology of liberty, justice, and equality that undergirds this civil religion, he does not look at how that religion may not function to incorporate Native Americans, African Americans, and other marginalized peoples into a cohesive population.

068 Berger, Peter L. *The Noise of Solemn Assemblies: Christian Commitment and the Religious Establishment in America.* Garden City, N.Y.: Doubleday, 1961.

Although he was trained as a sociologist, Berger provides both a theological and sociological critique of trends he observed in popular religious expressions in the 1950s, often seen as a period when religion was booming in American life. Berger concludes that the millions who identified with formal religious institutions did not have an abiding commitment to the beliefs ostensibly promoted by them, especially in the sense of seeing the ramifications of belief for personal and social behavior. Rather, Berger understood religious affiliation to be a matter of social convention, with individuals choosing to believe whatever they wished; such personal beliefs were often at variance with formal theology. When Berger wrote, few scholars were using the label of popular religion to describe this personal dimension, but what Berger discusses suggests that behind the presumed surface growth of religious institutions and religious influence in American life in the 1950s lay an idiosyncratic, syncretistic personal or popular religiosity.

069 Burns, G. Frank. "The Bible in American Popular Humor." In *The Bible and Popular Culture in America*, ed. by Allene Phy, 25-39. *The Bible in American Culture*, 2. Philadelphia: Fortress, 1985.

Burns makes the case that the Bible has been a major sources of popular humor, particularly in humor that seeks to call attention to the presence of God in human life and the accessibility of God to ordinary men and women. Among the examples he uses are several films, including "Oh God" that starred popular comedian George Burns in 1979 and "The Life of Brian." He does not address in depth whether the humor itself actually reflects the meaning of the biblical text.

070 Carnes, Mark C. *Secret Ritual and Manhood in Victorian America*. New Haven, Conn.: Yale University Press, 1989.

Carnes examines the rituals that developed among fraternal organizations with male memberships as such organizations became popular in the later nineteenth century. He argues that such rituals provided solace and psychological guidance for the Victorian male in the passage to adulthood. As the larger culture increasingly viewed religiosity as a domestic matter within women's sphere, fraternal organizations assumed a role parallel to that of evangelical Protestantism in securing male identity in a sphere that was removed from the home and the dominion of women. In Carnes's analysis, initiation into a fraternal order is akin to the classic experience of conversion in providing individuals with a new, viable identity and a symbolic framework on which to draw in giving enduring meaning to their unique experiences as men.

071 Chittister, Joan D., O.S.B., and Martin E. Marty. *Faith and Ferment: An Interdisciplinary Study of Christian Beliefs and Practices*. Minneapolis: Augsburg, and Collegeville, Minn.: Liturgical Press, 1983.

This book reports on a study conducted under the aegis of the Institute for Ecumenical and Cultural Research in Collegeville, Minnesota. The intent was to use questionnaires and interviews with a representative sample of Minnesotans to ascertain exactly what ordinary people actually believed and how their beliefs affected their daily behavior. The results revealed that Minnesotans drew on their religious belief to enable them to understand such matters as human suffering and also human shortcomings (sin). But they were also concerned with personal spiritual development. The study did demonstrate that although Minnesotans evidenced sincerity in their religious beliefs, those beliefs were in the last analysis ambiguous. The respondents were not asked specifically about what might be designated as popular religion, but the ambiguity in articulating personal belief is central to any understanding of popular religiosity and reflects its syncretism and highly individual character.

072 Cox, Harvey. *The Seduction of the Spirit: The Use and Misuse of People's Religion.* New York: Simon and Schuster, 1973.

When Harvard theologian Harvey Cox talks about people's religion in this book, he is referring to the "folk religion of ordinary people in its unsophisticated form and the popular religion that occurs outside formal ecclesiastical institutions" (p. 10). He also appraised various movements that gained prominence in the 1960s that had a religious function for participants, but were not identified with formal religious groups. Cox gives particular attention to the human potential movement that came to the fore thanks to such organizations as the Esalen Institute. The quest for maximizing human potential, according to Cox, was a new expression of pietism. It is also a part of popular religiosity in that persons may participate in such movements directly or indirectly without abandoning affiliation with conventional religions and draw on them in molding a personal religious world view, the heart of popular religiosity.

073 Ellwood, Robert S. *Alternative Altars: Unconventional and Eastern Spirituality in the United States.* Chicago: University of Chicago Press, 1979.

This volume, part of a University of Chicago Press series on American religion, offers a cogent look at many expressions of Eastern religions that gained currency in the United States in the 1960s and early 1970s. Ellwood is concerned not so much Asian immigrants and their efforts to transplant their religious traditions to the United States as with other Americans who were drawn to Asian religions and religious phenomena such as Theosophy that had some Asian connections. While millions of Americans dabbled in some sort of unconventional spirituality--Transcendental Meditation may have drawn the largest numbers--most did not become active adherents who completely abandoned other religious identification. Rather, they found in certain Eastern practices, especially meditation, a means of tapping into the realm of the inner self and of the supernatural. Such endeavors meant that much of the fascination with Eastern spirituality was an expression of popular religiosity.

074 Ellwood, Robert S. *The History and Future of Faith: Religion Past, Present, and to Come*. New York: Crossroad, 1988.

While this book has magisterial scope, it also contains a sensitive analysis of how the electronic media have changed not only the way religion is presented but the very understanding of religious faith. Because the media have contributed greatly to the increasing privatization of religiosity in twentieth-century American culture, Ellwood's study is especially valuable for illuminating the dynamics of popular religiosity in the contemporary period.

075 Ellwood, Robert S., and Harry Partin. *Religious and Spiritual Groups in Modern America*. 2nd ed. Englewood Cliffs, N.J.: Prentice-Hall, 1988.

This book, designed as a text for undergraduate courses, contains both historical and contemporary materials on numerous religious movements outside the orbit of the Christian and Hebrew traditions that have influenced American religious life in the last half of the twentieth century. The authors provide a brief narrative introduction about each group and excerpts from primary source materials that usually focus on the major beliefs of the group. End matter includes not only a helpful bibliography of key works about each group, but also addresses where individuals might contact the groups. As with the groups discussed in Ellwood's *Alternative Altars*, many of these are not exclusive in the sense that persons attracted to them do not necessarily become formal members of give up other religious affiliation. The value of the book is its cogent exposition and summary of many of those non-Western groups from which countless individuals have drawn ideas and practices that have been shaped into a personal, eclectic world view.

076 Elzey, Wayne. "Popular Culture." In *Encyclopedia of the American Religious Experience*, ed. by Charles H. Lippy and Peter W. Williams, 3:1727-41. New York: Scribners, 1988.

This essay is one of the best brief overviews of various materials designed for mass consumption that Americans have used in constructing a personal religiosity. Elzey ranges widely, looking at popular novels and personalities, Bible translations, religious artifacts intended for the home, and other media expressions that have a religious dimension. While Elzey views some of these as curiosities, he also argues that they are integral to the way ordinary men and women give expression to personal religious beliefs and styles. Elzey is among the most astute commentators on popular religion.

077 Fishwick, Marshall W. *Great Awakenings: Popular Religion and Popular Culture*. Binghamton, N.Y.: Haworth, 1994.

Fishwick in this study probes how popular culture has influenced American religion. He centers the book around five eras of religious revival. The final three focus on the period covered in this bibliography and constitute the bulk of the book: the modernist awakening, the celebrity preacher awakening, and the electronic awakening. Fishwick writes with witty engagement with the materials of popular culture, particularly when dealing with the twentieth century electronic explosion. Fishwick sees the interplay of popular religion and popular culture as a reflection of an ongoing yearning of the American people for a simple truth grounded in supernaturalism and revelation, yet affirming the gains of science and technology.

078   Flake, Carol. *Redemptorama: Culture, Politics, and the New Evangelicalism*. Garden City, N.Y.: Anchor, 1984.

Acknowledging her own Southern Baptist roots, Flake was spurred to scrutinize the rift between fundamentalism and secular culture by the surprise expressed by many media commentators over the mushrooming of Protestant evangelicalism in the United States in the 1970s. Writing for a lay audience, she claims that when evangelicals recognized their economic strength (Christian capitalism) and pursued engagement in the political arena, evangelicalism was transformed. Evangelical leaders such as Pat Robertson accepted the secular premises that "bigger is better" and that religious individuals should be regarded as consumers or tourists. Much of what comes within Flake's purview are expressions of an evangelical religiosity that cannot be tied to a particular religious institution. For example, she looks at the Christian Yellow Pages, a nondenominational booklet identifying businesses and commercial establishments owned by Protestant evangelicals that is intended to guide other evangelicals in their choice of merchants and the like. She also recognizes the import of much literature pitched to the masses that reinforces the broad contours of an evangelical way of looking at the world even though not all writers may themselves be evangelicals. Flake, for example, assesses the significance of the writings of Phyllis Schafly and Mirabel Morgan that call for adherence to traditional gender roles for women and non-denominational groups such as the Fellowship of Christian Athletes that advocate a muscular style of Christian religiosity for men.

079 Flowers, Ronald B. *Religion in Strange Times: The 1960s and 1970s*.
Macon, Ga.: Mercer University Press, 1984.

This book supplies chapters on the major currents that gave new shape to
popular religious consciousness during the "strange" decades of the 1960s and
1970s. Flowers singles out the beginnings of the evangelical resurgence, the
neo-charismatic movements, the fascination with alternative forms of spirituality
often dubbed the "cult" movement, the impact of both black theology and
feminist thought, and new issues in church-state relations for scrutiny. He also
includes two chapters that examine the larger social and cultural context that
gave these impulses credibility. Each chapter contains a brief, but helpful
bibliography of related works that offer more detailed examination of specific
topics.

080 Frankiel, Sandra Sizer. "California and the Southwest." In *Encyclopedia
of the American Religious Experience*, ed. by Charles H. Lippy and Peter W.
Williams, 3:1509-23. New York: Scribners, 1988.

Scholars have long recognized that geographical region is a significant factor in
influencing the shape and style of religious life. In this essay, Frankiel focusses
on California and the Southwest, noting how a sense of separation from much
of the rest of the nation and the character of those Euro-Americans attracted to
the region brought a lively interest in then unconventional forms of religious
expression.   Many experimented with religious alternatives of the day,
frequently crafting viable religious world views by mixing beliefs and practices
from many sources. Such eclecticism is basic to much popular religion.

081   Frankiel, Sandra Sizer.   *California's Spiritual Frontiers: Religious
Alternatives in Anglo-Protestantism, 1850-1910*.   Berkeley: University of
California Press, 1988.

Frankiel here expands treatment of many of the themes suggested in the essay
identified in the previous entry. For those interested in popular religion, the
most provocative sections deal with the appeal of metaphysical movements and
beliefs, particularly those associated with New Thought, Theosophy, and
Christian Science. Frankiel claims that when traditional religious institutions
were unable to provide the kind of personal and social stability that those who
were populating California needed, they turned to metaphysical movements
because they offered a sense of personal satisfaction and control in a setting
where much remained uncertain or tentative.

082 Gallup, George, and Jim Castelli. *The People's Religion: American Faith in the 90s*. New York: Macmillan, 1989.

Gallup and Castelli directly address several issues germane to the examination of popular religion, although that is not their stated aim. Their concern is to ascertain precisely what ordinary Americans actually believe, what impact those beliefs have on their daily life, and what Americans want to get from religion. They conclude that Americans remain committed to a belief in the supernatural, albeit somewhat nebulously defined, and that they look to religion to give them not only answers to situations that threaten to unravel whatever meaning they have in life, but also for a sense of personal comfort and satisfaction. Poll figures provide data documenting recent trends such as the increased popular belief in angels and other paranormal phenomena. Gallup and Castelli also include the results of polls treating such topics as abortion, political involvement, home schooling, gun control, and homosexuality.

083 Gallup, George, and Sarah Jones. *100 Questions and Answers: Religion in America*. Princeton, N.J.: Princeton Religion Research Center, 1989.

The 100 questions appraised in this book are drawn from various surveys conducted by the Gallup organization for the Princeton Religion Research Center. They reveal that by all measurable standards Americans remain among the most religious people on the planet. An extraordinarily high percentage of Americans claim belief in God, membership in a religious group, regular attendance at religious services, and a belief that religious values and ethics should play an important role in the larger society. What is significant is that particular religious affiliation matters little in all these matters; polls cited especially show that Protestants and Catholics are very similar in personal outlook. That suggests in turn that Americans may desire to have a religious label derived from membership in a particular religious group, but it matters little to which one a person belongs. The material here suggests that the lively sense of the supernatural basic to popular religion flourishes in the United States. At the same time, the statistics presented suggest several paradoxes. While Americans are more content than others with the religious groups to which they belong, fewer believe that religion is as able to offer solutions or resolutions of human problems than formerly. Although around one-third of American claim to have experiences a powerful personal religious Awakening, the percentage who believe that religion is an important influence in their lives dropped from three-quarters to just over a half since 1950.

084 Gallup, George, Jr., and David Poling. *The Search for America's Faith*. Nashville, Tenn.: Abingdon, 1980.

This study emerged from polls conducted in the 1970s and sought to project religious trends in the United States for the 1980s. Their efforts were predicated on the assumption that strong religious institutions are integral to maintaining a vital religious life within the larger culture. Hence they sought to identify what alienated people from religious groups in the expectation that the religious institutions would respond to consumer concerns in a way to keep them happy and involved. For example, Gallup and Poling found that American Catholicism was slowly recovering from the internal turmoil that followed on the Second Vatican Council of the 1960s, but that there remained a significant amount of dissent because self-identified Catholics disagreed with the official position of Catholicism as an institution on issues such as use of artificial means of birth control. At the same time, Gallup and Poling found that while those in adolescence and young adulthood distanced themselves from organized religion, they still saw themselves as being religious. So, too, the 41% of the population classified as "unchurched" or without formal religious affiliation: they were searching for some framework of meaning for their lives, but felt that the traditional religious organizations were incapable of providing it. Although Gallup and Poling were distraught over the proportion of Americans who were then without formal religious affiliation because they were convinced that the health of religion depended on traditional organizations, they unwittingly provided evidence for the pervasive presence of popular religiosity.

085 Goethals, M. Gregor. "In Search of Public Symbols." *Union Seminary Quarterly Review* 37 (1982): 230-38.

Goethals, who has written extensively about televangelism, here draws on sociologist Max Weber's notion that humans are constantly seeking to fulfill the basic need of the human mind to make sense of reality. He then explores the range of images used in television to promote Protestant evangelism. He concludes that there are many competing symbols, with none working effectively for the public as a whole. Goethals feels there should be a viable public symbolic structure, but questions whether American society has become so pluralistic as to render a single public symbol system an impossibility.

086 Hadden, Jeffrey K., and Theodore E. Long, eds. *Religion and Religiosity in America: Studies in Honor of Joseph H. Fichter*. New York: Crossroad, 1983.

Sociologist Joseph Fichter devoted much of his work in the 1960s and 1970s to new religious movements in an effort to dispel the aura of fear and anxiety that surrounded them as well as to understand why people from conventional religious backgrounds or no particular religious background were drawn to them. Hence several of the ten essays that comprise this book treat similar issues. For the student of popular religion, however, three of the essays (one each by Andrew Abbott, Theodore E. Long, and Michael Kearl) prove of special interest for they look at the so-called "new therapy." Taken together, these essays see the fascination with popular psychology and self-help movements as akin to magic in the religious sense. That is, the various new therapies allow practitioners to manipulate and control a realm of power (whether it be an inner power or an external supernatural one is irrelevant) in order to find inner happiness and a sense of self-fulfillment.

087 Harrell, David E., Jr., ed. *Varieties of Southern Evangelicalism.* Macon, Ga.: Mercer University Press, 1981.

Several essays in this collection deserve the attention of those interested in popular religion. Martin Marty gives an enlightening overview of the popular gains made by evangelicals in the 1960s and 1970s, linking them to the style of much Southern religiosity. Three other essays complement Marty's. Historian Wayne Flynt probes the diversity that prevails among Southern evangelicals when it comes to attitudes about how or even whether religion should be involved in social issues; David E. Harrell, Jr., reminds readers that Southern evangelical culture has been the seed bed for countless small sectarian movements that emerge initially from the people themselves; and Samuel Hill sketches in broad strokes some of the features of popular Southern white Protestant piety, calling particular attention to its certainty of its belief in the supernatural. Joseph R. Washington, Jr., argues that the style of Christianity that has developed among African Americans represents a folk religion (in the classic sense of being shaped by the experiences of common people) with a special emphasis on freedom, justice, dignity, and equal opportunity in this world predicated on a profound sense of the Ultimate. Finally, William Martin offers a penetrating appraisal of the work of evangelist Billy Graham, noting that much of Graham's stature stemmed from his uncanny ability to fathom the popular mind.

088 Hatch, Nathan O., and Mark A. Noll, eds. *The Bible in American Culture: Essays in Cultural History.* New York: Oxford University Press, 1982.

While the Bible has served as the official sacred text for the traditions of Christianity and Judaism that have dominated formal religious life in the United States, its impact has not been limited to them. The essays in this collection follow a chronological scheme, stretching from the colonial period to the twentieth century. Many were first developed as papers presented at a conference at Wheaton College in 1979. For the period since 1880, four offer insight into popular use of the Bible. Timothy Weber surveys fundamentalist attitudes and uses of scripture; Grant Wacker notes the demise of a cultural consensus grounded in a broad, evangelical Protestant notion of Christian civilization; Richard J. Mouw argues that twentieth century American Protestants have no single way of understanding the Bible; and Gerald P. Fogarty rehearses the saga of efforts to provide a vernacular text of the Bible for Catholics that would meet doctrinal norms set by the hierarchy as well as changing trends in Catholic biblical scholarship.

089 Heenan, Edward F., ed. *Mystery, Magic, and Miracle: Religion in a Post-Aquarian Age.* Englewood Cliffs, N.J.: Prentice-Hall, 1973.

Heenan brought together this collection of essays to provide insight into the new spirituality that appeared to be emerging in the United States in the late 1960s when the fascination with Eastern religions and other alternative forms of spirituality captured popular attention. Of particular interest for understanding some of the contours of popular religion is "Religion in the Age of Aquarius: A Conversation with Harvey Cox and T. George Harris" (pp. 15-28). In this piece, Cox attributes the renewed intrigue with astrology, long a dimension of popular religion because it holds out a means of coming into harmony with unseen supernatural forces that pervade the universe, to a need to recapture fantasy and festivity in a culture obsessed with rationalism.

090 Herberg, Will. *Protestant, Catholic, Jew: An Essay in American Religious Sociology.* Garden City, N.Y.: Doubleday, 1960.

First appearing in 1955, Herberg's study is now a recognized classic in probing the ways religion functions in American society and how certain cultural trappings have assumed religious functions. He argues that by the mid-twentieth century it no longer mattered whether one's formal religious identification marked the individual as a Protestant, Catholic, or Jew. Those labels had become functionally equivalent as badges of good citizenship; what mattered was that one had a label of some sort. Herberg goes on to demonstrate that beneath this functional equivalency lay a religion of the American way of life that others would call a civil religion. For Herberg, however, this common religion was marked by consumerism and threatened to erode an authentic, more prophetic faith and abiding commitment.

091 Hoge, Dean R., Benton Johnson, and Donald A. Luidens. *Vanishing Boundaries: The Religion of Mainline Protestant Baby Boomers.* Louisville,

Ky.: Westminster/John Knox, 1993.

Hoge, Johnson, and Luidens studied the religious beliefs and practices of several hundred early baby boomers (born between 1947 and 1956) who had been confirmed as Presbyterians. In middle age, although most were no longer Presbyterians, the majority did retain formal religious affiliation. The most important aspect of this study centers on the similarities these sociologists found between those who were still active Presbyterians and those who were not church members but regarded themselves as religious, groups that together counted for half of the sample. Both groups shared features of what the researchers called "lay liberalism': a concern for personal spirituality, insistence on individual choice in matters of belief, an abiding appreciation for pluralism and tolerance, very selective commitment to particular religious institutions (and other social institutions), and a willingness to draw on many religious traditions and belief systems in the construction of personal world views. All these features are also marks of popular religiosity, especially the eclecticism involved in developing individual constellations of belief.

092 Huber, Richard M. *The American Idea of Success*. New York: McGraw-Hill, 1971.

Huber contends that Americans have been captivated by the idea of success from the late nineteenth century onward because success brings with it power. In turn, power is thought to guarantee happiness and a feeling of inner peace and fulfillment. Several of the figures and phenomena that Huber analyzes are central to the story of popular religion in modern America. He looks, for example, at the popular preacher and lecturer Russell H. Conwell who purportedly delivered his "Acres of Diamonds" talk, in which he claimed that God demanded people to be successful, more than 6000 times. He also scrutinizes the many expressions of the Gospel of Wealth, noting that the fabulously rich such as Andrew Carnegie and John D. Rockefeller all believed that their religiosity contributed to their material success and that God had given them wealth for a purpose. Huber devotes a chapter to Dale Carnegie, whose *How to Win Friends and Influence People* represents one of the first expressions of what has become a voluminous literature on self-help and another chapter to Norman Vincent Peale whose writings on positive thinking, classic examples of popular religiosity, convinced millions that they could use God as a means of getting ahead in the larger society.

093 Jorstad, Erling. *Being Religious in America: The Deepening Crisis over Public Faith*. Minneapolis: Augsburg, 1986.

This monograph, which has a helpful bibliography at the end, questions whether the presumed common values that scholars have claimed provided social cohesion and a sense of common identity for the American people actually do work that way. Jorstad scrutinizes particularly at the connections between religion and patriotism, the way increasing religious pluralism has extended the boundaries of religious freedom, controversies over the legitimate role of religious bodies in influencing public policy-making, and the debates over the place of religion in the public schools. The implication is that a lack of consensus over common values ("public faith") has generated many of the contemporary controversies in both the religious and the political sectors.

094 Jorstad, Erling. *Holding Fast, Pressing On: Religion in America in the 1980s*. Westport, Conn.: Greenwood, 1990.

Jorstad identifies three trends that marked American religious life in the 1980s: struggles within the established Christian religious denominations, a different kind of struggle that ensued among evangelicals as they carved out a new prominence in American life that ignored institutional identity, and a very privatized, personal quest for meaning in life that drew on both mainline religion and evangelical currents, but also moved in a very eclectic and idiosyncratic fashion. For students of popular religion, the analyses of the latter two trends is of particular interest. Jorstad attributes some of the renewal of evangelicalism to deft use of mass media and believes it became a genuine popular movement as it found expression in so-called contemporary Christian music, parachurch groups, and best-selling mass market literature. The search for the self, albeit a very private one, Jorstad sees as part of a larger concern for fulfillment in human relationships spurred in part by the women's movement and sustained by the array of options captured under the designation "New Age."

095 Lippy, Charles H. "Waiting for the End: The Social Context of American Apocalyptic Religion." In *The Apocalyptic Vision in America: Interdisciplinary Essays on Myth and Culture*, ed. by Lois P. Zamora, 37-63. Bowling Green, Ohio: Bowling Green University Popular Press, 1982.

In this essay, Lippy looks at the millennialist impulse that has been a recurring feature of American popular religion. His particular concern is to discern what sorts of social conditions give greater plausibility to millennialist ideas. Lippy insists that popular expressions of millennialist thinking, ranging from hymnody to film, must be taken seriously as part of the way individuals seek to give the past, the present, and the future some overarching meaning.

096 McDannell, Colleen. *The Christian Home in Victorian America, 1840-1900.* Bloomington: Indiana University Press, 1986.

Scholars have long claimed that religion became domesticated in the Victorian era, that authentic religion flourished primarily in the private sphere of the home under the watchful eyes of women who had become seen as more spiritual than men and hence as wives and mothers had a duty to provide religious nurture to their children and families. McDannell probes the material culture of the Victorian era, including in her purview images of the ideal architectural design for both the Protestant and Catholic home, religious artifacts intended for use in decorating the home, and magazines and other literature designed to aid women in fulfilling their gender roles as spiritual voices. But because the home was the center of private life, relocating authentic religion to the domestic sphere promoted the privatization of religious experience and expression that is essential to popular religiosity.

097 Marty, Martin E. *The Public Church: Mainline--Evangelical--Catholic.* New York: Crossroad, 1981.

This book derives from numerous lectures Marty delivered on campuses and at other public forums in the late 1970s. Marty's concern here is in some ways the obverse of popular religiosity. He is content to recognize that modernization, among other forces, has made the particulars of religious belief increasingly a matter of the private sphere. Marty argues that one consequence of this relocation of religion has been a bewilderment in determining how what is essentially personal and private, even when shared with a tribe or group of like-minded others, can relate to the public sphere or realm of common life. Marty's efforts are directed to discerning ways in which Christians of many traditions and institutional backgrounds might regain a sense of common concern for the public arena, not necessarily in terms of types of political action or advocating single-issue political agendas, but rather in terms of a shared commitment to the common weal or common good of the citizenry. Students of popular religiosity will appreciate his struggle to develop a common ground from the highly pluralistic and idiosyncratic clusters of personal beliefs that prevail in contemporary American life.

098 Mead, Sidney. *The Nation with the Soul of a Church.* Reprint, Macon, Ga.: Mercer University Press, 1985.

Mead's well-known collection of essays wrestles with the subtle ways a religious consciousness that is not confined to any one formal religious tradition has pervaded American national identity from the arrival of the first Europeans in

North America. As the nation developed as a political entity, there remained a substratum that was distinctly religious. Within that substratum flourished a belief that the nation and its people had a mission ordained by divine providence and that its common values were not limited to the political realm but had a transcendent quality. One consequence has been the conviction of the American people, according to Mead, that they had a special destiny among nations that set them apart from other peoples. This constellation of ideas about morality, Deity, and providence, based on a radical monotheism rooted in reason and on the right of private judgment, constitute what Mead calls the "religion of the Republic."

099 Miller, Douglas. "Popular Religion of the 1950's: Norman Vincent Peale and Billy Graham." *Journal of Popular Culture* 9 (Summer 1975): 66-76.

Miller argues that religiosity permeated popular culture in the United States during the 1950s. For evidence he points to the tremendous increase in sales of the Bible, the religious lyrics of many popular songs, and the themes of numerous movies. Because none of these was denomination-specific, they represent genuine popular expressions of religiosity. Miller looks at two figures, Norman Vincent Peale and Billy Graham, to make the case that Americans wanted a sense of personal well-being from religion. In Peale's case, that came from a "cult of reassurance" fostered by the insistence that individuals could help themselves become happy and fulfilled; in Graham's, it emerged from the emphasis on an experience of personal conversion. But the essential feature that brings Peale and Graham together for Miller is their emphasis on the individual.

100 Moses, William J. "Civil Religion and the Crisis of Civil Rights." *Drew Gateway* 57 (Winter 1986): 24-42.

Critics have often claimed that the idea of an American civil religion spoke primarily to the experience of males of northern or western European ancestry. In this article, Moses examines how African Americans in the nineteenth and early twentieth centuries drew on the rhetoric of the developing civil religion to condemn slavery and call for racial integration in American society. At the same time, Moses rightly calls attention to the rejection of that rhetoric among black nationalists because of the conviction that language and ideology used to bolster oppression could never speak to the lived experience of African Americans.

101 Murphy, Larry. "Apocalypse and Millennium in America." *Explor* 4

(Spring 1978): 58-65.

In this very brief essay, Murphy challenges some of the traditional thinking that
sees apocalyptic themes as integral to American self-identity. He does not deny
their recurring presence, but questions whether millennialist images have been
more dominant in the minds of interpreters than in the minds of ordinary people
as they sought to make sense out of their lives.

102 Nye, Russell B. *The Unembarrassed Muse: The Popular Arts in America.*
New York: Dial, 1970.

Nye was among the first contemporary scholars to insist that popular culture and
its artifacts deserved careful analysis if one hoped to understand the dynamics
of culture. This work represents one of his many efforts to bring aspects of
popular culture to the forefront. Curiously, however, he gives relatively little
attention to popular arts with a specifically religious dimension. One chapter,
"Home and Jesus", traces the development of popular fiction, much of it
targeted to a female audience, concerned primarily with religious morality, but
rarely moving beyond the sentimental. Even when such literature became
melodramatic, as in the fiction of Harold Bell Wright who reached the zenith of
his popularity in the opening three decades of the twentieth century, the result
was still a simplistic affirmation that Christian faith and Christian principles
would cause all personal problems to fade. Nye gives considerable attention to
popular music and popular art, but, except for early American hymnody,
neglects to include religious music and omits a discussion of religious art that
was intended for domestic use (e.g., Warner Sallman's extraordinarily popular
magazine cover of the head of Christ). Those who wish to mine the fields of
popular religious music and art, however, do have in Nye's work an admirable
model.

103 Phy, Allene, ed. *The Bible and Popular Culture in America. The Bible
in American Culture* 2. Philadelphia: Fortress Press; Chico, Calif.: Scholars
Press, 1985.

This slim volume is so rich in its offerings that several of the essays will receive
individual entries. The introduction makes a compelling case for the careful
examination of Christian religious representations in many genres of popular
culture, claiming that their overall aim is to make Jesus a contemporary. That
is, popular religious forms transform the ancient or the eternal into the
contemporaneous. Editor Phy cites two examples to make her point. The
Broadway musical "Godspell" and the rock opera "Jesus Christ Super Star" both
drew on biblical and centuries-old religious stories to fashion a twentieth

century figure of Jesus. Phy's point is that popular culture serves as a vehicle to bring the supernatural into every day life in ways that ordinary men and women can appreciate and appropriate.

104 Princeton Religion Research Center and the Gallup Organization, Inc. *The Unchurched American*. Princeton, N.J.: Princeton Religion Research Center, 1978.

Using data compiled over several years as a result of numerous Gallup polls, this study sketches a provocative portrait of the 41% of the American population over eighteen years of age that in the mid-1970s claimed no affiliation with an organized religious group. The aim of the study was to provide religious institutions with clues about what they might do to gain some of that 41% as official members. Not surprisingly from the perspective of popular religiosity, however, the unaffiliated were by and large as personally religious as those who were formal members. That is, they still claimed belief in God and still espoused religiously-based values. Where the unaffiliated differed the most was in lacking confidence in traditional religious institutions to meet personal spiritual needs. In other words, the unaffiliated had developed a personal, popular religiosity in the wake of a perceived vacuum within traditional religion.

105 Real, Michael R. *Mass-Mediated Culture*. New York: Prentice-Hall, 1977.

Students of popular culture will take interest in the opening chapter on the significance of mass-mediated culture and the concluding one on theory. Those with a particular interest in popular religion will focus on the chapter titled "Billy Graham: Mass Medium" (pp. 152-205). Real uses six telecasts from different Graham crusades to define an ethnography and exegetical method for popular culture analysis. He wishes to make a distinction between mass culture and popular culture, claiming that Graham's deft use of media places him more in the former orbit. Real notes that Graham adapted the order of his crusade service for television in order to have greater audience appeal. He offers a scathing critique of Graham's message, insisting that Graham simply gives people what they want--a ready solution to everyday problems. By making religious and moral issues matters of individual, private concern, however, the Graham depicted by Real nourishes popular religiosity. But because this religiosity makes people feel good about themselves and their place in the world, Real insists that it is a powerful illustration of Marx's view that religion functions as an "opiate" for the masses.

106 Reichley, A. James. "Religion and the Future of Politics." *Political Science Quarterly* 101 (1986): 23-47.

Reichley in this essay covers territory now familiar to many. His interest is to probe how the religious identity of ordinary men and women relates to their political orientation. He looks at five clusters: white evangelical Protestants, Roman Catholics, Jews, African-American Protestants, and mainline white Protestants. Reichley argues that the surge in political strength of white evangelical Protestants could diminish should the economy take a drastic turn downward, that Roman Catholics have been drawn to the Republican Party because of its stand on social issues such as abortion, that Jews have likewise become more conservative but remain way of latent anti-Semitism among white evangelical Protestants, and that mainline Protestants have become increasingly conservative political even as their leaders have remained more liberal and chary of the motives of conservative politicians. Even the historic identification of African Americans with the Democratic Party, reinforced by fears associated with Barry Goldwater's Republican presidential race in 1964, has been weakened.

107 Reichley, A. James. *Religion in American Public Life.* Washington, D.C.: Brookings Institution, 1988.

In this carefully-documented study, Reichley traces the history of the interconnections between religion and politics in the United States. He follows the development of several models, ranging from the separationist that sees no place for religion trying to influence public life overtly to the interventionist, that is exactly the opposite. Reichley shows how the founding generations assumed that religious values would penetrate common life, but he then demonstrates how that assumption has been challenged as he looks at how the First Amendment has been interpreted and at examples of religious involvement in political action from 1790 to 1985. In an insightful concluding chapter, Reichley makes the case that democracy requires a moral basis to be effective, claiming that religion has historically provided that base. However, he also warns against religious fanaticism as indicative of the way religion can also undermine democracy.

108 Roof, Wade Clark. "American Religion in Transition: A Review and Interpretation of Recent Trends." *Social Compass* 31 (1984): 273-89.

Of contemporary sociologists, Roof has been among the most adamant that the period since the 1960s has witnessed an amazingly increased privatization of religion in America linked to the ostensible decline in commitment to particular religious institutions unleashed by, for example, the Second Vatican Council (1962-1965) in Roman Catholicism and the American youth culture of the 1960s. The mobility of American society over the last three decades has also generated more switching between religious institutions among those who maintain formal membership and more dropping out (at least on a temporary basis) of active involvement in a formal religious organization. Yet Roof, as others, notes that those who drop out as well as those who remain unaffiliated do not differ greatly from the rest of the population when it comes to personal beliefs, suggesting again the deep imprint of popular religiosity on the larger culture.

109 Roof, Wade Clark. *A Generation of Seekers: The Spiritual Journeys of the Baby Boom Generation.* San Francisco: HarperSanFrancisco, 1993.

Based on extensive surveys and representative, in-depth interviews, this portrait of the post-World War II baby boom generation shatters some long-held ideas, but confirms the powerful presence of popular religiosity in the United States. Characterized as defiant of traditional authority, including religious authority, during their formative years, boomers were thought to have cast aside religion because they tended not to maintain formal religious affiliation. Yet in coming to maturity, many took on some identification with organized religious groups. At the same time, Roof's study confirms that the absence of formal religious affiliation did not mean an absence of spirituality or spiritual concerns. Rather, the boomers were carving out personal world views of an eclectic sort, thus sustaining the role of popular religiosity in American life. Roof also demonstrates that what the boomers want out of religion is very much on par with what others have claimed to seek, namely a sense of personal fulfillment and inner peace. What set the boomers apart was their willingness to probe alternative forms of spirituality and their readiness to construct idiosyncratic and highly personal belief systems. Yet, as Roof also demonstrates, the individualism inherent in this understanding is not necessarily antagonistic to participation in religious communities; but boomers define the extent and limits of their participation rather than letting the communities do it for them. All this is also consistent with the assertion that an undercurrent of popular religiosity pervades American life.

110 Roof, Wade Clark, ed. *Religion in America Today.* *Annals of the American Academy of Political and Social Sciences* 480. Beverly Hills, Calif.: SAGE Publications, 1985.

Several essays in this anthology attend to matters of popular religion. Three especially merit comment. Patrick McNamara looks at American Catholicism and finds that Catholics are increasingly able to construct personal belief systems that may be at variance with the official doctrine and teaching of the church as an institution, yet draw on a wider range of Catholics sensibilities. He cites, for example, the diverse views of American Catholics on issues such as papal infallibility and birth control. What this means is that Catholics are shaping a popular religiosity that is related to but not identical with the religiosity endorsed by the church as an institution. Sociologist Robert Wuthnow scrutinizes what he calls the new religious pluralism, the range of popular religious expression that crosses institutional lines in a variety of ways: the Moral Majority phenomenon, the pro-life clusters, the charismatic movement. While Wuthnow believes that all these may revitalize formal religious institutions, he attributes their emergence in part to the bureaucratic inertia of established religious bodies that makes them unable to respond to the changing needs and concerns of their own constituencies. Finally, pollster George Gallup calls attention to a rising interest in religion among Americans who are yearning for spiritual moorings, many because they seek a way to increase personal self-esteem and in turn gain greater inner peace and happiness. But traditional religious institutions do not seem to offer the kind of spiritual thrust that people are seeking; hence they turn to alternatives. Or, although Gallup does not make this point, they construct private, personal belief systems that work for them.

111 Roof, Wade Clark, and William McKinney. *American Mainline Religion: Its Changing Shape and Future*. New Brunswick, N.J.: Rutgers University Press, 1987.

Spurred by the steady erosion of membership among the Protestant denominations once designated as "mainline" because of their dominance and widespread cultural influence, Roof and McKinney here echo themes articulated by numerous commentators on the contemporary religious scene for they attribute much of the loss to a failure of the mainline groups to address matters of personal spirituality. The immersion of mainline religious groups in social issues such as the civil rights movement of the 1960s apparently deflected attention to matters of personal spirituality. The result has been an ongoing relegation of spirituality to the private sphere (where popular religion flourishes). As well, Roof and McKinney highlight the growing attraction of special interest groups that meet specific needs but whose participants are not restricted to a single religious group. To survive, they suggest that the mainline groups must more directly meet the needs of Americans for a deep, inner spirituality.

112 Ruthven, Malise. *The Divine Supermarket: Shopping for God in America*. New York: Morrow, 1989.

Ruthven, who hails from Britain, sets out on a journey in the United States that will retrace the route taken by the Mormons from their genesis in upstate New York to their establishment of a near theocracy in Utah and surrounding areas. Along the way, there are many detours. What baffles the openly agnostic Ruthven is the pluralism and individuality that mark contemporary American religious life. The former he views as alien and exotic, perhaps because his own native culture has long been under the sway of an officially-established Church of England, and from that negative perspective he derives the appellation of the divine supermarket. The latter he cannot really comprehend for he assumes that authentic religion is that captured in the formal teachings and practices of a recognized religious institution. Thus he claims that a place like Dallas, Texas, is not religious, despite the presence of megachurches and despite the obvious presence of what he labels the stuff of religion (personal piety and devotion). Rather, he sees personal religiosity merely as "lip service" paid to religion precisely because it is so individualistic. In other words, Ruthven offers an outsider's glimpse of popular religiosity, although he fails to appreciate its power and its function.

113 Schroeder, W. Widick, *et al.* *Suburban Religion: Churches and Synagogues in the American Experience.* Chicago: Center for the Scientific Study of Religion, 1974.

Two chapters of this work are relevant for understanding the pulse of popular religiosity. The second chapter, "America's Public Religion: The Privatization of Suburban Churches and Synagogues," notes how the mobility of the American population has diminished loyalty to particular religious traditions. The result has been to minimize doctrinal distinctiveness; such in turn fosters popular religiosity seen as the individual construction of a religious belief system that may draw in part, but not exclusively, on established religious traditions. Another dimension of the privatization of congregations stems from the racial and economic homogeneity of many suburban enclaves; religious groups are comprised of persons of similar racial and economic status than persons committed to formal doctrine. The sixth chapter, "Private Morality," touches much more directly on the foundations of popular religiosity in its claim that for most suburban Americans, religious institutions are of little influence in determining morals and ethics; they are regarded purely as personal and private matters.

114 Smith, Timothy L. "Lay Initiative in the Religious Life of American Immigrants, 1880-1950." In *Anonymous Americans: Explorations in Nineteenth-Century Social History,* ed. by Tamara Hareven, 214-49. Englewood Cliffs, N.J.: Prentice-Hall, 1971.

Smith's essay is part of an anthology intended as a source book of supplementary readings for courses in American social history. Smith calls attention to the vitality of religion in village life in central and Eastern Europe, the major sources of immigration to the United States in the later nineteenth century. One result was the adding of layers of ethnic overlay to the beliefs and practices of formal religion in the village context. When immigration came, this fusion of the ethnic and the religious was maintained, largely because of lay initiative. Many priests and religious leaders in the United States frowned on that which was peculiarly ethnic. Yet in the American context, the ethnic took on a new dimension, for ethnic identity led to the formation of many voluntary mutual aid societies that provided assistance of many sorts to new or recent immigrants. Instructive for students of popular religion is Smith's discussion of the interconnection of the ethnic and the religious, for from that fusion emerged many of the strains of popular piety that marked immigrant life.

115 Speak, David M. "The Renascence of Civil Religion in the U.S.: Weber, Lincoln, Reagan, and the American Polity." In *Religion and Philosophy in the United States of America*, ed. by Peter Freese, 2:697-711. Essen, Germany: Verlag Die Blaue Eule, 1987.

Speak suggests that part of the appeal of Ronald Reagan was his charismatic ability to inspire ordinary Americans to revive the symbols and rhetoric associated with the American civil religion. Using Max Weber's classic distinction between charisma of person and charisma of office, Speak suggests that Reagan's popularity clearly resulted from his exhibiting charisma of person. Although Reagan theoretically possessed charisma of office as President, he was not able to function in the priestly role that went with the office.

116 Szasz, Ferenc Morton. *The Divided Mind of Protestant America, 1880-1930*. University, Ala.: University of Alabama Press, 1982.

Szasz identifies the main issues dividing Protestant America between 1880 and 1930 as evolutionary theory, the value of comparative religion, and the use of higher criticism in the analysis of scripture. He gives attention, for example, to how all of these played into the fundamentalist-modernist controversy of the 1920s. But Szasz also argues that the debates only slowly reached the popular level; for most of the period they were of primary concern to religious professionals and bureaucrats. Ordinary folk went about the business of being religious much the same as they had done for generations. Hence Szasz looks at some of the literature that shaped the popular religious mind, particularly the novels of Margaret Deland and Mrs. Humphrey Ward as well as the best-selling *In His Steps*. When the arguments over higher criticism did come into popular view, they reached people in the pew more through articles in popular magazines like *Cosmopolitan* than the pronouncements of religious authorities. Szasz's analysis is valuable in pointing out that there is frequently a gap between the issues that rage among intellectuals and what concerns folk in their daily lives. It is also helpful in ferreting out the processes by which those issues are gradually mediated to ordinary women and men.

117 Tate, Allen. "Remarks on Southern Religion." In *I'll Take My Stand: The South and the Agrarian Tradition*, by Twelve Southerners, 155-75. Baton Rouge: Louisiana State University Press, 1930.

Although he does not use the term, Tate sketches some features of a distinctively Southern civil religion linked to antebellum agrarian culture. Basic to that regional civil religion was a popular belief in a God possessed of inscrutable power. He suggests that a gradual bifurcation between reason and religion had left Southerners without a viable religious mythology, substituting an emphasis on a practical, workable "half-religion" for a faith that had once been prevalent. Still controversial is Tate's claim that had Southerners maintained sufficient faith in their own kind of God, their agrarian culture would be have suffered defeat.

118 Tyson, Ruel W., Jr., James L. Peacock, and Daniel W. Patterson, eds. *Diversities of Gifts: Field Studies in Southern Religion*. Urbana: University of Illinois Press, 1988.

This collection of essays offers a valuable look at elements of popular religiosity that prevail among Protestants who belong to independent congregations. That is, their churches are not affiliated with larger denominations. The field work that buttresses these studies was conducted in North Carolina, but rightly assumes that they are a microcosm for a larger regional religious culture. All the studies highlight the way gesture, often expressed in ecstatic experience, serves to express an abiding belief in the reality of a supernatural realm of power, as do the emphasis on both subjective, inner experience as the locus of authentic spirituality and an understanding of scripture, although varied, as a divinely-mandated guide for individual belief and behavior.

119 Weber, Timothy. *Living in the Shadow of the Second Coming: American Premillennialism, 1875-1982*. Enl. ed. Grand Rapids, Mich.: Zondervan, 1983.

Millennial currents have long been part of the popular religious consciousness in the United States. Weber gives a penetrating analysis of the premillennialist strand that became prominent in the later nineteenth century in the wake of the fury over higher criticism and evolution. His study is particularly germane to understanding popular religiosity for it appraises in detail some of the ways in which premillennialism filtered down to ordinary folk. Among the most important was the publication of the *Scofield Reference Bible*, based on clear premillennialist assumptions. For millions of American Protestants, this study Bible became the edition of choice for generations. Weber also highlights the way premillennialist advocates developed a network of auxiliary institutions, many not affiliated with a particular denomination, that trained church workers who in turn etched the premillennialist viewpoint into the minds of those with whom they labored. Among the more well-known is the Moody Bible Institute in Illinois. Weber examines as well some of the recent literature intended for a mass audience that perpetuates a premillennialist understanding of history, such as Hal Lindsey's best-selling *The Late, Great Planet Earth*.

120 Wilson, Charles Reagan. "American Heavens: Apollo and the Civil Religion." *Journal of Church and State* 26 (Spring 1984): 209-226.

The Apollo in the title refers to the moon mission, not the ancient Greek god. Wilson argues that the mission to land Americans on the moon reveals much about American public religion. For example, it served to demonstrate how science and technology had created an ideological framework for American culture as a scientific "city on a hill." It thus cast the apocalyptic, millennialist dimension of American self-understanding in a new way. Wilson notes, however, that ordinary Americans did not necessarily respond to the religious ramifications of the Apollo mission.

121 Wilson, Charles Reagan. *Baptized in Blood: The Civil Religion of the Lost Cause, 1865-1920.* Athens: University of Georgia Press, 1980.

Wilson persuasively argues that in the decades following Southern defeat in the Civil War there emerged a distinct, regional civil religion that sought to endow that defeat with a redemptive quality. By looking at such diverse phenomena as celebrations commemorating the service of Confederate veterans, funeral and memorial orations for Confederate heroes, and movements to erect monuments and the like in their honor, white Southerners were developing a cultural religion, albeit one rooted in nineteenth century evangelical Protestantism. Among its assumptions were the salvific role of suffering, the transformation of defeat into victory, and the purification of a way of life through the sacrificial shedding of blood. While all these are part of orthodox Christian understanding, white Southerners used them to affirm the validity of their antebellum values and way of life despite the transformations that were coming to their culture after the Civil War.

122 Wilson, Charles Reagan. "'God's Project': The Southern Civil Religion, 1920-1980." In *Religion and the Life of the Nation: American Recoveries*, ed. by Rowland A. Sherrill, 64-83. Urbana: University of Illinois Press, 1990.

Wilson here extends themes first advanced in his *Baptized in Blood*. He looks first at the Southern literary renaissance that perpetuated what became known as the agrarian tradition and flourished between 1920 and 1950. Allen Tate is one representative of that tradition, which continued to see the "lost cause" as creating a redemptive community. Next, Wilson turns attention to the civil rights movement and its impact on the entrenched patterns of segregation that prevailed in the South, showing that in the midst of the upheaval, there remained a conviction that Southerners were a chosen people, but a tragic people as well. Finally he comments on the events marking the centennial of the Civil War between 1960 and 1965 that once again reinforced a distinct regional identity, albeit without sentimentalization of the past.

123 Wilson, John F. *Public Religion in American Culture*. Philadelphia: Temple University Press, 1979.

Historian John Wilson is interested in the proposal that there is a civil or public religion in the United States, arguing that analysis of such constructs is a prerequisite to developing responsible study of American religion. He concludes that there is not a full-blown public religion, but that many dimensions of the common life of the American people may have religious aspects or functions. More to the point of Wilson's contention about the role of interpretive constructs, he makes the case that the very notion that there might be a civil religion, advanced so compellingly by Robert Bellah and others, represents what cultural anthropologists have called a revitalization movement. In other words, when Bellah made his proposal in the late 1960s, American culture was in a time of transition and crisis, and the hypothesis that there was a civil religion prompted a rethinking of the nature of the nation and the meaning of being an American that would bring renewed vitality to public life.

124 Woodrum, Eric, and Arnold Bell. "Race, Politics, and Religion in Civil Religion among Blacks." *Sociological Analysis* 49 (Winter 1989): 353-67.

Woodrum and Bell argue that African Americans have been less involved in American civil religion than whites because of the way that civil religion has

been used to perpetuate racism and discrimination.   While religiously
conservative whites are more likely to see their religiosity as implying a
sanctification of American government, the opposite holds true among African
Americans, except where political accommodationism has held sway. As well,
the more personally devout African Americans are, the more they are likely to
be critical of a civil religion for they are more attuned to the gaps between the
presumed ideology of the civil religion and the empirical realities of American
society.   Woodrum and Bell claim that the opposite holds true for white
Americans.

125 Wuthnow, Robert. *Christianity in the Twenty-First Century: Reflections
on the Challenges Ahead.* New York: Oxford University Press, 1993.

Princeton sociologist Wuthnow has been a prolific commentator on currents
marking the late twentieth-century religious scene in the United States. In this
book he assesses the implications of several trends he has highlighted in
numerous other works, such as the increasing privatization of religion in
American culture, the growing importance of special interest or single interest
small groups for religious life, and the expectation of ordinary men and women
that whatever religious beliefs and practices they espouse must function to give
them a sense of inner well-being and contentment. In this particular study,
Wuthnow looks at institutional, ethical, doctrinal, and political trends, arguing
that in each area what transpires in the twenty-first century will depend on
where Americans and religious institutions locate themselves on four continua:
individual-community,   diversity-uniformity,   liberalism-conservatism,   and
public-private.

126 Wuthnow, Robert. *God and Mammon in America.* New York: Free
Press, 1994.

Based on extensive survey data, Wuthnow seeks to unpack precisely what
ordinary Americans think about the connections between religion and economics.
But he goes well beyond attitudes toward particular economic systems to probe
how religious beliefs affect honesty on the job, links between economics and
social justice, whether religious views influence decision-making in the work
place, how beliefs may or may not influence charitable activity, and a host of
related issues. For the student of popular religiosity, the greatest asset of this
book is its demonstrating that ordinary Americans do not necessarily look to
organized religion for guidance or teaching about ethical behavior, attitudes
about work, and the like. Rather, they expect religion to confirm the rightness
of whatever ethical choices they have made, whatever actions they have taken,
and whatever attitudes they already hold. In other words, the private, highly

individualistic character of popular religiosity prevails over the doctrine and systematic ethical teaching of religious institutions.

127 Wuthnow, Robert. *The Restructuring of American Religion: Society and Faith Since World War II*. Princeton, N.J.: Princeton University Press, 1988.

This book represents Wuthnow's most sustained analysis of currents that have brought change to American religion in the last half century. He highlights the declining significance of denominationalism, the increasing relegation of morals and ethics to the arena of individual choice, the proliferation of special purpose groups as diverse as the Fellowship of Christian Athletes and the Freedom from Religion Foundation, the erosion of a civil religion that works to bring cohesiveness to the American people, and the rising significance of a strident religious conservatism. Many of these currents reinforce the understanding of popular religiosity, for as Wuthnow argues in chapter seven, "The Great Divide: Toward Religious Realignment", the formal categories of theology and religious labels have never reflected the religious pulse of ordinary people. Rather, personal experience, however defined, and seeing religion as an individual matter have always been paramount for the rank and file.

128 Zaretsky, Irving I., and Mark P. Leone, eds. *Religious Movements in Contemporary America*. Princeton, N.J.: Princeton University Press, 1974.

The essays in this book, unusual in being of uniformly high quality, deal with topics that range from the ritual structures of African-American music to religious dimensions of altered states of consciousness. Authors also discuss magical therapy, health, shamanism, faith healing, glossolalia, modern witchcraft, contemporary Pentecostalism, as well as specific groups such as the Hare Krishna movement and the devotees of Meher Baba. Several essays are more theoretical in nature, probing methods for analyzing religious currents and religious change.

4

Evangelicalism, Fundamentalism, and the Religious Right

129 Ammerman, Nancy Tatom. *Bible Believers: Fundamentalists in the Modern World.* New Brunswick, N.J.: Rutgers University Press, 1987.

Sociologist Ammerman provides an engaging look at the resurgent fundamentalism that has marked American religious life since the 1970s. She argues that some of the attractiveness of the fundamentalist style is its clear sense of authority, whether that authority is placed in the sacred text of the Bible or the preacher/pastor of a congregation. That authority perpetuates belief in a lively sense of supernatural power that ultimately governs human life in the present, as well as providing hope for its future destiny. The security that results enables fundamentalists to have a firm sense of control over their lives.

130 Anderson, Robert Mapes. *Vision of the Disinherited: The Makings of American Pentecostalism.* New York: Oxford University Press, 1979.

Anderson's study has become one of the standard works looking at the historical roots of contemporary Pentecostalism. His title implies his essential thesis: through an ecstatic experience of the power of the Holy Spirit, Pentecostalism brings those who are devoid of power in terms measured by society into an arena of superior power. As Pentecostalism has mushroomed in the twentieth century, the economic nuances of that thesis have become more muted, but the sense of submitting to the control of the supernatural has remained strong.

131 Baker, Tod A., Robert P. Steed, and Laurence W. Moreland, eds. *Religion and Politics in the South: Mass and Elite Perspectives.* New York: Praeger, 1983.

The authors identify the "mass" or popular perspective with evangelicalism, while fundamentalism forms the basis for the elite perspective. Using intricate sociological statistics, they claim that only a minority of evangelicals are thorough-going political conservatives and that the recent political activism among fundamentalism represents an unusual break in the modern fundamentalist avoidance of overt political involvement. At the same time, they call attention to the history of the interplay of popular religiosity and political life in the South that stretches back to the colonial period.

132 Balmer, Randall H. *Mine Eyes Have Seen the Glory: A Journey into the Evangelical Subculture in America.* New York: Oxford University Press, 1989.

Balmer's brilliant study, which formed the basis for a series by the same name that aired on public television, takes the reader to a range of local congregations and communities that serve as case studies to appraise the dynamics of contemporary evangelicalism. Balmer blends astute historical, sociological, and anthropological analysis with the appreciation of the participant-observer as he moves from group to group. He concludes that there are affective ties that link evangelicals together in their conviction of the reality of the divine presence in daily life.

133 Bird, B. "FGBMFI: Facing Frustrations and the Future." *Charisma* 11 (June 1986): 25-26, 28.

The Full Gospel Businessmen's Fellowship International (FGBMFI) is one of the flourishing parachurch movements that brings together primarily professional men of a Pentecostal persuasion across denominational lines. The group meets regularly for prayer and praise in those communities where it exists. One result is a network of like-minded business persons who, it is assumed, will support each other's professional endeavors. Another is the assumption that those who share common religious views and experiences, regardless of formal religious affiliation, are all honest and trustworthy persons. Dilemmas arise, however, when occasionally denominational particularities bring minor differences to the fore.

134 Bird, B. "The Legacy of Demos Shakarian." *Charisma* 11 (June 1986): 20-25.

This brief article highlights the work and personal religious experience of Demos Shakarian, who founded the Full Gospel Businessmen's Fellowship International in 1953. Shakarian was intent on forming an association where men would be free to express their spirituality in personal terms, for he believed that popular perceptions saw true, vibrant religiosity almost exclusively as a feminine phenomenon. In other words, Shakarian sought to provide a means for the expression of a male popular religiosity that was not limited to formal religious traditions or institutions.

135 Bloch-Hoell, Nils. *The Pentecostal Movement*. London: Allen and Unwin, 1964.

Appearing just as the neo-pentecostal movement was gaining ground, Bloch-Hoell's work is one of the better historical accounts of modern Pentecostalism, from the Azusa Street revivals in Los Angeles in 1906 to the mid-twentieth-century. He gives attention to some of the theological debates surrounding the validity of Pentecostal experience, noting that giving free rein to the power of the Holy Spirit makes it difficult for human institutions such as the church to control the results.

136 Bromley, David G., and Anson Shupe, eds. *New Christian Politics*. Macon, Ga.: Mercer University Press, 1984.

This collection contains several important essays that help illuminate the connection between popular evangelicalism and politics in contemporary America. By and large, evangelicalism is associated with televangelism, and several authors probe the political import of the use of religious television in both stirring political activism among viewers and shaping their political views. Hence the books is as much about the electronic church as it is about the resurgence of political conservatism connected to religion.

137 Bruce, Steve. *The Rise and Fall of the New Christian Right: Conservative Protestant Politics in America, 1978-1988*. New York: Oxford University Press, 1988.

A British sociologist, Bruce analyzes the emergence of the Christian right in American politics using interpretive constructs developed to study social movements. In his appraisal, much of the perceived strength of the Christian right was tied to Ronald Reagan. He concludes that by 1988, the Christian right had essentially failed in its hopes to transform American culture into a conservative Christian society because it had an exaggerated estimate of the support given to conservative politics by persons who were evangelicals and it underestimated the residual strength of more liberal viewpoints. Bruce issued one word of caution, however, in noting that he was describing the demise of a social movement that had not yet died when he wrote.

138   Carpenter, Joel A.   "Fundamentalist Institutions and the Growth of Evangelical Protestantism, 1929-1942." *Church History* 49 (1980): 62-75.

Carpenter is among the more astute analysts of contemporary fundamentalism who argues that, contrary to much traditional interpretation, fundamentalism was neither totally discredited nor forced into oblivion by its apparent defeat in the 1920s.   Rather, the intervening decades witnessed a quiet regrouping and mobilization. Carpenter shows how Chicago became the center of a developing evangelical network and how evangelicals used institutions ranging from schools and periodicals to Bible institutes and summer conferences to stem erosion and pave the way for later gain.

139   Carpenter, Joel A.   "The Fundamentalist Leaven and the Rise of an Evangelical United Front."   In *The Evangelical Tradition in America*. ed. by Leonard I. Sweet, 257-88.   Macon, Ga.: Mercer University Press, 1984.

In this piece, Carpenter offers more evidence for the diverse ways fundamentalists in the 1930s and 1940s especially were developing a broadly-based coalition. Although consigned to the religious margins by the media and most denominational bureaucracies, fundamentalists were forming associations and establishing connections through organizations such as the Christian Business Men's Committee and the National Association of Evangelicals that would provide a strong base for the contemporary resurgence of a conservative religious style. He also gives attention to some of the internal debates among fundamentalists, particularly those concerning whether maintaining doctrinal purity required separation from the larger society and religious world or whether there could be co-operation with other religious leaders and groups to achieve shared goals.

140   Carpenter, Joel A.   "Revive Us Again: Alienation, Hope, and the Resurgence of Fundamentalism, 1930-1950."   In *Transforming Faith: The Sacred and Secular in Modern American History*, ed. by M. L. Bradbury and James B. Gilbert, 105-125.   Westport, Conn.: Greenwood, 1989.

Carpenter calls attention to the use of popular periodicals such as *Our Hope* and *Revelation* in sustaining the dispensationalist premillennialism that undergirded fundamentalism. He also notes that fundamentalists were quick to use the results of modern technology for their own purposes, despite the fundamentalist antipathy to modernity. As one example, he points to the early use of radio by fundamentalist evangelist Charles E. Fuller. He concludes that fundamentalism supports historian Martin E. Marty's contention that evangelicalism exists in a symbiotic relationship with modernity, rejecting modernity in theory but using its benefits to advantage.

141 Conway, Flo, and Jim Siegelman. *Holy Terror: The Fundamentalist War on America's Freedoms in Religion, Politics and Our Private Lives.* Garden City, N.Y.: Doubleday, 1982.

The title of this book betrays its polemic nature. Conway and Siegelman attack what they dub the "syndrome of fundamentalism," accusing fundamentalists of using propaganda in the same way as German Nazis or Soviet and Chinese Communists. They regard fundamentalism as a manifestation of spiritual imperialism, a dangerous fanaticism that demands surrender of the intellect and thereby destroys thought. As evidence, they recount cases of persons presumably driven to suicide because of fundamentalist harangues. While Conway and Siegelman may identify some of the dangers of extremism in any form, they evince little understanding of the dynamics of fundamentalism as a religious phenomenon.

142 D'Antonio, Michael. *Fall from Grace: The Failed Crusade of the Christian Right.* New York: Farrar, Straus, Giroux, 1989.

D'Antonio, a journalist by profession, provides a breezy account of the emergence of the Christian right as both a political and a religious force in American life in the 1980s, propelled primarily by televangelists such as Jerry Falwell, Pat Robertson, Oral Roberts, Jimmy Swaggart, and Jim and Tammy Faye Bakker. He asserts that the scandals that surrounded the Bakkers and Swaggart in the latter part of the decade, along with the growing rift in the Southern Baptist Convention between moderates and conservatives, effectively ended the crusade to recast American society in a conservative Christian mold.

143 Daugherty, Mary Lee. "Serpent Handling as Sacrament." In *Icons of America*, ed. by Ray B. Browne and Marshall Fishwick, 124-38. Bowling Green, Ohio: Popular Press of Bowling Green State University, 1978.

An earlier version of this essay appeared in *Theology Today* 33 (October 1976). Daugherty has long been one of the more perceptive commentators on features of Appalachian religion. In this piece, she shows how snake handling is a symbolic celebration of the power of life, death, and resurrection that emerges from a longing for holiness. From the perspective of popular religiosity, Daugherty also calls attention to how the practice gives snake handlers a sense of power in a world where social conditions are likely to limit their own freedom and power in an empirical sense.

144   Dayton, Donald W., and Robert K. Johnston, eds.   *The Variety of American Evangelicalism.* Knoxville: University of Tennessee Press, 1991.

Dayton and Johnston organized this book to show the many faces of evangelicalism and thereby to help dispel the myth that evangelicalism is monolithic. Several essays focus on the diverse roots of evangelical belief, noting connections to premillennialism, fundamentalism, Pentecostalism, Adventism, and the Holiness movement. Others look at the evangelical style as it has been expressed in various denominations and movements such as Restorationism, Black religion, Baptist groups, Pietism, the Reformed tradition, and Lutheranism. Attention is also given to a critique of evangelicalism from a Mennonite perspective, discussion of the usefulness of the label "evangelical" given its diverse expression, and the claim that evangelicals constitute an extended religious "family."

145   DeBerg, Betty A.   *Ungodly Women: Gender and the First Wave of American Fundamentalism.* Minneapolis: Fortress, 1990.

DeBerg's monograph is a provocative analysis of the popular appeal of early fundamentalism because of its defense of middle-class Victorian domestic conventions against the challenges of modernity. She demonstrates that fundamentalism through the 1920s was particularly hostile to changes in the role of women that had become fixed in the Victorian era when the home became the only acceptable sphere for women's activity. As evidence, she notes that virtually all fundamentalist periodicals opposed the woman's suffrage movement, that fundamentalist attacks on popular entertainment media such as film were based on the portrayal of women in such media, and that fundamentalists argued repeatedly that anything that challenged the traditional role of women was a sign of the nearness of the apocalypse. She concludes that fundamentalism was antimodernist not because of theological objections but because modernism was thought to lead to immorality since it was believed to encourage a breakdown of established social gender roles.

146 Dobson, Edward. *In Search of Unity: An Appeal to Fundamentalists and Evangelicals.* Nashville, Tenn.: Thomas Nelson, 1985.

Dobson's essays, several of which are based on articles that first appeared in the *Fundamentalist Journal*, are a plea for conservative Protestant Christians to end the divisions that separate those who call themselves fundamentalists and those who call themselves evangelicals. Both, he claims, tend to marginalize the other through the creation of separate organizations and structures. Dobson argues that only through healing the divisions that separate evangelicals and fundamentalists can genuine religious revival come to American society.

147 Enlow, David R. *Men Aflame: The Story of the Christian Business Men's Committee International*. Grand Rapids, Mich.: Zondervan, 1962.

Fundamentalist radio evangelist Charles E. Fuller formed the Christian Business Men's Committee International in 1937, more than a decade after he began his radio ministry. As such, it is one of the older parachurch organizations to span denominational boundaries. Enlow's book is an uncritical account of the growth of Christian Business Men's Committee in its first quarter century of existence, but it does show how groups such as this enabled fundamentalists to build strong networks during the years when they were generally consigned to the religious fringe.

148 Fowler, Robert Booth. *Religion and Politics in America*. ATLA Monograph Series 21. Metuchen, N.J.: Scarecrow, 1985.

Originating as a Harvard doctoral dissertation, Fowler's study asserts that although there has been much involvement of religious leaders such as Billy Graham and religious institutions in public life in the United States, their influence has been minimal in the twentieth century. He attributes the relative lack of influence to an abiding suspicion of politics and politicians among the churches and clergy and to the pluralism that marks American religious life, making it difficult for one person or group to assume a position of political power.

149 Frank, Douglas W. *Less Than Conquerors: How Evangelicals Entered the Twentieth Century*. Grand Rapids, Mich.: William B. Eerdmans, 1986.

Written from an evangelical perspective, Frank's study focuses on the dispensationalist premillennialism, victorious life theology, and revivalism of Billy Sunday that dominated the evangelical strains which supported Protestant fundamentalism. A recurring theme is that a major weakness of this strand of evangelicalism was its over emphasis on personal moralism and its confusing the gospel of Jesus Christ with its own idealized image of American culture. For example, Frank criticizes the victorious life movement for employing "privatized and spiritualized means of dealing with a wicked world" (p. 167) to the exclusion of other approaches. Although it is not his intention, Frank provides abundant evidence to sustain the contention that the evangelicalism that issued in fundamentalism was essentially a form of popular religiosity with its focus on the individual, personal religious experience, and private access to a realm of supernatural power.

150 [Frankiel], Sandra Sizer. "Politics and Apolitical Religion: The Great Urban Revivals of the Late Nineteenth Century." *Church History* 48 (1979): 81-98.

Frankiel looks closely at the religious revivals of 1857-1858 and those linked to Dwight L. Moody in 1875-1877. She argues that while Moody stressed the conversion of individuals in his preaching, there were clear social and political implications that followed. On the one hand, converted persons made good workers in an industrializing nation and brought stability to home and family life. But the larger political dimension came in the assumption that only through individual conversion could the nation (society and the political order) be cleansed and purified. Hence Frankiel claims that there were important political nuances since the Moody revivals transpired in an age of political scandal, fears of the consequences of industrialization, and growing apprehension of immigrants who were viewed as alien and who also were overwhelmingly non-Protestant (and therefore targets for conversion).

151 Geiger, Annamaria. "Born-Againism: Popular Religion in Contemporary America." In *Religion and Philosophy in the United States of America*, ed. by Peter Freese, 1:321-43. Essen, Germany: Verlag Die Blaue Eule, 1987.

Geiger argues that the development of a common language to talk about religious experience that separates those who are born again (insiders) from those who cannot use that vocabulary to describe their personal religiosity (outsiders) is a central dynamic of contemporary American evangelicalism. She notes that this language does not depend on formal denominational structures, but is perpetuated by popular media such as published devotional materials, newspaper columns, and television and radio evangelists, as well as by parachurch phenomena such as prayer breakfasts and revivals. She notes that the common vocabulary, along with the prevalence of seeing charismatic experience as essential, tends toward dogmatism.

152 Gilbert, J.E. "Ballot Salvation." *Journal of Popular Culture* 18 (Summer 1984): 1-8.

Gilbert's article presents an overview of the political concerns articulated in the early 1980s by Jerry Falwell and Falwell's assertion of the need for a "moral revolution" in the United States.　Gilbert takes note of the strident criticism of Falwell advanced by mainline religious personnel, but also insists that part of Falwell's appeal results from the attractiveness to Americans of a call to experience vital religion directly rather than simply consigning religion to the realm of intellectual belief.

153　Gillespie, Paul F., ed.　*Foxfire 7*.　Garden City, N.Y.: Anchor Books, 1982.

With more than 200 photos and other illustrations, this volume provides a rich resource for understanding the popular religiosity that prevails in much of the rural South and in Appalachia.　Included in its purview are camp meetings, the prevalence of the sacrament of foot washing, snake handling, and the tradition of shape note singing.　What makes this particularly valuable for students of popular religion is its reliance on interviews and other first person narratives, mostly from persons living in Appalachia.

154　Harrell, David E., Jr.　*All Things Are Possible: The Healing and Charismatic Revivals in Modern America*.　Bloomington: Indiana University Press, 1975.

Harrell presents this book in two distinct sections.　The first, focusing on the period from 1947 to 1958, deals with the revivals that emphasized faith healing and with figures such as Oral Roberts and William M. Branham.　Harrell notes that the most frequent criticisms of the healing revivals concerned questions about financial abuse and doctrinal debates over whether gifts of the Spirit such as faith healing had ceased with the close of the apostolic age.　The second section, treating the period from 1958 through 1974, looks at the broader interest in charismatic phenomena that went well beyond faith healing.　Of especial value to those wishing to pursue further study is Harrell's splendid bibliographical essay.　The book also benefits from many photographs.

155　Hefley, James.　*God Goes to High School*.　Waco, Tex.: Word Books, 1970.

This book is an uncritical account of the founding of Youth for Christ, an evangelical ministry targeted to high school age adolescents that was founded in the mid-1940s.　Its unabashed aim was to gain converts to a fundamentalist-style of Protestant Christianity among high school youth and young adults through Bible study groups, rallies, and other evangelical media.　Interdenominational in focus, Youth for Christ counted Billy Graham among its early staff members. It illustrates the penchant within popular religiosity to see simple reliance on supernatural power as the pivot for endowing life with meaning.

156 Hill, Samuel S., and Dennis E. Owen. *The New Religious Political Right in America*. Nashville: Abingdon, 1982.

One of the first scholarly inquiries into the fundamentalist foray into political life with the formation of groups such as the moral majority, Hill and Owen argue that the millennialist impulse behind fundamentalist visions for a Christian America are essentially pessimistic. They reflect both despair and fear, sometimes reaching the level of paranoia, because of a perceived void at the heart of American culture. Hence the religious political right tends to see polar opposites at every turn, reducing the choices to their own authoritarian persuasion or social chaos.

157 Hollenweger, W. J. *The Pentecostals: The Charismatic Movement in the Church*. Minneapolis: Augsburg, 1969.

Hollenweger's encyclopedic study looks at the Pentecostal movement in the United States, South AFrica, Europe, and areas of Latin America such as Brazil. While his primary interest is tracing the history of modern Pentecostalism, Hollenweger gives careful attention to matters of belief such as the understanding of Scripture, the doctrine of the Trinity, the idea of justification, the belief in the Holy Spirit, the insistence on the reality of miracles, and eschatology. He also argues that Pentecostalism serves as one means of offering help and positive identity to those who are on the fringes of society through its emphasis on the personal friendship of Jesus and through the leadership of modern shaman-like figures. Hollenweger also discusses how Pentecostalism has sought to shore up its intellectual foundations through the founding of schools and colleges and how in recent years, Pentecostals have increased their social commitment.

158 Hunt, Keith, and Gladys Hunt. *For Christ and the University: The Story of InterVarsity Christian Fellowship of the U.S.A., 1940-1990*. Downers Grove, Ill.: InterVarsity Press, 1991.

Founded by C. Stacey Woods to provide religious nurture (as well as to gain possible converts) to conservative Christian students enrolled as "secular" colleges and universities, IVCF remains a strong parachurch movement on many campuses where it sponsors Bible study groups and other activities. This sympathetic, uncritical look at the first half century of IVCF tells the story primarily by looking at key figures and personalities who have provided IVCF with leadership. The Hunts do note, however, that in recent years IVCF has made a more conscious effort to reach a multi-ethnic student audience.

159 Hunter, James Davison. *American Evangelicalism: Conservative Religion and the Quandary of Modernity.* New Brunswick, N.J.: Rutgers University Press, 1983.

Part of the "quandary" that Hunter examines is the tension between the personal and the public that marks much of the evangelical style. At the base of evangelicalism lies a very private, personal religious experience, but events in recent years have drawn evangelicals into the political sector and therefore given it a much more public cast. Hunter uses this private-public paradox to examine the history of evangelicalism in the United States in the twentieth century, giving careful consideration to the ways evangelicals have sought to propagate their message through popular media. There is a good discussion, for example, of the work of evangelical publishing houses in which Hunter concludes that books produced for a popular evangelical audience give extraordinary treatment to the emotional and psychological dimensions of ordinary human experience.

160 Hunter, James Davison. *Evangelicalism: The Coming Generation.* Chicago: University of Chicago Press, 1987.

Sociologist Hunter argues that contemporary evangelicalism is a tradition in the process of transformation. The current and coming generations, he asserts, are redrawing the boundaries of faith by devoting more attention to social concerns, rethinking the ascetic strand popularly associated with evangelicalism, and having to come to grips with changes in family structure and the political manifestations of the evangelical style. Hunter regards both the efforts at cultural accommodation and the defensiveness that resists such as signs of transformation within the evangelical subculture that has resulted in part from gains in education and the emergence of an evangelical elite.

161 Johnson, Weldon T. "The Religious Crusade: Revival or Ritual?" *American Journal of Sociology* 76 (1971): 873-90.

Johnson uses the crusades of Billy Graham as a case study. His primary interest is to determine whether these crusades actually deserve to be labelled as a revival, since that term carries a connotation of spontaneity. He concludes that fixed ritual patters are integral to the dynamics of the modern religious crusade, often making the results a foregone conclusion. Hence what appears to be a spontaneous response to the preaching of the evangelist is actually a well-orchestrated ritual.

162 Jorstad, Erling. *Evangelicals in the White House: The Cultural Maturation of Born Again Christianity, 1960-1981*. New York: Edwin Mellen, 1981.

One of a trio of books Jorstad has written assessing the conservative religious influence in contemporary American politics, this monograph examines the evangelical style associated in public life with Jimmy Carter. Jorstad looks to the 1960s with its social upheavals as a time when a new evangelicalism was taking shape. Rather than eschewing political involvement as had earlier evangelicals, those of the ilk of Jimmy Carter sought to bring their religious faith to bear on public policy. Jorstad briefly takes note of the shift of the "new evangelicals" to the political right by 1980.

163 Jorstad, Erling. *The New Christian Right, 1981-1988: Prospects for the Post-Reagan Decade*. Lewiston, N.Y.: Edwin Mellen, 1987.

In some ways a sequel to *Evangelicals in the White House*, this book is Jorstad's appraisal of the long-term impact of the alliance of conservative evangelicals with the political right during the Reagan administrations. Jorstad calls attention to the difficulties in implementing the political agenda of the religious right and the way the pragmatism of political reality tempers the possibilities of radical changes in the short run. He suggests that the "single issue" character of the politics associated with the religious right will prove problematic in the long run, but claims that it would be mistaken to underestimate the prospect for change if the religious right remains politically active.

164 Jorstad, Erling. *The Politics of Moralism: The New Christian Right in American Life*. Minneapolis: Augsburg, 1981.

This brief study is targeted for a lay audience. Jorstad looks at both the phenomenon of televangelism and the political activity of groups such as the Moral Majority, Christian Voice, Religious Roundtable, and the National Christian Action Coalition. He argues that the emergence of the new Christian right represents a response to the far-reaching social and technological changes of recent decades, even as those of the Christian right appropriate the results of change (e.g., use of computer technology to generate massive direct mailing programs to target potential supporters). Jorstad concludes that working from confrontation rather than seeking consensus, while posing threats to religious freedom, will perpetuate stalemates in effecting responsible change in political programs and public policy for the foreseeable future.

165 Jorstad, Erling. *Popular Religion in America: The Evangelical Voice*. Westport, Conn.: Greenwood, 1993.

In this book, Jorstad expands considerably on the second of the three themes he identified in the work discussed in the preceding entry. Jorstad believes that evangelicalism is virtually synonymous with popular religion in contemporary American culture because it is not restricted to a particular religious denomination, has spawned its own voluminous literature and other media expressions that are targeted to a mass audience, and reflects a deep desire among ordinary people for experience of and access to the supernatural. Students of popular religion will find this book particularly helpful because of the sources Jorstad has painstakingly consulted: a dazzling array of popular religious periodicals and other literary genres, the music of evangelicalism from new gospel to Christian rock, and the popular secondary treatments of evangelicalism as the news media became captivated by its domineering presence in public life. The notes and bibliography alone make this book valuable.

166 Kater, John L., Jr. *Christians on the Right: The Moral Majority in Perspective*. New York: Seabury, 1982.

Kater's work provides both historical and religious scrutiny of the forces that led Jerry Falwell to found the Moral Majority. Written for a general audience, this book rehearses much now familiar territory. For example, Kater provides some background understanding for why evangelicals such as Falwell feel that American society has lost its religious moorings, given the perception of rapid social change in the 1960s and 1970s and the belief that secular forces have come to dominate public life.

167 Laurentin, Rene. *Catholic Pentecostalism*. Translated by Matthew J. O'Connell. Garden City, N.Y.: Doubleday, 1977.

A Frenchman, Laurentin connects the recent surge of charismatic expression within American Catholicism to the larger story within the history of Christianity when there have been groups and movements that claimed their authority came from a direct experience of the Holy Spirit. He suggests that church authorities have always had difficulty in responding to such phenomena because they can be interpreted in so many ways. Some always see charismatic expression as a legitimate sign of the presence of the Spirit; others always regard it as a fraud. Yet others find in charismatic experience the liberation of the depth of the human psyche. Laurentin attempts to make a place for Catholic Pentecostalism by grounding it in Marian devotion and piety.

168 Liebman, Robert C., and Robert Wuthnow, eds. *The New Christian Right: Mobilization and Legitimation.* New York: Aldine, 1983.

Liebman and Wuthnow bring a sociological slant to this collection of essays that investigate forces that enabled Christian evangelicals of a conservative political bent to build coalitions and organizations. Essays are grouped under five topical categories: descriptions of the movement, strategies of mobilization, identifying the constituency, the ideology behind the Christian right, and the cultural environment that has helped sustain the Christian right. A concluding essay by Liebman suggests that the emergence of the Christian right in late twentieth century America provides sociologists with raw materials for rethinking the traditional analysis of social movements and the way they carve a place for themselves in the larger culture.

169 Lovett, Leonard. "The Spiritual Legacy and Role of Black Holiness-Pentecostalism in the Development of American Culture." *One in Christ: A Catholic Ecumenical Review* 23 (1987): 144-56.

Lovett demonstrates the connections between the worship and style stemming from slave religion, with its amalgamation of African and Christian dimensions, and the worship and style associated with Holiness-Pentecostalism. He does not claim that the two necessarily share identical belief systems, but places emphasis on the role of sacred dance, spirit possession, call and response, and ecstatic experience such as glossolalia. Both have at their heart, Lovett claims a "poor people's theology" that is designed to give power to those who lack it.

170 Maguire, Daniel. *The New Subversives: Anti-Americanism of the Religious Right.* New York: Continuum, 1982.

The title of Maguire's book reveals its core thesis. In Maguire's view, the Christian right has perverted both religion and politics, using the Bible as an oracle like a ouija board to determine whether God is for or against any given political program or policy. He finds the religious understanding that undergirds the politics of the religious right to be grounded in a magical understanding of divine power and a literal interpretation of sacred texts. As an example, Maguire scrutinizes the development of creation science and the efforts of the religious right to use political power to bring creation science into school curricula.

171 Marsden, George M. *Fundamentalism and American Culture: The Shaping of Twentieth Century Evangelicalism, 1870-1925.* New York: Oxford University Press, 1980.

Notre Dame historian Marsden provides one of the more incisive and insightful accounts of the origins of fundamentalism in American culture. He looks at the form of evangelicalism that prevailed in the later nineteenth century before fundamentalism had taken clear shape and then shows how clusters of beliefs that came from millennialism, common sense realism, dispensationalism, and the Victorious Life strand of the Holiness movement came together in American fundamentalism. Marsden gives careful attention to how fundamentalism revolved around a concept of civilization, particularly of an American Christian civilization, as much as it did around particular theological doctrines. To understand fundamentalism, he demonstrates that one must view its expression not only from social, political, and intellectual perspectives, but also as a distinctly American religious phenomenon.

172 Marsden, George M. *Understanding Fundamentalism and Evangelicalism.* Grand Rapids, Mich.: Eerdmans, 1991.

Marsden here offers revised versions of several essays that originally appeared independently. Because popular and academic writers have tended to use "fundamentalism" and "evangelicalism" as interchangeable terms, Marsden sketches their similarities and differences both historically and in the present. Part of the definitional dilemma arises, he claims, from their representing religious styles as well as particular sets of beliefs. He also gives historical perspective to evangelical involvement in politics as well as the concern for interaction with science (ranging from Enlightenment science to creation science).

173 Moen, Matthew C. *The Christian Right and Congress.* Tuscaloosa: University of Alabama Press, 1989.

Although most commentators have claimed relatively minor success for the religious right in implementing its political agenda during the Reagan administrations, Moen offers a contrary view. By looking at the sophisticated lobbying techniques used by the religious right, Moen makes a case that the right was much more successful in bringing its agenda into the consciousness of members of Congress, especially during the first Reagan administration. He uses as examples the Congressional debates over tuition tax credits and Constitutional amendments that would permit prayer in public schools. Moen notes, however, that the direct influence of the religious right waned in the second Reagan administration, leading to a change of strategy that would emphasize local rather than national political activity.

174 Morris, James. *The Preachers*. New York: St. Martin's, 1973.

Written with some scholarly sophistication for a mass audience, Morris's book contains biographical vignettes of popular evangelists and revivalists. Morris based his work in part on field observations from attending several hundred preaching services at which his subjects spoke. He is more interested in the personalities of these preachers than in their theologies. Morris also is especially taken by the financial intrigue that has surrounded many popular evangelists. Among the subjects included are A. A. Allen, Herbert W. and Garner Ted Armstrong, C. W. Burpo, Billy Graham, Billy James Hargis, Kathryn Kuhlman, Rev. Ike, Carl McIntire, and Oral Roberts.

175 Murphy, Cullen. "Protestantism and the Evangelicals." *Wilson Quarterly* 5 (Autumn 1981): 105-116.

Murphy argues that the evangelical upsurge in American religious life is the most important development within Protestantism since the 1970s, although he also notes that evangelical groups have had a consistent rate of growth since the 1930s. What has made the difference is the way fundamentalists and other evangelicals had exploited use of popular media and recognition that labelling some long-established denominations as "mainline" was a myth. Murphy suggests that evangelicalism of some stripe constitutes the bulk of American popular religion.

176 Quebedeaux, Richard. *By What Authority: The Rise of Personality Cults in American Christianity*. New York: Harper and Row, 1982.

Quebedeaux was among the first scholars to take seriously the new breed of evangelicalism that has become a prominent feature of American religion in the last quarter century. In this book, after an opening chapter on popular religion in America, he directs attention to the fascination the public has long had with flamboyant religious figures from the days of Dwight L. Moody to the present. He suggests that "converted criminals, drug addicts, sports heroes, beauty queens, and the like, and those in the mass media who give them a stage, are the new leaders of popular religion in America." Others have sustained their popular authority not only through the power of their personalities, but through advancing a crass pragmatism that deals with the self-centeredness Quebedeaux finds at the heart of popular religion, what he calls a "psychological homelessness" following Peter Berger.

177 Quebedeaux, Richard. *The New Charismatics: The Origins, Development, and Significance of Neo-Pentecostalism.* Garden City, N.Y.: Doubleday, 1976.

This study emphasizes the heritage of the fundamentalist Bible school tradition, the challenge presented to traditional religion by secularism, and the rediscovery of a sense of the supernatural as basic to the emergence of neo-Pentecostalism. Quebedeaux gives sustained treatment to issues of authority, especially the personal authority of key individuals in recent Pentecostalism. Among those whose personal dynamism he highlights are Kathryn Kuhlman, Oral Roberts, and Demos Shakarian.

178 Quebedeaux, Richard. *The Worldly Evangelicals.* New York: Harper and Row, 1978.

Quebedeaux's basic thesis in this appraisal is that the current generation of evangelicals is intent on providing a solid intellectual base for their beliefs and practices as well as a new sense of public discipleship. To this extent, contemporary evangelicals are less separatist than those of earlier generations. For evidence, he points to the spate of new evangelical colleges and seminaries that have been founded; the work of groups such as InterVarsity Christian Fellowship, Young Life, and Youth for Christ; the growth of a new evangelical style within the Southern Baptist Convention and the Lutheran Church-Missouri Synod; and the ministry of individuals such as Billy Graham. Quebedeaux also calls attention to the way evangelicals have fostered a greater appreciation of the arts that were once dismissed as inimical to authentic religious faith and wrestled with controversial issues such as those surrounding feminism and homosexuality.

179 Quebedeaux, Richard. *The Young Evangelicals: Revolution in Orthodoxy.* New York: Harper and Row, 1974.

This study, among the earlier of several that Quebedeaux has devoted to evangelicalism, concentrates on the new concern for issues of social justice among younger evangelicals. He also notes that contemporary evangelicals appear willing to abandon the rigid dispensationalism that marked an earlier age. Instead, they are looking for new intellectual roots by drawing on ideas advanced by theological writers such as C. S. Lewis and Dietrich Bonhoeffer.

Quebedeaux also notes that contemporary evangelicals are distressed by what often appears to be a cavalier rejection by liberals.

180 Ribuffo, Leo P. "God and Jimmy Carter." In *Transforming Faith: The Sacred and Secular in Modern American History*, ed. by M. L. Bradbury and James B. Gilbert, 141-59. Westport, Conn.: Greenwood, 1989.

Because Carter was the first United States president to insist that his evangelical religious identification was central to the way he approached public policy, Ribuffo seek to understand how religion actually affected Carter's abilities to be an effective political leader. He concludes that the public misconstrues Carter's evangelical humility as a weakness and his expressions of uncertainty whether God could always be identified with the position taken by the government as casting doubts on Carter's ability to be a strong leader.

181 Rosenberg, Ellen MacGilvra. *The Southern Baptists: A Subculture in Transition.* Knoxville: University of Tennessee Press, 1989.

Some commentators who see evangelicalism as the heart of contemporary popular religion also regard the Southern Baptists as a prime example of an institution that reflects popular religion. While several scholars have looked at the tensions within the Southern Baptist Convention as fundamentalists have gained control of denominational bureaucracy, Rosenberg casts a wider net. She is sensitive to the ways in which Southern Baptists have represented a cultural style as much as a religious one. Consequently, her study also looks at transformations in the Southern Baptist ethos that have ensued as the denomination became national rather than just regional in scope and as it lost its sectarian identity in becoming the epitome of a dominant evangelical presence in American religion.

182 Sandeen, Ernest R. *The Roots of Fundamentalism.* Grand Rapids, Mich.: Baker Book House, 1970.

Sandeen's study has become a standard history of the forces that gave birth to fundamentalism in the United States. Sandeen is particularly sensitive to the larger context of American fundamentalism as an ideology, calling attention to the connections between American and British currents in shaping the early fundamentalist belief system. Hence he highlights especially the links between the fundamentalist perspective and the premillennial dispensationalism that began in Britain with John Nelson Darby and his followers.

183 Shakarian, Demos. "FGBMFI Struggles Toward the Future." *Charisma* 13 (March 1988): 24.

Shakarian, founder of the Pentecostal-oriented Full Gospel Business Men's Fellowship International, offers a very brief statement about trends he sees marking this parachurch movement. Shakarian believes that hostile forces will always seek to undermine the work of the Spirit, but remains convinced that this cross-denominational movement represents an authentic, popular manifestation of supernatural presence and has the potential to transform the world of business.

184 Shriver, Peggy L. *The Bible Vote: Religion and the New Right.* New York: Pilgrim, 1981.

Shriver's book is among the earliest to examine the surge of political interest and activity among religious conservatives. Writing for a general audience, Shriver traces the greater public attention given to religion by political candidates beginning with the presidential candidacy of Jimmy Carter and the subsequent greater appeal to evangelicals of Ronald Reagan in the 1980 presidential campaign. At the time Shriver wrote, religiously conservative groups like the Moral Majority were still focussing primarily on the national level. Shriver makes a case for the importance of having religiously-based ethical values inform personal political choices, but argues that such should not be restricted to religious conservatives alone.

185 Shupe, Anson, and William A. Stacey. *Born Again Politics and the Moral Majority: What Social Surveys Really Show.* New York: Edwin Mellen, 1982.

As the subtitle indicates, Shupe and Stacey based their appraisal on an analysis of survey materials that purport to show the actual political beliefs of Americans and the correlation between political beliefs and personal religiosity. Shupe and Stacey conclude that even among those who identify themselves as born again evangelicals, the Moral Majority and similar political groups did not have the depth of support that their leadership claimed and that there was much more diversity among born again evangelicals than suggested in the popular media.

186 Silk, Mark. *Spiritual Politics: Religion and America since World War II.* New York: Simon and Schuster, 1988.

Silk's aim is to understand the connections between religion and public life (politics) in the United States since World War II. He recognizes that the gnawing question is to determine precisely in what way religion should influence public life, a matter complicated in the later twentieth century by the increasing and tenacious individualism that marks spirituality in America. If patriotism has spawned a national philosophy supporting democracy, the prevailing religious pluralism and individualistic spirituality have not always undergirded that philosophy in the same way, according to Silk. Looking primarily at responses to the Cold War, the civil rights movement, the antiwar crusade of the Vietnam era, and the alliance between religious and political conservatives during the Reagan years, Silk argues from the perspective of a journalist that tension is basic to the American way when linking religion and the public order.

187 Viguerie, Richard A. *The New Right: We're Ready to Lead*. Rev. ed. with introduction by Jerry Falwell. Falls Church, Va.: Viguerie Co., 1981.

Done without such scholarly apparatus as notes or bibliography but illustrated with photographs, Viguerie's book is an unabashed apology for intense political action on the part of the religious right.   Those seeking to understand the religious rationale for this political action will find chapter 11 especially helpful, for here Viguerie develops the claim that God supports only the political agenda of the religious right because the right is committed to the creation of a Christian culture where, for example, prayer will be a regular part of public education.

188 Wacker, Grant. "The Holy Spirit and the Spirit of the Age in American Protestantism, 1880-1920." *Journal of American History* 72 (1985): 45-62.

Wacker scrutinizes the "higher life theology" that was a major current in late nineteenth century American evangelicalism and finds interesting parallels with the more liberal theology identified with the Social Gospel. Both, for example, were concerned to develop a theology sensitive to the practical ways one could discern the presence of the Holy Spirit in everyday life. Both kept a focus on religious experience. The new, more liberal theology tended to see such as experience as a gradual process, while higher life advocates talked about conversion as a series of discrete events. Both were attentive to eschatology, basing their passion for the inbreaking of God's kingdom on analysis of the rapid social change that marked the era, but they developed their eschatology in different directions. Both, claims Wacker, were nourished by the Reformed tradition, although the conventional interpretation sees the Wesleyan Holiness heritage as more prominent with the higher life theology.

189 Wacker, Grant. "Pentecostalism." In *Encyclopedia of the American*

Religious Experience, ed. by Charles H. Lippy and Peter W. Williams, 2:933-45. New York: Scribners, 1988.

This essay provides the best brief overview of Pentecostal developments in American culture. Wacker traces the history of American Pentecostalism from the Azusa Street revivals of 1906 through the ministry of Oral Roberts. He shows how Pentecostalism moved from the sectarian fringe, where a sense of prophetic vision and commitment to pure truth prevailed, to the mainstream of American religious life. In the process, Wacker argues that Pentecostalism assumed an uncritical identification with the values associated with middle-class America and muted its critique of modernity as it appropriated the benefits of technological advance to promote itself.

190 Wacker, Grant. "Searching for Norman Rockwell: Popular Evangelicalism in Contemporary America." In *The Evangelical Tradition in America*, ed. by Leonard I. Sweet, 289-315. Macon, Ga.: Mercer University Press, 1984.

Wacker turns his analytic lens on contemporary evangelicalism in this penetrating essay, arguing for the necessity of making a distinction between two strains of evangelicalism. One, the Evangelical Right, is wedded to a notion of a Christian civilization for America based on its commitment to ideals deriving from Victorian culture and immortalized popularly in the magazine covers drawn by Norman Rockwell. The other, the Evangelical non-Right, is committed to active engagement with current cultural forces, striving to develop appropriate modes of social action informed by evangelical principles. Wacker argues that it is the first strain of evangelicalism that has witnessed great growth, while the latter (dismissed by the Evangelical Right as hardly worthy of the evangelical label) has simply held its ground among American Protestants for the past few decades.

191 Wagner, Melinda Bollar. *God's Schools: Choice and Compromise in American Society*. New Brunswick, N.J.: Rutgers University Press, 1990.

Wagner's study is among the first scholarly examinations of the Christian schools movement, the endeavor of religious conservatives to establish private academies where a fundamentalist world view informs all instruction. She looks at the myriad legal issues that have surrounded the movement and the efforts of the religious right to gain tax advantages for Christian schools parallel to those granted public schools. The dimension of compromise enters the picture in part when Christian academies are forced to adhere to standards set by governmental educational agencies.

192 Wells, David F., and John D. Woodbridge, eds. *The Evangelicals: What They Believe, Who They Are, and Where They Are Changing*. Nashville: Abingdon, 1975.

     This collection of essays appeared during the time when the media had first begun to trumpet evangelicalism as the epitome of popular religion in the United States. Hence the authors look at the theological distinctiveness of evangelicalism, its manifestations in black religion, tensions within evangelicalism, and the historical links between fundamentalism and evangelicalism. Essays also examine the resurgence of social concern among evangelicals who once saw themselves as separated from the larger society and the rethinking of the relationship between evangelicalism and science prevalent in some intellectual circles. An annotated bibliography, incisive in its comments on what is now somewhat dated material, concludes the volume.

193   White, James W., and John G. Hallsten.   "Campus Crusade Goes Suburban." *Christian Century* 89 (10 May 1972): 549-51.

At its origin, the evangelistic program of Campus Crusade was oriented to college students. But in 1972, Campus Crusade organized the Lay Institute for Evangelism (LIFE) to train persons from mainline and fundamentalist Protestant churches to use the techniques developed by Campus Crusade in working with college students in their own suburban communities. White and Hallsten are critical of this endeavor, claiming that its doctrinal base is biblically suspect and theologically inadequate and that its proselytizing methods are ethically questionable as well as both ecclesiastically and psychologically problematic.

194 Wilcox, Clyde. *God's Warriors: The Christian Right in Twentieth Century America*. Baltimore, Md.: Johns Hopkins University Press, 1992.

Wilcox begins with a chapter surveying the political interests of religious conservatives in the first half of the twentieth century, particularly the strident opposition to communism. He then sifts through much survey and sociological data to understand more precisely the ways in which religious conservatives have been politically active (e.g., looking at which candidates received financial contributions from religious conservatives). Among his more interesting conclusions is that there is far more widespread support for a conservative political platform among religious conservatives than there is support for the individuals and groups that identify themselves as voices of the religious right (e.g., Pat Robertson, Christian Voice, Moral Majority). Wilcox includes an extensive bibliography of literature published through the 1980s that deals with the new Christian right on both national and local levels.

195   Young, Perry Deane.   *God's Bullies: Power Politics and Religious Tyranny*.   New York: Holt, Rinehart, and Winston, 1982.

Young offers a scathing critique of the religious-political right, as evidenced by the title of his book.   He regards televangelists who equate their political perspective with divine truth as tyrants who use scare tactics to badger their listeners to support a radical agenda.   In Young's view, the goal of the religious-political right is little short of establishing a police state that would use governmental power to coerce conformity to prescribed behavior.   He regards such as a dangerous threat to personal freedom and the democratic process.

196 Zeik, Michael.   *New Christian Communities: Origins, Style, and Survival*. Williston Park, N.Y.: Roth Publishing, 1973.

Zeik's work looks at several recent experiments in Christian community formation, not all of which were or are communitarian in organization.   He describes, for example, the Reba Place community in the Chicago area, a Catholic Pentecostal community in Indiana, the Free Church of Akron, Ohio, and a coeducational monastery.   Many of these experiments were short-lived, and Zeik does not detail reasons why women and men saw these communities as meeting personal religious needs.   Hence the value of the book rests primarily in its identifying alternative communities established to support individual spiritual quests.

197 Zweir, Robert.   *Born Again Politics: The New Christian Right in America*. Downers Grove, Ill.: InterVarsity, 1982.

Zweir writes from an evangelical perspective in sketching the history of the numerous political action groups that are identified with the Christian right, noting that the religious groups in their early days benefited greatly from mailing lists and the like that had been amassed by their secular counterparts. Zweir more than some others points to the problems encountered in several states by Christian schools and academies when they sought appropriate licensing as a primary catalyst in sparking greater political activity among fundamentalists who once eschewed direct involvement in the political process because it was regarded as inherently corrupt.

5

Radio and Television Ministries

198 Abelman, Robert, and Kimberly Neuendorf. "How Religious Is Religious Television Programming?" *Journal of Communication* 35 (1985): 98-110.

Scrutinizing random five minute segments of 27 of the leading religious television programs, Abelman and Neuendorf concluded that 75 percent have religious themes and that only 2 percent were overtly political. Many of the programs addressed personal problems that viewers might confront, such as divorce and family violence, although some of these issues, such as abortion and pornography, also had potential political dimensions. Abelman and Neuendorf also notes that nearly three-quarters of the programs offered products for sale, with Jerry Falwell's program at the time offering the largest variety. They also realized that despite requests for donations from viewers, no program revealed the total amount that had been received from such appeals.

199 Armstrong, Ben. *The Electric Church.* Nashville: Thomas Nelson, 1979.

One of the first books to survey the development of televangelism and give a historical sketch of religious broadcasting, Armstrong's study is written from an evangelical perspective. Armstrong argues that the use of media such as radio and television has brought unparalleled opportunities for Christianity to propagate the gospel to the masses. Although uncritical in analysis, this book is valuable for its factual information, especially regarding the early use of radio for religious purposes.

200 Babson, Roger. "83 Stations Send Sermons by Air." *New York Times,* 4 February 1922, 7:12.

An economist by profession, Babson surveys the earliest use of radio by American religious groups. At the time of writing, the 83 stations that carried some religious broadcasting, usually sermons preached in local congregations, reached 65.2 percent of the United States population. Babson expressed concern that increased use of the airwaves would be detrimental to organized religion because persons would choose to listen to broadcasts in the comfort of their homes rather than become active participants in a religious group by attending services.

201 Berkman, Dave. "Long Before Falwell: Early Radio and Religion--As Reported by the Nation's Periodical Press." *Journal of Popular Culture* 21, 4 (1988): 1-11.

Berkman focuses on the period between 1919 and 1924. He notes that the most frequent concern about religious use of radio was the conviction that listening to religious broadcasts would replace actual attendance at worship services. At the same time, he found that those religious leaders who advocated use of the then new medium saw distinct advantages, such as being able to reach the homebound and those who were not members of a religious organization.

202 Bissett, J. Thomas. "Religious Broadcasting: Assessing the State of the Art." *Christianity Today* 24 (12 December 1980): 28-31.

Bissett analyzes polls that examined the nature of the audience of religious television and the attitudes viewers had of what they watched. He notes that the audience is heavily evangelical by self-definition, with 85 percent declaring themselves already converted. Viewers regarded religious telecasts much as they regarded churches since they promoted voluntarism in terms of financial support, reflected some of the pluralism of religious institutions, and advocated an experiential expression of personal faith that is central to evangelicalism. Although Bissett concluded that most viewers who send donations to the organizations sponsoring religious television programs also contribute to local religious organizations, the money sent to the televangelists represents a potential financial loss for local churches. Bissett concluded that while religious television may reinforce Christian values and offer a Christian interpretation of world affairs, there is too much duplication of style and content among popular programs.

203 Bourgault, Louise M. "The PTL Club and Protestant Viewers: An Ethnographic Study." *Journal of Communication* 35 (1985): 132-48.

Bourgault bases her study on 43 interviews conducted in a southeastern Ohio community with a population of 4400. She found that the most positive views of religious television programs came from those who also appreciated fundamentalist attitudes and worship styles but felt estranged from local churches because they were regarded as too lax. For fundamentalist viewers, religious television had great merit because it provided "safe" entertainment that reinforced their own beliefs and values.

204 Buddenbaum, Judith M. "Characteristics and Media-Related Needs of the Audience for Religious TV." *Journalism Quarterly* 58 (1981): 266-72.

Buddenbaum documents the Protestant preference of most viewers of religious television. Her study also found that viewers tended to come from lower income homes, hold low-status jobs, and had relatively low levels of educational attainment. Most were women over the age of 62. Although the correlation was weak, she did find that many viewers watched religious television because they believed they could come to know themselves better as a result and they could avoid loneliness. Based on a 1978 survey in Indianapolis, Buddenbaum's study estimated that 44.2 percent of the population watched some religious television, a figure lower than that suggested earlier by religious broadcasters.

205 Cardwell, Jerry D. *Mass Media Christianity: Televangelism and the Great Commission.* With contributions by Jack L. Thorpe. Lanham, Md.: University Press of America, 1984.

Beginning the introduction and each section of his book with a biblical quotation, Cardwell believes that televangelism has great potential for the expansion of Christian influence in American society. He assumes that the appeal of media religion stems from a crisis in society in which liberals have forgotten the importance of religion and conservatives had forgotten the power of addressing social issues in preaching. Television, he claims, beings a sense of both belonging and participation to viewers who have not been able to internalize religious commitment in traditional modes. Cardwell argues that television could transform American society. The books includes brief biographical vignettes on individuals Cardwell believes have made effective use of television in their ministries. Included, among others, are Billy Graham, Oral Roberts, Rex Humbard, Jerry Falwell, Jim Bakker, Jimmy Swaggart, Pat Robertson, and Robert Schuller.

206 Clements, William M. "The Rhetoric of the Radio Ministry." *Journal of American Folklore* 87 (October 1974): 318-27.

This article argues that the broadcasts of radio preachers are folklore events. Based on a study done in a predominantly white rural area of northeastern Arkansas, Clements found that radio preachers had to adapt their rhetoric to the medium. Because they could not interact directly with their audience or adapt the form and content of their message to the response of the audience, they had to develop a different delivery style. Clements also examines how time constraints influenced style; communicating a message within the limits of a single program required preachers to streamline their radio sermons.

207 Coakley, Thomas F. "Preaching by Wireless." *Catholic World* 72, 5 (January 1922): 516.

Coakley, aware that the earliest use of radio for religious purposes came from Protestants, urges Catholics to explore the possibilities of the medium for their own purposes. He suggests that were Catholics to establish their own stations, they could reach the masses with the truth of Roman Catholicism. He notes that the first use of radio by Catholics in the United States was a two week series of sermons by Paulists carried on Pittsburgh's KDKA starting on 2 November 1921.

208   Eskridge, Larry K.   "Evangelical Broadcasting: Its Meaning for Evangelicals." In *Transforming Faith: The Sacred and Secular in Modern American History*, ed. by M. L. Bradbury and James B. Gilbert, 127-39. Westport, Conn.: Greenwood, 1989.

Eskridge attributes the attractiveness to evangelicals of using broadcast media to the potential for nurturing values and for drawing non-evangelicals into the evangelical ranks.   He also claims that evangelical broadcasting, while representing an appropriation of modern technology, is actually a hedge against modernity among evangelicals since the content of programs promotes traditional beliefs and values.

209 Fore, William F. "Religious Broadcasting." In *International Encyclopedia of Communication*. New York: Oxford University Press, 1989.

This entry is a brief, but helpful historical survey of the development of religious broadcasting, going from the early days of radio to the rise of televangelism in the 1970s and 1980s. It is a valuable starting point for further study in providing much accurate factual information.

210 Fore, William F. *Television and Radio: The Shaping of Faith, Values, and Culture*. Minneapolis: Augsburg Publishing House, 1987.

Fore's essential thesis in this provocative book is that television is taking over the role of the church if not of religion in general in shaping values, embodying faith, and expressing the essence of American culture. Written from a Christian perspective, the book argues that television presents a world view in that it creates a shared culture of what is of ultimate value. In turn, that shared culture becomes a basis for how individuals justify personal behavior and their own way of life. The problem, as Fore sees it, is that the culture generated by television is based utilitarian and relativistic principles. Fore also claims that television has fostered a new colonialism in that by relying on programming from the United States, television in the Third World becomes a medium for imposing American values. Fore also includes helpful chapters on the history of religious programming on radio and television and on the televangelism phenomenon of the later twentieth century.

211 Frankl, Rozelle. *Televangelism: The Marketing of Popular Religion*. Carbondale, Ill.: Southern Illinois University Press, 1987.

Frankl links the emergence of televangelism to the heritage of urban revivalism in the United States. As the revivalism promoted by Charles G. Finney, Dwight L. Moody, and Billy Sunday fused use of established means, careful organization, and entertainment, so televangelism operates on the assumption that religious conversion can be stimulated and encouraged by conscious planning and appropriate entertainment. The content of televangelism, Frankl argues, is distorted to fit the medium and competitive marketing demands. As many other studies, this one traces the early exclusion of fundamentalists from subsidized religious broadcasting, discusses the problem of financial accountability of televangelists, and confirms that the primary audience consists of women over the age of 50 who belong to ultraconservative churches.

212 Fuller, Mrs. Charles E. *Heavenly Sunshine: Letters to the "Old-Fashioned Revival Hour"*. Westwood, N.J.: Fleming H. Revell, 1956.

The letters submitted by viewers that Grace Fuller read as part of each "Old-Fashioned Revival Hour" radio broadcast were perhaps the most popular feature of this early example of religious radio. This collection offers testimony to the prevalence of belief in supernatural intervention in daily life as the bulk of the letters report instances in which listeners recount how a simple but absolute faith in God turned tragedy to triumph and enabled them to gain confidence in their ability to cope with whatever they confronted.

213 Gaddy, Gary D., and David Pritchard. "When Watching Religious TV Is Like Attending Church." *Journal of Communication* 35 (1985): 123-31.

Using data from a Gallup poll commissioned by the popular evangelical magazine *Christianity Today*, Gaddy and Pritchard analyze the extent to which watching religious programs on television becomes a substitute for attending religious services. They conclude that Protestants are more likely than others to make this substitution and that the more hours per week that individuals watch religious programming, the less they actually attended formal religious services. They attribute the reason for lowered attendance to the functional similarity between the programs and formal services, noting that they both provide the same kind of gratification. Gaddy and Pritchard do not address such issues as whether advancing age or declining health might also lead viewers to watch religious programs instead of attending services in person.

214 Gerbner, George, and Kathleen Connoly. "Television as New Religion." *New Catholic World* 221 (March-April 1978): 52-56.

The title of this article is misleading for it deals primarily with a study of how television exaggerates and glorifies violence and materialism, while claiming to tell stories of everyday life. The religious dimension comes into play when the Gerbner and Connoly argue that the result of this emphasis is the creation of a symbol system, a set of cultural images that individuals use like a religious world view to give meaning and order to their lives.

215 Gitlin, Todd. *Inside Prime Time*. New York: Pantheon, 1983.

The twelfth chapter of this book, "The 'Far Righteous' Shake the Temple of Commerce" (pp. 247-63), is of some interest to students of popular religiosity. It focuses on the attacks led by Donald Wildmon on television advertisers who sponsor programs that are believed to undermine "traditional values" or on advertising that Wildmon believes satanic in origin. Gitlin notes that Wildmon often launches his attacks without having seen or screened the programs to which he objects on religious grounds and that the traditional values Wildmon espouses are often cast in extraordinarily vague terms.

216 Goethals, Gregor. "Religious Communication and Popular Piety." *Journal of Communication* 35 (1985): 149-56.

Goethals makes the case that in American culture, the integrative function of religion is now found in popular culture and the mass media; only the salvific function remains private and personal. He builds his argument not from explicit religious programming, but from how the communication coming from such phenomena as press conferences and the evening news bolsters a civil religion and uncritically supports the inchoate values identified with the "American way of life." Goethals believes that this form of civil religion is more dangerous to traditional religion than more explicit religious programming.

217   Hadden, Jeffrey K.   "The Rise and Fall of American Televangelism."   In *Religion in the Nineties*, ed. by Wade Clark Roof, 113-30. *Annals of the American Academy of Political and Social Science 527*. Newbury Park, Calif.: Sage Periodicals, 1993.

Hadden's essay is one of the more perceptive analyses written after scandal had brought the demise of televangelists Jimmy Swaggart and Jim and Tammy Faye Bakker in the late 1980s.   After providing a capsule history of religious broadcasting, Hadden assesses the impact of the scandals as well as shifts in the political impact of televangelists. He argues that although the immediate result was a decline in both the number of religious programs and financial support for them, religious television has moved in new directions that provide the base for continuing religious and political influence.   The two new approaches that Hadden emphasizes are the use of cable networks and the expansion of locally-owned religious stations that serve particular regions.

218   Hadden, Jeffrey K.   "Soul Saving via Video."   *Christian Century* 97 (28 May 1980): 609-613.

Sociologist Hadden in this article probes the ways in which televangelists are able to use technological media targeting the masses in such a way as to make viewers think they are important as individuals. He notes, for example, how the use of simple form letters generated by computer allows televangelists to provide a "personal" response to viewer letters. Hadden claims that there was in 1980 a ready audience for this type of personalized approach composed of those who were disaffected from or by society by the events of the 1960s and who longed for a more traditional, conservative culture.   He also calls attention to the standard anxiety expressed by religious leaders over the expansion of religious television programming, namely that it will compete with local religious organizations for financial and other support.

219   Hadden, Jeffrey K., and Charles E. Swann.   *Prime Time Preachers: The Rising Power of Televangelism*. Reading, Mass.: Addison-Wesley, 1981.

This book is one of the earliest scholarly studies and critiques of televangelism. Besides demonstrating that the typical regular viewer of religious television is a Southern white female over the age of 50, Hadden and Swann present statistical data suggesting that televangelists have consistently exaggerated the size of their viewing audience. They also argue that there is much overlap in viewership so that the number of those who are regular watchers of religious television is not the aggregate of the audiences of individual programs.

220 Hill, George H. *Airwaves to the Soul: The Influence and Growth of Religious Broadcasting in America.* Saratoga, Calif.: R & E Publishers, 1983.

This brief, but perceptive monograph is more descriptive than analytical. It summarizes information gleaned from a variety of surveys conducted between 1942 and 1979 and thus covers both religious radio and the phenomenon of the "electric church." Hill offers a barrage of valuable statistics for further study and gives information of many personalities, several of them not well known, who have been critical in the development of religious broadcasting. Valuable too is Hill's attention to black gospel, especially in radio. Most other studies restrict themselves to broadcasting aimed primarily at a white audience.

221 Hill, George H., and Lenwood G. Davis. *Religious Broadcasting, 1920-1983: A Selectively Annotated Bibliography.* New York: Garland, 1984.

This is a helpful reference work that covers not only key personalities in the history of religious radio and television broadcasting in the United States, but also works these broadcasters have written themselves. Hill and Davis also include material about the National Association of Religious Broadcasters as well as other organizations that have influenced the development of religious radio and television.

222 Hoover, Stewart N. *Mass Media Religion: The Social Sources of the Electronic Church.* Newbury Park, Calif.: SAGE Publications, 1988.

Following chapters that trace the historical origins of the fundamentalist and neoevangelical response to modernity, the history of religious broadcasting in the United States, and the history of CBN and the "700 Club" program, Hoover turns to interviews with viewers and members of Pat Robertson's "700 Club." He concludes that many are attracted to this program because it allows them to recover their own evangelical roots, either through having a personal religious experience as a result of watching the program or because they were viewing the "700 Club" at a time of personal crisis. Hence Hoover argues that religious television may be part of a larger revitalization movement in American religion emerging as a response to both the dislocation of modernity and the failure of the mainline churches to provide an authentic faith for members that works to give meaning to their lives. As with cognate analyses, this one confirms that most viewers are also involved in some organized religious group; those groups may be informal Bible studies as well as churches or similar organizations.

223 Horsfield, Peter G. "Evangelism by Mail: Letters from the Broadcasters." *Journal of Communication* 35 (1985): 89-97.

Horsfield wrote to five religious broadcasters claiming that he was a convert because of their media ministry. In this study he examines the responses he received. Over a nine month period, the five broadcasters sent him 54 mailings, including letters, magazines, and books. Only four of 45 letters made direct reference to his presumed conversion, but 44 asked for financial contributions. Horsfield concluded that the broadcasters were more interested in securing supporters for their own organizations and media ministries than they were in nurturing new converts by connecting them to local religious organizations.

224 Horsfield, Peter G. *Religious Television: The American Experience.* New York: Longman, 1984.

Horsfield provides a solid historical exposition of the development of religious television in the United States going back to the popular programs of Roman Catholic Fulton J. Sheen in the 1950s. He reviews the concern of religious leaders over whether religious television constitutes competition for organized religion and summarizes much prior research on the nature of the audience for religious programs. As with others, he concludes that the audience is larger in those areas of the United States where cognate polls indicate a higher degree of church attendance. Horsfield includes a helpful bibliography for further study.

225 Loveless, Wendell P. *Manual of Gospel Broadcasting.* Chicago: Moody Press, 1946.

Written in the peak epoch for religious radio broadcasting, this manual offers practical advice from an evangelical perspective for those who wanted to develop radio ministries. Loveless addresses such basics as how to train the voice for most effective use on the air and how to use a microphone. Five chapters are devoted to the unique techniques required of writing for radio. Today this book is of interest primarily for historical purposes. Yet it is valuable also because it appeared as part of a conscious effort to persuade evangelical Christians to use radio as a vehicle for proclamation of the gospel at a time when many evangelicals believed that radio itself was a threat to religious values and beliefs.

226 Martin, William C. "The God-Hucksters of Radio." In *Side-Saddle on the Golden Calf: Social Structure and Popular Culture in America*, ed. by George H. Lewis, 49-55. Pacific Palisades, Calif.: Goodyear, 1972.

Sociologist Martin, a recognized authority on the religious use of media technology, appraises in this essay the content of radio sermons. Most, he concludes, emphasized a practical religion that promoted health and wealth. Radio preachers offered simple, if not simplistic, definitions of right and wrong, good and evil, in an effort to appeal to the values of working class Americans.

227 Marty, Martin E. *The Improper Opinion: Mass Media and the Christian Faith*. Philadelphia: Westminster Press, 1961.

Marty's purview encompasses the larger world of mass media, including books, magazines, newspapers, film, radio, and television. Marty argued that the religious use of mass media was a greater threat to authentic faith than the secular use because the media fashioned a religion out of proximate social values and a common "faith" of self-help. Media religion, in his estimate, was deficient because it lacked the dimensions of worship and service that he regarded as central to genuine religiosity.

228 Marty, Martin E. "The Invisible Religion: A Closer Look at the Theology of the Electric Church." *Presbyterian Survey* 69 (May 1979): 13.

In this brief opinion piece, Marty criticized religious television for its failure to nurture faith, noting that the converts claimed by televangelists had not been confirmed by increases in the membership rolls of local congregations. He suggested that persons were drawn to the electric church because they found a personal fulfillment in this "invisible" (non-institutionalized) religion. Marty also expressed concern that the mainline religious groups lacked the financial resources to compete with the televangelists in developing alternative programming that would be more in keeping with historic Christian faith and practice.

229 Miller, Spencer, Jr. "Radio and Religion." *Annals of the American Academy of Political and Social Science* 177 (January 1935): 135-40.

This early analysis of religious use of radio surveys the policies then in effect for religious broadcasting among the major networks and their desire to have programs with a "non-sectarian" appeal. Miller articulates the recurring concern that religious broadcasting should not be construed as a substitute for corporate worship and the common anticipation that the medium nevertheless held great potential for spreading religion and reaching those who were not identified with an organized religious group.

230   Parker, Everett C., David W. Barry, and Dallas W. Smythe.   *The Television-Radio Audience and Religion*.   New York: Harper, 1955.

Written in the early days of commercial television, these three authors conclude that there was then no program that had the mass appeal of the urban revivalists of earlier generations.   They argued, however, that there was a danger should such develop for they believed that broadcasting would ultimately ignore or deny the fundamental purposes of the Christian church, especially in terms of its historical combination of worship, nurture, and service.   Their analysis of the audience revealed what have been continuing characteristics: the typical listener and/or viewer was an older female who was already a member of an organized religious group.

231   "Preaching by Wireless."   *Literary Digest* 72, 5 (1922): 650.

This unsigned piece appeared shortly after the first religious radio broadcast of January 1921.   It is one of the earliest statements of the recurring fear that those who listened to religious radio would evidence a lower rate of attendance at religious services and would be less likely to remain members or become members of an organized religious group.   The same concern a generation later shifted to religious television.   The author advances the criticism that became commonplace over the years that broadcasting eliminated the corporate dimension integral to traditional religion.

232   Roozen, David A., guest ed.   *Analyses of Religious Television*.   Special symposium issue.   *Review of Religious Research* 29, 2 (Winter 1987).

This special theme issue includes several articles pertinent to assessing the import of religious television for understanding the dynamics of popular religiosity.   Robert Wuthnow, for example, addresses "The Social Significance of Religious Television" (pp. 125-34), arguing that the growth of the electronic church has spurred the privatization of religion in American life.   Robert Abelman and Kimberly Neuendorf, in "Themes and Topics in Religious

Television Programming" (pp. 152-74), conclude that some explicit religious content dominates, although there has been an increase in raising social and political concerns. Stewart M. Hoover's essay, "The Religious Television Audience: A Matter of Significance, or Size?" (pp. 135-51), demonstrates that the aggregate audience is actually much smaller than televangelists have claimed and that the most religious viewers watch the most programming.

233 Schwarz, Hans. "The Electronic Church as an Expression of the American Religious Mind." In *Religion and Philosophy in the United States*, ed. by Peter Freese, 1:673-83. Essen, Germany: Verlag Die Blaue Eule, 1987.

Schwarz offers a critical appraisal of the way religious television actually works in American culture. He insists that the electronic church reinforces prevailing trends in popular belief; it does not induce change. His most potent criticism concerns the way religious programming offers instant gratification. Television preachers gear their message and their programs to what viewers want. To this extent, they minimize the prophetic dimension of religion and many of the central doctrines of traditional religious faith.

234 Starr, Michael E. "Prime Time Jesus." In *Popular Culture in America*, ed. by Paul Buhle, 163-73. Minneapolis: University of Minnesota Press, 1987.

Starr believes that the drama of salvation is played out on television because of the growth in religious broadcasting from the 1950s to the early 1980s. He argues that the American phenomenon of revivalism has found a new location in television, giving celebrity status to revivalists such as Billy Graham and Oral Roberts. Starr also demonstrates that much religious television is theologically ambiguous, if not simplistic, in an effort to appeal to larger audiences. He also notes that in the 1950s, religious television personalities consciously avoided mention of social issues in order not to offend viewers, but that the most prominent programs of the 1980s often addressed current social issues.

235 Swann, Charles. "The Electric Church." *Presbyterian Survey* 69 (May 1979): 9-12, 14-16.

Swann is highly critical of the simplistic theology articulated by televangelists; he stridently argues that the electric church tells people what they want to hear rather than challenging them. At the same time, Swann suggests that religious programming has been a bonanza to the broadcast industry because of it popularity. He notes that the televangelists have readily availed themselves of the most sophisticated methods the medium offers. Swann also attacks the emphasis placed on appeals for financial support from viewers, noting that little if any of the contributions received go to benevolent activities.

236 Thomas, Sari. "The Route to Redemption and Social Class." *Journal of Communication* 35 (1985): 111-22.

Thomas's thesis is that the content of religious television programs varies depending on the social class of the intended audience. Studying 186 episodes of 23 nationally-syndicated Protestant programs shown on Philadelphia television channels between 1981-and 1983, Thomas concluded that fourteen were aimed at the working class, six at the working middle class, and three primarily at those who were upwardly mobile. For example, those targeted toward the working class placed the greatest emphasis on the idea that having money generated negative results, did not produce happiness, and was rarely put to good use. Those aimed at an upwardly mobile audience never identified wealth with evil, more positively associated money with happiness, and stressed that money could be put to good use. Similar correlations occurred when program content stressed salvation. For the working class, stress was placed on personal piety; for the working middle class, on Christian living; for the upwardly mobile, on both Christian living and worldly accomplishments.

237 Tweedie, Stephen W. "Viewing the Bible Belt." *Journal of Popular Culture* 11 (1978): 865-76.

Tweedie advances a new method for defining the parameters of the "Bible belt." Whereas in popular perception the Bible belt is associated broadly with the South, in Tweedie's view a new configuration emerges is one uses the concentration of the audience of religious television as the basis for definition. He concludes that there are in reality two Bible belts, one more eastern that stretches from northern Florida through Alabama, Tennessee, North and South Carolina, and into Virginia, and another that is more western (though actually central), moving from central Texas to the Dakotas, but concentrated in Texas, Arkansas, Louisiana, Oklahoma, Missouri, and Mississippi.

6

Expressions of Popular Religion in the Arts

238 Allitt, Patrick. "The American Christ." *American Heritage* (November 1988): 128-41.

Allitt reviews images of Jesus found in popular novels and other writing intended for a mass audience. He deals with such familiar works as *Ben Hur* and *In His Steps*, as well as Henry Ward Beecher's *The Life of Jesus, the Christ* (1870) and the more recent *The Messiah* by Marjorie Holmes that appeared in 1987. He recognizes that the American Jesus tends to be a benevolent figure whose supernatural power is accessible to believers. Americans, Allitt concludes, want a Jesus who is with them wherever they go. This American Jesus, however, bears little resemblance to the far more complex figure portrayed in the New Testament, but much more reflects the cultural values of the time period in which the particular fictional portrayal was written.

239 Baker, Paul. *Contemporary Christian Music*. Rev. ed. Westchester, Ill.: Crossway Books, 1985.

Baker writes from an evangelical, conservative position in this brief commentary on contemporary Christian music. On the one hand, he sees great value in the appropriation of popular musical forms by Christian artists since they can be used to proclaim an evangelical gospel targeted primarily to a younger audience. On the other hand, he is also somewhat cautious in his appraisal, for he recognizes that there is a thin line between adopting and adapting popular culture forms and "selling out" to a popular culture that remains inimical to evangelical Christianity.

240 Baker, Paul. *Why Should the Devil Have All the Good Music?* Waco,

Tex.: Word Books, 1979.

In this work, Baker looks primarily at the "Jesus Music" of the 1970s as manifested in the compositions and artistry of such individuals as Andrae Crouch, Debby Boone, and Amy Grant. He also examines how this music was a catalyst in drawing thousands of young Americans to various Jesus festivals at that time. He praises the musicians for their technical achievements and applauds the appeal of Jesus music to the youth culture. At the same time, he repeats the often-stated fear that too eager appropriation of secular popular musical forms will lead to an abandonment of an authentic evangelical perspective.

241 Barkowsky, Edward Richard. "The Popular Christian Novel in America, 1918-1953." Ed.D. diss., Ball State University, 1975.

This dissertation represents one of the few secondary studies of popular religious fiction of the first half of the twentieth century. For the early period, the most sustained treatment is that of Ralph Connor's *Sky Pilot*. Barkowsky includes a valuable discussion of the work of Lloyd C. Douglas, whose religiously-based novels not only frequently made the best-seller lists, but in many cases provided the subject matter for feature-length commercial films. Barkowsky argues that the early novels of Douglas were designed to alleviate the economic distress wrought by the Depression by holding out religious faith as a means to gain material reward, but that the later novels began to look more to a mythic past and ancient values as the clues to attaining happiness in the present. For the period since 1939, Barkowsky documents an increase in the number of pro-Catholic religious novels, a reflection of the increased religious tolerance that is one concomitant of pluralism. But in all the works examined, Barkowsky concludes, religion is presented in simplistic terms, offering tools for persons to live well in the present and attain happiness in the here-and-now. What is missing is a concern for eschatology and the afterlife. That popular novels should have a practical, this-worldly focus is in keeping with the functional nature of much popular religiosity as an inchoate mixture of beliefs and practices that enable persons to make sense out of their lives in the present and gain a feeling of control over their own destinies in this life.

242 Ben-Yehuda, Nachman. "The Revival of the Occult and of Science Fiction." *Journal of Popular Culture* 20, 2 (Fall 1986): 1-16.

In this article, Ben-Yehuda attributes the resurgence of interest in the occult to its proclaimed ability to understand, use, and control supernatural power and thus to give order to life--all part of the dynamics of popular religiosity. He sees a parallel between intrigue with occult phenomena and the blossoming of science fiction since science fiction is likewise predicated on the assumption that there is power to transform the empirical world. Both, he believes, betoken a serious return to a lively sense of the sacred.

243 Bode, Carl. "Lloyd Douglas: Loud Voice in the Wilderness." *American Quarterly* 2 (1950): 340-58.

Because scholars have tended to dismiss literature targeted to a mass audience as being by definition of less value than presumed "great" writing, they have too readily ignored the novels of Lloyd C. Douglas. According to Bode, Douglas's novels merit more serious consideration for their implicit theological content. Bode believes that Douglas himself moved from a liberal theological position that marked his early years as a pastor and writer to espouse the tenets of Protestant neo-orthodoxy as the latter gained ascendancy in the 1930s and 1940s. The novels are therefore important vehicles in the transmission to a popular level of those theological currents moving through the larger Protestant traditions.

244 Bredeck, Martin J., S.J. *Imperfect Apostles: The Commonweal and the American Catholic Laity, 1924-1976*. New York and London: Garland, 1988.

The *Commonweal* began publication in 1924 as a magazine offering commentary on current events and religious issues written from a Catholic perspective and targeted for the educated Catholic laity. Bredeck's study focusses on the editorials that appeared over a period of 45 years when the magazine was under the direction of Michael Williams, Edward S. Skillin, and James O'Gara. Bredeck discerns an increasing acceptance of the tenets of democracy as a legitimate base for both church and government and a gradual espousal of the validity of religious pluralism. By the end of the period covered, the *Commonweal* had adopted an editorial stance that frequently criticized the Catholic Church and its hierarchy for failing to accept a greater voice for laity within the church and to recognize that laity had a responsibility to participate actively in society as Catholics even when their personal views might not mirror the official teachings of the church. Although Bredeck does not discuss popular religiosity directly, his argument supports the contention that American Catholics, as others, maintained a private, personal religiosity that was vital in giving direction to their lives even when formal doctrine was only one source sustaining that religiosity.

245 Brock, Van K. "Assemblies of God: Elvis and Pentecostalism." *Bulletin of the Center for the Study of Southern Culture and Religion* 3 (April 1979): 9-

15.

Brock argues that the Pentecostal style of the Assemblies of God was as vital a force in shaping Elvis Presley as were the jazz of Memphis's Beale Street, the Grand Old Opry, and Hollywood. Brock sees in the idiosyncratic body movement inextricably linked to Presley the movement of the Pentecostal preacher and the "automatisms" of Pentecostal experience of the power of the Spirit. Pentecostal experience fosters the same ecstatic release that Presley articulated in his music. Brock also suggests that the Pentecostal understanding of grace as freedom contributed to Presley's apparent sense of liberation from the constraints imposed by traditional morality.

246 Brown, David H. "Garden in the Machine: Afro-Cuban Sacred Art in Urban New Jersey and New York." Ph.D. diss., Yale University, 1989.

Brown offers an extraordinarily provocative study of how persons of Afro-Cuban descent developed an indigenous art in urban enclaves in the New York metropolitan area. Much of that art was rooted in a rural, agrarian culture where a lively appreciation of the supernatural prevailed. In turn, much of the sense of the supernatural was shaped by enduring threads of the African experience. One of the major contemporary religious influences is Santeria. Although Brown is also sensitive to the reasons why this expression of popular religiosity was perceived as threatening especially by Euro-Americans, he makes a compelling case for its authenticity and legitimacy as a genuine expression of spirituality.

247 Burton, Laurel Arthur. "Close Encounters of a Religious Kind." *Journal of Popular Culture* 17 (Winter 1983): 141-45.

This article advances the thesis that print advertisements, television commercials, and certain commercial films actually function as a medium for religious revelation. Many of those studied revolve around a sense of present evil that, if left unchecked, will bring eschatological catastrophe; but they also offer a means of salvation. One example must suffice: Burton uses popular advertisements for toothpaste in which the threat of tooth decay and plaque mark a realm of evil that has potentially catastrophic results, but use of a particular brand of toothpaste serves as a means of grace to bring release from evil. Burton finds similar themes in the series of "Star Wars" films.

248 Butler, Ivan. *Religion in the Cinema*. New York: A. S. Barnes, 1969.

Butler looks for religious themes in commercial films form the 1920s through the 1960s. Some of his subjects are obvious (e.g., DeMille's "King of Kings"). He is particularly interested in cinematic portrayals of Bible stories, the figure of Christ, and religious professionals such as priests, preachers, evangelists, and missionaries. At the same time, he is attuned to the theological dimensions in films like "The Inn of Sixth Happiness" and cinematic representations of religious controversy such as the depiction of the Scopes trial and debates over the teaching of theories of evolution in "Inherit the Wind." Butler operates on a fairly sophisticated level and tends to be more interested in theological implications than in matters of popular religiosity.

249 Cohen, Stanley. "Messianic Motifs, American Popular Culture, and the Judeo-Christian Tradition." *Journal of Religious Studies* 8 (Spring 1980): 24-34.

Cohen develops the well-known perceived congruence between the history of ancient Israel and the creation of the United States as a nation that was prominent in Puritan thinking. He is particularly interested in popular messianic figures. For example, he regards the "Lone Ranger" as a popular messiah of a non-apocalyptic sort whose mission was to restore an erring culture to its core values. Cohen also makes a case for seeing "Superman" and "Batman" as messianic figures of a different sort because their struggles against forces of evil take on a distinctly apocalyptic cast.

250 Crawford, David. "Gospel Songs in Court: From Rural Music to Urban Industry in the 1950's." *Journal of Popular Culture* 11 (1977): 551-67.

In the 1920s, according to Crawford, many song books containing gospel music appeared, but many lacked appropriate copyrights since the songs themselves often emerged in slightly variant forms in different places, all reflecting their popular roots in rural America. As radio became an important entertainment medium in the 1930s, the appeal of gospel expanded. But by the 1950s when gospel music had become a big business, there were numerous court cases over who held legal rights to particular gospel songs. Crawford is on target in distinguishing the early gospel song from the hymn, regarding the message of the gospel song as more directed to popular religiosity and often intended to be an agent of proselytizing.

251 Cusic, Don. *Sandi Patti: The Voice of Gospel*. New York: Dolphin Books, 1988.

Patti has established herself as both a major performer and arranger in the field of contemporary Christian music. Cusic has written an appreciative, uncritical popular biography that emphasizes the connections between Patti's personal religiosity and her work as a musician. In his view, Patti has a divine call to a specialized ministry that makes her much more than simply a professional musician.

252 Dawidoff, Nicholas. "No Sex. No Drugs. But Rock 'n' Roll (Kind of)." *New York Times Magazine*, 5 February 1995, 40-44, 66, 68-69, 72.

Dawidoff looks at the boom in the contemporary Christian music industry, noting that it rapidly approaching becoming a billion dollar business annually. He uses several groups and individuals as case studies to emphasize the tensions that pervade the field as performers are expected to lead model religious lives even as they compete with secular performers for recognition as musicians. Dawidoff notes that contemporary religious music was once dismissed by the larger popular music industry until it became a major economic force in the field. Now that it has gained economic stature, the field of contemporary Christian music, according to Dawidoff, faces the constant threat of compromise as industry magnates gradually take over its management and promotion.

253 Delloff, Linda Marie, Martin E. Marty, Dean Peerman, and James M. Wall. *A Century of the Century*. Grand Rapids, Mich.: Eerdmans, 1984.

In 1884 the *Christian Century* began publication as a popular magazine broadly reflecting the tradition of the Disciples of Christ. It quickly assumed a more ecumenical stance, becoming a voice for a middle-of-the-road to liberal mainstream Protestant perspective on current political and religious issues. The four contributors to this centennial volume all had intimate association with the *Century* in some sort of editorial capacity. Their essays note how the *Century* has consistently called for persons of religious faith to be actively engaged society, but the positions the *Century* has supported over the years reveal some continuity and some change. The *Century* has been a steady supported of civil rights for all Americans and called for Christian unity and a more vibrant appreciation of the global dimension of many social issues. At the same time, the *Century* supported the movement for national Prohibition, adopted an anti-Catholic position in the presidential election of 1928, and was nearly silent on the devastation of the Holocaust during World War II. The import of the *Century* lies in its being both a mirror and shaper of social attitudes informed by a more sophisticated popular Protestant religiosity.

254 DeMarr, Mary Jean. "Agnes Sligh Turnbull and the World of the Pennsylvania Scotch Presbyterians." *Journal of Popular Culture* 19, 4 (Spring 1966): 75-83.

Turnbull (1888-1982) was a novelist whose works include *The Day Must Dawn*, *Remember the End*, *The Rolling Years*, and *The Crown of Glory*. Although none was widely acclaimed by literary critics, all were designed for a popular audience whose religiosity was rooted in the Calvinistic base undergirding American Presbyterianism. According to DeMarr, Turnbull stressed the importance of personal religious faith as a way of coping with everyday life, tended to idealize the past as a time when true faith flourished, and communicated a subtle, but obvious anti-Catholicism.

255 DeMott, Benjamin. "Rock as Salvation." In *Popular Culture in America*, ed. by David Manning White, 191-204. Chicago: Quadrangle Books, 1970.

Originally appearing as an article in the *New York Times Magazine* in August 1968, DeMott's essay revolves around the question of whether rock music can be construed as a religious force because of much of its lyric content seems to offer something akin to mystical experience. The force of DeMott's argument is to dismiss the apparent religious dimension, seeing secular rock as offering transient escape from the quandaries that individuals confront in life rather than salvation from them. DeMott claims that the primary motivation behind rock music, however imaginative it may be musically, are market pressures.

256 Detter, Raymond Arthur. "A Ministry to Millions: Lloyd C. Douglas, 1877-1951." Ph.D. diss., University of Michigan, 1975.

This dissertation, running nearly 1000 pages, is an exhaustive scholarly analysis of popular novelist Lloyd C. Douglas and his work. Detter not only draws on all of Douglas's published work, he makes extensive use of private papers and cognate materials housed at the University of Michigan. Its greatest strength is the way it locates Douglas contextually in the larger cultural milieu. For example, Detter shows how Douglas's novels published in the 1920s portrayed religious faith as a necessary ingredient to economic success that was not captive to materialism, while those appearing during the years of the Great Depression held out personal religious faith as a source of personal peace in the midst of frustration. Detter suggests that Douglas consciously wrote to satisfy the needs of his perceived audience, primarily Protestants of a liberal bent and those who were successful in business but wrestling with the ethical dilemmas of that success.

257 Duncan, The Rev. Canon Joseph. *Popular Hymns: Their Authors and Teaching.* London: Skeffington House, 1910.

This older study, although based on sermons preached in Britain rather than in the United States, does examine the religious content of hymns popular in Protestant circles on both sides of the Atlantic in the opening decades of the twentieth century. While many today are less familiar, several are still found in many hymnals that are widely used, including "Rock of Ages," "Jesus, Lover of My Soul," "Just as I Am," and "Nearer, My God to Thee." The thrust of Duncan's commentary is that such hymns offer a simple faith or trust in divine power as an antidote to the pressures of daily life and become a means to grant individuals access to this realm of supernatural power. This sense of power pervades popular religiosity.

258 Egan, James. "Sacral Parody in the Fiction of Stephen King." *Journal of Popular Culture* 23, 3 (Winter 1989): 125-41.

Egan believes that King's best-selling fiction stands in the lineage of the Gothic which in turn carries an implicit religious meaning. Egan marshals examples to demonstrate that King finds organized religion spiritually bankrupt. He notes that in both *The Dead Zone* and *Carrie* King parodies fundamentalist obsessions, while *Cycle of the Werewolf* holds up clergy, sacraments, and religious rites to ridicule. But Egan also feels that there is a dimension of mysticism in some of King's work, especially *The Dead Zone* and *The Shining.*

259 Ellsworth, Donald P. *Christian Music in Contemporary Witness: Historical Antecedents and Contemporary Practice.* Grand Rapids, Mich.: Baker Book House, 1979.

Ellsworth's book, written from a self-conscious evangelical viewpoint, provides a useful look at precedent and historical background for the current surge of interest in adapting popular musical forms for Christian purposes. Ellsworth is aware, for example, that in all ages religious music has had a symbiotic relationship with more popular forms of musical expression and has always been subject to the criticism that drawing on secular forms carries the inherent danger of abandoning religion's traditional posture as a force transcendent to and wary of popular culture.

260 Elson, Ruth Miller. *Myths and Mores in American Best Sellers, 1865-1965.* New York and London: Garland, 1985.

Ruth Miller Elson devotes one chapter to "Religion: This World and The Next" in which she surveys best sellers with an explicit religious focus. As the rest of the book, this chapter presumes that best sellers are one means of discovering "what ideas were held by ordinary people in any period" (p. 1), although she recognizes that literature reveals more about what concepts were available to readers in their efforts to construct their own world views, not what they actually did with those ideas. In the century of materials that she surveys, Miller notes that there has been a small decline in the number of religiously-oriented best sellers although religion was a major element in virtually all novels until the 1920s. Between 1865 and 1965, the religious emphases changed. Early in the period, there was a concern for redemption. That gradually gave way to an understanding that the main role of religion was to offer comfort and consolation in times of difficulty, particularly in dealing with death. Religion is consistently portrayed as a positive moral force in early twentieth century writing, and even at mid-century was viewed as playing a key role in providing social stability. At the same time, Miller underscores the broad Christian tone of most of the best sellers, even those that portrayed clergy in less than favorable terms; until the mid-twentieth century nearly all religious best sellers were written by Christians, and many perpetuated antisemitic stereotypes of Jews.

261 Elzey, Wayne. "'What Would Jesus Do?' *In His Steps* and the Moral Codes of the Middle Class." *Soundings* 58 (1975): 463-89.

Elzey offers a critical reading of Charles M. Sheldon's best-selling *In His Steps* that concerns members of a Protestant congregation who agree for one year to ask themselves what Jesus would do in every situation they confront personally and professionally and then gear their own actions accordingly. Elzey uses interpretive constructs drawn particularly from the cultural anthropology of Claude Levi-Strauss to show that the novel in essence sees the values and interests of the upper class and those of the lower class as bipolar opposites, both of which are inherently dangerous, yet alluring, to persons who wish to live as Jesus would. In this way, the novel becomes a means of giving religious sanction to the morals and values identified with the urban middle class that was coming into its own in the 1890s when *In His Steps* first appeared. At the same time, by making the primary religious question ("What would Jesus do?") intensely personal, the novel reflects the increasingly common relegation of authentic religion to the private sphere, a hallmark of popular religiosity.

262 Fackre, Gabriel. "Archie Bunker: Vision and Reality." *Christian Century* 89 (19 July 1972): 772-74.

Theologian Fackre wrote this article when the television program "All in the
Family" was at the peak of its popularity. He begins by depicting Archie
Bunker, a leading character in the program, as a symbol of the alienation
experienced by many middle-aged, middle class Euro-Americans. But the heart
of the essay moves from analysis of the television program to an argument that
such "middle Americans" need liberation from bondage to the status quo and
that a Christian theology of God's reign must foster alliances with, not
alienation from, the poor, African Americans, and the young to be truly
inclusive.

263 Ferreira, James. "Only Yesterday and the Two Christs of the Twenties."
South Atlantic Quarterly 80 (1981): 77-83.

The two Christs that Ferreira compares and contrasts in this article are taken
from popular biographies of Jesus published in the 1920s: Bruce Barton's *The
Man Nobody Knows* and Giovanni Papini's *Life of Christ*. Barton's book
quickly became a best seller after it appeared in 1925; its portrayal of Jesus as
the consummate businessman and most popular dinner guest in Jerusalem struck
a chord with the reading audience of the day. As a result, most appraisals,
epitomized by Frederick Lewis Allen's in his *Only Yesterday*, have seen Barton
as creating a Jesus who mirrored the successful capitalist and thereby endorsing
the *laissez-faire* capitalism of the decade. To the contrary, Ferreira argues that
neither Barton nor Papini sought to give their readers a religious justification for
capitalist economics, but a Jesus who was believable because he seemed more
real and human.

264 Finley, Ruth E. *The Lady of Godey's*. Philadelphia: Lippincott, 1931.

For decades after it began publication in 1837, *Godey's Lady's Book* was among
the most popular of magazines geared to a mass audience of American women;
in its first 25 years of publication, it attained a circulation approaching 150,000,
and even after its demise remained a model for other popular women's
magazines. In its own way, particularly in the years following the Civil War,
Godey's Lady's Book undergirded many strands of popular religiosity. The
"lady of Godey's" that Finley examines was a woman nurtured a genteel
refinement in her husband and children. But that refinement came largely
through the inculcation of religious values, broadly construed, in the home. To
this extent, *Godey's Lady's Book* echoed the Victorian tendency to relegate
authentic religiosity to the domestic sphere which was seen as the domain of
women. But this shift of authentic religion away from established religious
institutions is also central to sustaining currents of popular religiosity.

265 Ford, James E. *"Battlestar Gallactica* and Mormon Theology." *Journal of Popular Culture* 17 (Fall 1983): 83-87.

Ford offers a speculative piece in which he examines the once popular television series "Battlestar Gallactica" with its portrayal of a future cosmic struggle between good and evil. His claim is that the approach taken by the series reflects the concept of salvation advanced by the Church of Jesus Christ of Latter-Day Saints, more commonly known as the Mormons. However, the aim of the series was not to proselytize, according to Ford. But he claims that the parallel between the series and Mormon thinking is intentional because the executive producer and principal writer was a practicing Mormon.

266 Forshey, Gerald E. "Popular Religion, Film, and the American Psyche." *Christian Century* 97 (30 April 1980): 489-93.

Forshey for many years has written occasional commentary for the *Christian Century* on the religious dimensions of popular film and literature. In this piece, he claims that over the decades, American films with an explicit religious subject have addressed a relatively narrow range of topics that represent problems pervading the collective American psyche. He notes, for example, that the figure of Pharaoh in Cecile B. DeMille's "The Ten Commandments" fits the image of the evil Communist that pervaded popular consciousness at the time the film appeared. Forshey also argues that the three most popular religious films of the late 1960s and early 1970s ("Rosemary's Baby," "The Exorcist," and "The Omen") all depicted popular dissatisfaction with the limits of empirical epistemology. Other films perpetuated a sense of corporate righteousness ("Ben Hur," "Quo Vadis"), while many simply reinforced popular culture values, especially those revolving around the idealized family and individual conscience ("A Man Called Peter," "One Foot in Heaven," "Friendly Persuasion").

267 [Frankiel], Sandra Sizer. *Gospel Hymns and Social Religion: The Rhetoric of Nineteenth-Century Revivalism*. Philadelphia: Temple University Press, 1978.

Frankiel demonstrates that the language of what are now regarded as the "old" gospel hymns that originated in the later nineteenth century revivals had more than just a religious function. Besides encapsulating the evangelical message, they worked to create a community of feeling, affective bonds that drew together those who found in the revivals keys to personal and social identity. Frankiel's work is also a solid model for looking at the multifaceted functions of religious music in more recent years.

268 Gambone, Robert L. *Art and Popular Religion in Evangelical America,*
1915-1940. Knoxville: University of Tennessee Press, 1989.

Gambone looks primarily at paintings, drawings, and lithographs with explicitly
religious themes that were influenced by the revivalism of Billy Sunday, the
movement that led to Prohibition, the Harlem Renaissance, and popular
evangelical hymn texts. All these phenomena, according to Gambone, were
vital to the popular culture of the day and all had a base in Protestant
evangelical understanding. Among the artists whose work he analyzes are
Thomas Hart Benton, Grant Wood, John Stuart Curry, George Bellows, Wyman
Adams, and Paul Sample. The book is richly illustrated with color plates and
figures

269 Gill, Jerry H. "The Gospel According to Bruce." *Theology Today* 45
(April 1988): 87-94.

The "Bruce" in the title of Gill's article is popular singer Bruce Springsteen.
Gill suggests that Springsteen's music speaks especially to blue collar young
adults for whom the personal experience of the American dream has gone sour.
Gill finds this particularly in lyrics that describe the drudgery of labor and
disappointments in romantic love. At the same time, he argues that Springsteen
offers a gospel of hope and redemption through the energy of the music itself,
an emphasis on individual decision and responsibility, descriptions in the songs
of a more realistic approach to love, and words that talk about cleansing and
renewal.

270 Gold, Mike. "Wilder: Prophet of the Genteel Christ." *New Republic* 64
(22 October 1930): 266-67.

This brief essay critically reviews several of Thornton Wilder's works, including
The Cabala, The Bridge of San Luis Rey, The Woman of Andros, and *The Angel*
That Troubled the Waters. Gold builds this review around Wilder's own claim
that he was attempting to restore the spirit of religion to American literature.
Gold insists, however, that the figure of Christ that emerges in Wilder's writing
is akin to a proper British gentleman and that the religion Wilder espouses is
simply a "parlor Christianity" because Wilder's rhetoric is too neat to reveal
both the agony and the exaltation that accompany the biblical Christ. The image
that Wilder gives to the popular mind, according to Gold, is one where the
function of religion is to perpetuate good manners.

271 Goldsmith, Marlene. "Video Values Education: *Star Trek* as Modern

Myth." *Religious Education* 78 (Summer 1983): 421-22.

This brief report summarizes the main thesis of Goldsmith's 1981 doctoral dissertation at the University of Minnesota. She claims that even though the "Star Trek" series was filmed in the 1960s, the shows reflect the values of the 1950s in their unquestioned faith in freedom and progress, their ambivalent view of gender equality, and their portraying non-Americans as subservient despite a rhetoric of equality.

272 Graham, Stephen R. "Bill and Gloria Gaither." In *Twentieth-Century Shapers of American Popular Religion*, ed. by Charles H. Lippy, 155-62. Westport, Conn.: Greenwood, 1989.

There is a dearth of secondary literature about Bill and Gloria Gaither, two of the leading vocalists, composers, and arrangers of contemporary Christian music. Graham's piece is one of the few to offer some analysis and appraisal. Graham notes how the Gaithers consciously seek to relate their understanding of the gospel to the routine events encountered by ordinary people in everyday life, while avoiding what might be controversial or confrontational.   In summarizing the few published interviews with the Gaithers, Graham discusses how they, as other artists in the field of contemporary Christian music, have been forced to defend their appropriation of popular musical forms.

273 Greeley, Andrew. "The Catholic Imagination of Bruce Springsteen." *America* 158 (6 February 1988): 110-15.

Catholic sociologist Greeley makes a case that Springsteen's music reveals the singer and composer's early Catholic background. He looks at Springsteen as a liturgist with a minstrel ministry who emphasizes the conflict between good and evil and indirectly calls for redemption through the use of symbols of rebirth such as water and light. Greeley admits, however, that this Catholic imagination is implicit rather than explicit.

274 Gruver, Rod. "The Blues as Secular Religion." *Blues World* 29 (April 1970): 3-6; 30 (May 1970): 4-7; 31 (June 1970): 5-7; 32 (July 1970): 7-9.

Gruver claims that contemporary blues presents a religion of self-affirmation that is set over against traditional Christian moralism. In the lyrics of blues, Gruver finds the apotheosis of men and women in a mythologizing of sexuality. In particular, Gruver sees blues lyrics as turning women into gods.

275 Hackett, Alice Payne. *Seventy Years of Best Sellers, 1895-1965.* New York and London: R. R. Bowker, 1967.

Hackett's work is more expository than critical, more a cataloguing of works classified as best sellers than an analysis of what cultural forces made them so attractive to the American reading public. Yet not all the works identified here necessarily appeared on the lists of best selling works assembled by the literati, although some did. Hackett notes, for example, that in the twentieth century several works that offered aids to private devotion and personal religious reflection sold in excess of a million copies each in the year of publication. Among them are Mary W. Tileson's *Daily Strength for Daily Needs* (1901), *Bible Readings for the Home Circle* (1914), and *Streams in the Desert* (1931) by Mrs. Charles E. Cowman. Such works, intended for domestic use apart from the ministrations of religious professionals or the doctrines of religious institutions, are major sources for understanding the sense of the supernatural that underlies popular religiosity as well as its practical bent; devotion is meant to empower individuals to get through life.

276 Harris, Michael W. *The Rise of Gospel Blues: The Music of Thomas Andrew Dorsey in the Urban Church.* New York: Oxford University Press, 1992.

Harris's careful study is one of the few to examine the music of Dorsey, most well-known for his "Precious Lord, Take My Hand." Harris builds a strong argument that one cannot understand the gospel blues that Dorsey developed without also appreciating the dynamics of African American Christianity. In particular, Harris highlights the urban black church of the opening years of the twentieth century, when migration of African Americans to cities brought both religious dislocation and adaptation. That milieu, according to Harris, provided the ethos for the gospel blues genre associated with Dorsey.

277 Hart, James D. *The Popular Book: A History of America's Literary Taste.* New York: Oxford University Press, 1950.

As the title suggests, this book surveys popular literature from the colonial period to the mid-twentieth century. Hart gives particular attention to *Ben Hur*, not only as a book but as a play and film. He notes, for example, that over two decades around 20 million persons saw the stage version. How they appropriated its message into their personal religiosity, however, he leaves for other analysts. He also highlights works such as Ralph Waldo Trine's *In Tune With the Infinite*, which sold in excess of one and a quarter million copies in the half century after its publication in 1896. Trine's work is a prime example of the precursor of contemporary self-help literature.

278 Heilbut, Tony. *The Gospel Sound: Good News and Bad Times*. Garden City, N.Y.: Anchor Books, 1975.

This study, now somewhat dated, provides a good history of the development of gospel as a distinctive musical genre. Heilbut gives some of the flavor of the religious background for gospel, as intimated in the subtitle. The essence of gospel was to offer a vision of hope to a people who were oppressed and excluded. Heilbut also explicates connections between gospel and other musical genres such as jazz and the blues.

279 Herx, Henry. "Religion and Film." In *Encyclopedia of the American Religious Experience*, ed. by Charles H. Lippy and Peter W. Williams, 3:1341-58. New York: Scribners, 1988.

The opening section of this essay looks at the development of film as an entertainment medium and as an industry. Herx also directs attention to the religious spectacles made by American film makers in the 1920s before examining images of clergy and organized religion in films made in the United States since 1930 as well as the biblical epics produced since then. Some treatment is given to religious themes and subjects in European film. Herx provides an intriguing discussion of the connections between religion and censorship, particularly the attempts to use religious and traditional morality as a standard for what is appropriate in commercial films.

280 Hollinger, Dennis P. "American Individualism and Evangelical Social Ethics: A Study of *Christianity Today*, 1956-1976." Ph.D. diss., Drew University, 1981.

Christianity Today began publication in 1956 as an evangelical alternative to the *Christian Century*, which was perceived as too liberal in its focus. What stands out when Hollinger examines its coverage and treatment of ethical issues, particularly those with a social dimension, is the individualistic social philosophy that runs through the magazine's pages. When social problems were discussed, their resolution was found in individual behavior, not changes in social structures. Hollinger finds this particularly true in the area of economics, where *Christianity Today* during the years covered consistently saw both wealth and poverty as resulting from individual behavior. Both *Christianity Today* and this dissertation offer insight into the personal religiosity informed by an evangelical perspective as evangelicalism was understood at mid-century.

281 Hulteen, Bob. "Of Heroic Proportions: Fifty Years of Captain America."
Sojourners 19 (August-September 1990): 39, 41-43.

Hulteen rightly suggests that comic books are a mirror of society and its values.
Hence he offers in the neo-evangelical *Sojourners* a brief analysis of the Captain
America comic book character, assuming that Captain America echoes the values
of an American civil religion. Hulteen notes that in the first three decades of
the cartoon character's history, Captain America was a staunch defender of an
abstract freedom and a white, middle class American way of life. But Captain
America retreated in the 1970s in the wake of the Watergate scandals, a time
when even academicians mourned the erosion of common values that exerted a
religious function in providing a broadly-based social cohesion.

282 Hurley, Neil P., S.J. "Christ-Transfigurations in Film: Notes on a Meta-
Genre." *Journal of Popular Culture* 13 (Spring 1980): 427-33.

Hurley focuses on more elusive Christ figures or, as he calls them, Christo-
morphic figures, in film. He is interested in characters that model Christ's life
that do not have obvious or direct parallels because he assumes that such reveal
the underlying cultural penetration of Christianity. Among his examples are
Paul Newman's title role in "Cool Hand Luke" and the character of Calvero
played by Charlie Chaplin in "Limelight."

283 Hurley, Neil. "Hollywood's New Mythology." *Theology Today* 39
(January 1983): 402-408.

In this article, Hurley draws on the various "Superman," "Star Wars," and "Star
Trek" films as well as those such as "ET" to argue that cinema has created a
mythology that departs from that advanced by traditional religion. In the
Hollywood mythology, science, technology, and organizational advances become
forces that have the power to effect fundamental changes in human nature. In
this sense, the mythology of film represents a decisive break with traditional
religious values and approaches.

284 Hustad, Don. "The Explosion of Popular Hymnody." *The Hymn* 33 (July
1982): 159-67.

This essay is one of the first to offer critical appraisal of the surge in popular
hymnody that has occurred since 1960 when Beaumont's "Twentieth Century
Folk Mass" appeared. Hustad notes that different styles of popular hymns,
which he defines as sacred music sung by a congregation, have developed in the

liturgical and more liberal churches than in those of a more evangelical bent where "minihymns" and Scripture songs are more prevalent. He looks at the contribution made by musicians as diverse as Richard Avery and Donald Marsh on the one hand, and Bill and Gloria Gaither on the other.

285 Jennings, Willie J. "When Mahalia Sings: The Black Singer of Sacred Song as Icon." *Journal of Black Sacred Music* 3 (Spring 1989): 6-13.

Jennings draws on the Eastern Orthodox understanding of the religious icon to argue that the singer becomes a sacramental vessel with a transcendent, eschatological dimension when communicating a message of suffering and oppression leading to redemption. Mahalia Jackson serves as a case study to illustrate the thesis.

286 Jones, G. William. *Sunday Night at the Movies*. Richmond, Va.: John Knox, 1967.

Jones derives his title from the perception that going to see commercial films has replaced attendance at formal Sunday evening worship services for many American Christians. He wants to take film seriously as an art form. Even more, he argues that film often functions as a parable to make a statement about the human condition in much the way the parables recounted in the New Testament do. For examples, he draws on films such as "The Hustler," "The Edge of the City," and "Blue Denim."

287 Karr, Jean. *Grace Livingston Hill, Her Story and Her Writings*. New York: Greenberg, 1948.

Grace Livingston Hill (1865-1947) published 79 novels targeted to a popular female audience. All in one form or another extolled the practical value of a nebulously defined Christian faith for resolving life's problems or providing a way to deal with crisis situations. In many respects, Hill's novels are the direct forerunners of contemporary Christian romance and mystery novels. None of Hill's books made the best seller lists, although they sold more than 3 million copies during Hill's lifetime. Many have been updated and reissued or reprinted. Karr's study is the only full-length treatment of Hill's life and work. It is hardly analytical, but does contain a complete bibliography of the works Hill published under her own name or pseudonymously. Hill's writing grants access to many of the currents sustaining the religiosity of American women in the early twentieth century.

288 Kreuziger, Frederick A. *The Religion of Science Fiction.* Bowling Green, Ohio: Bowling Green State University Popular Press, 1986.

Kreuziger regards science fiction has being essentially religious. He bases this understanding on a functionalist approach to religion; that is, whatever individuals use to create a world view that gives meaning to life has a religious dimension or function. In this analysis, the apocalyptic aspect of science fiction is paramount. Apocalypticism in this context refers not only to some cataclysmic doomsday that will bring history to a close, but the vision of a positive future when the vagaries of the present have been resolved. Apocalyptic therefore offers hope. According to Kreuziger, the apocalyptic base of science fiction "comforts and gives hope to those who are disillusioned by the failure of science and technology to deliver the world from ignorance, poverty, disease, famine, plague, war and death" (p. 15).

289 Long, Kathryn. "Godey's Lady's Book." In *Popular Religious Magazines of the United States,* ed. by P. Mark Fackler and Charles H. Lippy, 240-46. Westport, Conn.: Greenwood, 1995.

This brief essay offers a sketch of the publication history of one of the nineteenth century's most popular magazines for women. Long is particularly sensitive to the ways that *Godey's Lady's Book* sought to buttress Victorian notions of female religiosity and thus how it helped give its readership a personal religious identity that supplemented whatever religious nurture and guidance women received from traditional religious institutions.

290 Mable, Norman. *Popular Hymns and Their Writers.* 2nd ed. London: Independent Press, 1951.

This study provides an uncritical, but very appreciative look at many hymns regarded as "old favorites" among Protestant Christians at mid-century. Each two-to-three page exposition, arranged alphabetically by the last name of the writer of the hymn lyrics, gives a brief synopsis of the circumstances that led to the writing of the hymn and of the theological points it makes. Although Mable is a British writer working from British hymnals, many of the ones he discusses still appear in hymnals used in American Protestant circles. Among the hymns discussed are "Blest Be the Tie That Binds," "Faith of Our Fathers," and "Just As I Am."

291 Mander, Mary S. "*Dallas*: The Mythology of Crime and the Moral Occult." *Journal of Popular Culture* 17 (Fall 1983): 44-50.

Mander sees the prime-time television series "Dallas," which reached the peak of its popularity in the early 1980s, as portraying the moral ambiguity that pervades the modern world. Such ambiguity pervades both the business ventures portrayed on the program as well as the personal relationships among members of the Ewing family, the central characters on the show. The emphasis on a moral void and a resulting despair, according to Mander, transforms the program into a study of the ongoing conflict between good and evil that undergirds popular religiosity.

292 Marsh, Spencer. *God, Man, and Archie Bunker.* New York: Harper and Row, 1975.

Marsh's brief commentary focuses on the once popular "All in the Family" television program. In Marsh's view, Archie Bunker, the central character in the series, is a classic representation of "everyman" in his struggles to hold to absolutes in a relativistic world. Often Archie's situation seems hopeless, but time and again he is set in the right by his wife, Edith, whom Marsh regards as a prototypical Christ figure.

293 Martin, Bernice. "The Sacralization of Disorder: Symbolism in Rock Music." *Sociological Analysis* 40 (Summer 1979): 87-124.

The social anthropology of Mary Douglas and Victor Turner informs this analysis. Following Turner, Martin argues that youth represents a liminal stage in the life process where people turn to symbols of antistructure to create "communitas." This antistructure Martin finds in the dress and behavior of rock stars and their musical techniques for all seem to promote anarchy, taboo-breaking, and ambiguity. By turning rock stars into totem figures and using the beat of rock music as a ritualized symbol, youth create communitas.

294 Maus, Cynthia Pearl. *Christ and the Fine Arts: An Anthology of Pictures, Poetry, Music, and Stories Centering in the Life of Christ.* New York: Harper and Brothers, 1938.

The aim of this book is both devotional and pedagogical. In the introduction, Maus explains her conviction that the fine arts can be used to teach religion, communication truths, and make spiritual values creative. The various topical sections of the book trace the life of Christ from the nativity through the ascension. Maus offers devotional commentary on various popular poems, paintings, and hymns that sometimes includes valuable information on the circumstances that led to their creation. Most of the works of art she discusses have been popular among American Protestants of the early twentieth century.

295 Maus, Cynthia Pearl, in collaboration with John P. Cavarnos, Jean Louise Smith, Ronald E. Osborn, and Alfred T. DeGroot. *The Church and the Fine Arts: An Anthology of Pictures, Poetry, Music, and Stories Portraying the Growth and Development of the Church through the Centuries*. New York: Harper and Brothers, 1960.

A companion volume to Maus's *Christ and the Fine Arts*, this book organizes its meditative and expository pieces around the apostolic church, the Eastern Orthodox church, Roman Catholicism, the Protestant Reformation, American Protestantism, and Christianity in the non-western world. Although the book has this historical format, many of the paintings, poems, and songs or hymns that the writers examine were the work of Americans of the nineteenth and twentieth centuries. The various articles offer insight into many strands of the popular piety of American Protestants.

296 May, John R., and Michael Bird, eds. *Religion in Film*. Knoxville: University of Tennessee Press, 1982.

May and Bird adopt a functional definition of religion in that they regard the role of religion as giving meaning to life. That understanding underlies the three sections that structure the collection of essays: religious interpretation of film through dramatic action and structure, film as a cinematic genre that gives power to viewers through portrayal of cultural currents and tensions, and discussion of film directors such as Stanley Kubrick, Ingmar Bergman, Federico Fellini, and others who have been open to using film as a forum for communicating religious concerns.

297 Medved, Harry, and Michael Medved. *The Golden Turkey Awards*. New York: Berkeley, 1981.

Harry and Michael Medved are highly critical of much of the film industry, offering dubious awards for what they regard as poor performances or bad films. Their evaluative criteria are not always obvious. One section bears on popular religion: a short discussion of the "Worst Performance by an Actor as Jesus Christ." For this honor, they single our Ted Neeley, who played Jesus in "Jesus Christ Super Star." Neeley, according to the authors, created a "screaming Jesus" in a "hysterical performance."

298 Messbarger, Paul R. *Fiction with a Parochial Purpose: Social Uses of American Catholic Literature, 1884-1900.* Boston: Boston University Press, 1971.

Messbarger examines fiction written by and for American Catholics at a time when the Catholic population was growing at an extraordinary rate thanks to heavy immigration. Much of the fiction extolled private devotion, a central feature of popular religiosity. And like all popular religiosity, this devotion had numerous practical purposes. Messbarger demonstrates, for example, how fiction saw private devotion as valuable in resolving marital difficulties, ensuring material success, protecting the faithful from physical danger, enabling the pious to avoid temptation, giving guidance on proper social behavior, and the like. In other words, Catholic fiction was intended to facilitate the accommodation of Catholics to American culture in a way that sustained their Catholic identity. Messbarger looks not only at novels, but also at such popularly-oriented magazines as the *Young Catholic*, a Sunday School paper that was designed to raise the religious sensibilities of Catholic children. As well, Messbarger comments on the anti-Catholic attitudes that pervaded much other popular writing of the day.

299 Montgomery, Edrene S. "Bruce Barton's *The Man Nobody Knows*: A Popular Advertising Illusion." *Journal of Popular Culture* 19, 3 (Winter 1985): 21-34.

Montgomery reminds readers that Barton's immensely popular biography of Jesus was first published in serial form in *Women's Home Companion*. The articles reviews the contemporary criticism of Barton's work by the theological elite on the grounds that it emphasized the humanity rather than the divinity of Jesus and followed a modernist perspective in playing down such matters as the virgin birth, resurrection, and second coming. What made Barton's book so popular, Montgomery argues, was its concreteness; a middle-class adrift from its Victorian moorings found the physical description of Jesus a source of personal inspiration in that fed their hunger for wholeness. Photocopies of advertisements used to promote *The Man Nobody Knows* accompany the article.

300 Morgan, David. "Imaging Protestant Piety: The Icons of Warner Sallman." *Religion and American Culture* 3 (Winter 1993): 29-47.

Morgan opens with a perceptive methodological statement regarding the importance of understanding how art in any form is received if one is to grasp the impact of popular religious art. Morgan then examines numerous accounts by ordinary Americans discussing what they found in Sallman's "Head of

Christ," leading him to conclude that the image had a transparent quality. That is, the portrayal of Christ ceased to call attention to itself as an image, but revealed what others found to be vital truths about their own lives. Morgan finds a similar process with other illustrations and work by Sallman, buttressing his conclusion that Sallman's art, as virtually all popular religious art, depicted "sentiments, values, and ideals that millions of Christians felt were under siege in American life" (p. 36).

301 Morgan, David. "Sallman's *Head of Christ*: The History of an Image." *Christian Century* 109 (7 October 1992): 868-70.

Perhaps no painting of Jesus has been more popular among American Protestants than the "Head of Christ" fashioned by Warner Sallman, by profession an illustrator.   Designed as a cover for the religious periodical *Covenant Companion*, this representation of Christ, according to Morgan, was influenced by the earlier work of a French artist. Morgan captures well the way in which this painting took on a role among Protestants akin to that of the crucifix among American Catholics as a popular decoration for the home, Sunday school room, and the like.

302 Mott, Frank Luther. *Golden Multitudes: The Story of Best Sellers in the United States*. New York: R. R. Bowker, 1947.

Defining a best seller as any book with sales totalling one percent of the population at the time of publication, Mott not only identifies key titles from 1638 to 1947, he also offers extended comment and analysis of several of them. For example, there is critical exposition of Lew Wallace's *Ben Hur*, Charles M. Sheldon's *In His Steps*, and the several best selling novels by Harold Bell Wright. Mott notes that nearly one-third of all best sellers prior to 1915 had an overt religious theme and that nearly 15 percent of the best selling authors came from the ranks of the clergy. Mott singles out the way religious faith can be a source for individual self-improvement as the most frequently recurring religious theme.

303 Northcott, Cecil. *Hymns We Love: Stories of the Hundred Most Popular Hymns*. Philadelphia: Westminster, 1954.

Although it is not clear by what means Northcott determined which hymns were indeed the most popular among American Protestants, he offers a series of one-to-two-page vignettes explaining the circumstances that led to the writing of the hymn lyrics and in many cases also of the writing of the tune associated with them. Northcott's work is clearly intended for a lay audience and designed to inspire as much as to inform. His interest is exclusively directed to songs found in hymnals of the larger Protestant denominations. Hence he is not concerned with the genre of the gospel hymn or chorus. Among the hymns he examines are "Abide with Me," "Beneath the Cross of Jesus," and "The Church's One Foundation."

304 Pascal, Richard. "Walt Whitman and Woody Guthrie: American Prophet-Singers and Their People." *Journal of American Studies* 24 (April 1990): 41-59.

Despite the title, this essay has minimal discussion of religion per se, although Pascal does claim that both Whitman and Guthrie became religious prophets of sorts because of their imaginative use of language and their exaltation of egalitarianism as Christ-like. The thrust of the article, however, is an argument seeking to demonstrate the influence of Whitman on the lyrics and writing of Woody Guthrie.

305 Phelps, Elizabeth Stuart. *The Gates Ajar*. Edited by Elizabeth Sootin Smith. Cambridge, Mass.: Harvard University Press, 1964.

While this annotated bibliography concentrates almost exclusively on secondary sources, this popular novel is included because of the critical introduction provided by the editor, Elizabeth Sootin Smith. *The Gates Ajar* was not a best seller, but it did attract much popular attention since it sold an estimated 80,000 copies in the United States between its publication in 1868 and the end of the century. The introduction offers insight into exactly how Phelps's domesticated view of heaven was a means of linking empirical reality and the realm of the supernatural. One of the functions of popular religion is to create precisely that kind of bridge.

306 Phy, Allene Stuart. "The Bible as Literature for American Children." In *The Bible and Popular Culture in America*, ed. by Allene Phy, 165-91. *The Bible in American Culture* 2. Philadelphia: Fortress, and Chico, Calif.: Scholars Press, 1985.

This article looks at how the Bible was presented in materials written primarily for children, regardless of formal religious background. It concentrates on the period after the publication of the *Child's Bible Reader* (1898). Phy notes that there has been a tendency to focus on stories from the Hebrew Bible (Old Testament) in order to appeal to an audience that might include Jews as well as

Christians.   But the major emphasis, until quite recently, was on promoting a commitment to private, personal devotion in children by holding up models of religious faith such as Moses. Really only after the mid-twentieth century did more accurate attention to detail mean that the materials became more appropriate for instructional use.

307 Phy, Allene Stuart.   "Retelling the Greatest Story Ever Told: Jesus in Popular Fiction." In *The Bible and Popular Culture in America*, ed. by Allene Phy, 42-83. *The Bible in American Culture* 2. Philadelphia: Fortress, and Chico, Calif.: Scholars Press, 1985.

Phy's essay in this important book gives very brief, but trenchant commentary on numerous fictional portrayals of Jesus in American literature published between 1850 and 1980. In addition to treating titles one would expect such as *Ben Hur*, several of the works of Lloyd C. Douglas, and Fulton Oursler's *The Greatest Story Ever Told*, Phy also looks at lesser known portrayals, such as those found in selected writings of Upton Sinclair, Taylor Caldwell, Frank Slaughter, Jim Bishop, and others. Although many of the books discussed were artistic failures according to the canons of elite literature, they did emphasize how private, personal faith even in a fictionalized Jesus could give a sense of power to the individual.   To that extent, they are, according to Phy, fictionalized versions of the more overt self-help literature produced by Norman Vincent Peale, Joshua Liebman, Fulton J. Sheen, Catherine Marshall, and others.

308 Pollard, Alton B., III. "Religion, Rock, and Eroticism." *Journal of Black Sacred Music* 1 (Spring 1987): 47-52.

Primarily using rock star Prince as a case study, Pollard argues that contemporary rock music highlights the dilemma of youth who confront faltering authorities that were once absolute (government, the church, technology). In the absence of such authorities, youth turn to the only area where they have control, their bodies, and transform biological orgasm into a religious phenomenon in which the transcendent becomes incarnate.

309 Raphael, Marc Lee. "From Marjorie to Tevya: The Image of the Jews in American Popular Literature, Theatre, and Comedy, 1955-1965." *American Jewish History* 74 (September 1984): 66-72.

Raphael's examples range from Herman Wouk's *Marjorie Morningstar* to the musical *Fiddler on the Roof* and the comedy of Alan Sherman. He is particularly appreciative of the novels of Leon Uris because he finds in them solid portrayals of Jews who are worthy hero and heroine figures. Sherman's comedy is likewise viewed in a positive vein for the way in which it uses popular cultural stereotypes of Jewish parents to show a genuine underlying humanity.

310 Real, Michael R. "Trends in Structure and Policy in the American Catholic Press." *Journalism Quarterly* 52 (Summer 1975): 265-71.

Real examines the amazing growth of a popular Catholic press in the nineteenth century when 1822 to mid-century a new Catholic newspaper was established at the rate of one per year. Even by the later twentieth century, several diocesan papers maintained circulations in excess of 100,000. Hence the papers provide a critical key to understanding the signals Catholic readers received about Catholic belief and practice, signals they could use in forging their own religious identities. Real notes that for much of the nineteenth century, the papers were independent of institutional control, although there has been a trend, especially pronounced in the years since Vatican II (1962-1965) to bring the papers under more direct control of the church hierarchy. The reason for the church leadership's desiring greater control was the controversial position some papers often took, occasionally criticizing if not rejecting the formal teaching of the church as an institution. Such criticism helped bolster the private popular religiosity of Catholic laity who remained intent on developing their own private beliefs, including some that were at odds with formal Catholic doctrine, while retaining a Catholic identity.

311 Ribuffo, Leo P. "Jesus Christ as Business Statesman: Bruce Barton and the Selling of Corporate Capitalism." *American Quarterly* 33 (1981): 206-231.

Ribuffo provides a carefully crafted statement of the familiar critique of Barton's *The Man Nobody Knows*. Because Barton was himself a successful advertising executive, he created a Jesus who exemplified the latest in corporate leadership styles in the way he mustered the loyalty of the disciples and captivated the masses, who readily adopted what a business age would call advertising techniques to promote his message, and in his teaching gave a strong endorsement to the values that perpetuated capitalism and were especially prominent in the 1920s.

312 Rice, Milburn. "The Impact of Popular Culture on Congregational Song." *The Hymn* 44, 1 (January 1993): 11-19.

Rice argues that an implicit incarnational theology lies behind contemporary Christian music. Aware that critics have panned such music, Rice demonstrates that there is ample historical precedent in American Christianity for using forms taken from popular culture and that one aspect of American religious music has long been directed to filling consumer desires. Among the historical precedents that he uses to bolster his argument are the use of praise choruses in movements such as Youth for Christ in the 1940s and 1950s, the long heritage of African-American gospel music with its connections not only to the spiritual but also to blues and jazz, and the folk musicals that were popular among youth in the 1960s.

313   Rosenberg, Ann Elizabeth. *Freudian Theory and American Religious Journals, 1900-1965*. Studies in American History and Culture 17. Ann Arbor, Mich.: University of Michigan Research Press, 1980.

Rosenberg's work aids students of popular religion in understanding when and how sophisticated psychological theories began to filter down to ordinary religious folk. She looks particularly at pastoral psychologists who were writing for religious periodicals. Many of them, such as Seward Hiltner, also wrote for a popular audience. Rosenberg claims that in the twentieth century, these psychologists drew increasingly on the psychoanalytic theories of Freud, although not uncritically, and prior to 1965 were prone to combine psychoanalytic constructs with those drawn from existential philosophy. Gradually, the theories of Jung gained ascendancy. She argues that Roman Catholic writers were harsher in their criticism of Freud, but that Jewish writers were the most accepting. She attributes the latter in part to the immense popularity of Rabbi Joshua Liebman's best-selling *Peace of Mind* that appeared in 1946.

314   Russell, Mary Ann Underwood. "Lloyd C. Douglas and His Larger Congregation: The Novels and a Reflection of Some Segments of the American Popular Mind of Two Decades." Ph.D. diss., George Peabody College for Teachers, 1970.

This dissertation provides a comparative analysis of the novels written by Douglas in the 1930s with those written in the 1940s. As other commentators on Douglas's work, Russell believes that Douglas sought to shape his work around the perceived religious and emotional needs of the reading public. Hence those of the earlier decade mirror the ethos of the Great Depression and speak particularly of how religious faith can offer individuals an abiding hope, while those of the 1940s address the concerns of men and women whose lives revolve around issues emerging from World War II. The later novels tend to emphasize how religious faith provides strength and courage to believers.

315 Sanjik, Russell. *American Popular Music and Its Business*. 3 vols. New York: Oxford University Press, 1988.

Several chapters scattered throughout the first two volumes deal with popular religious music. One touches on the period covered in this bibliography, "The Music of God's Americans, 1865-1909" (2:247-68). Besides looking at the continuing influence of shape note singing, particularly in the religious culture of the American South, Russell also gives attention to the emerging popular hymnody associated with urban revivalism from the time of Dwight L. Moody on. His major examples center on the work of Homer Roheheaver.

316 Short, Robert L. *The Gospel According to Peanuts*. Richmond, Va.: John Knox, 1965.

The popular cartoon strip "Peanuts," created by Charles M. Schulz, receives interpretation as an exposition of neo-orthodox Protestant theology in this book. Short introduces his study with a discussion of the church and the arts. He then proceeds to demonstrate how the characters in the cartoon strip illustrate the Christian doctrine of original sin and also the consequences of sinful behavior. Snoopy, the dog, emerges as a Christ-figure who aids the hapless Charlie Brown in turning stumbling-blocks into supports.

317 Short, Robert L. *The Parables of Peanuts*. New York: Harper and Row, 1968.

This book is a sequel to Short's *The Gospel According to Peanuts* and develops its themes in greater detail. As well, Short shows how relationships among the characters in the cartoon strip become paradigms for illustrating the ethics of the New Testament and also how their disappointments and frustrations are those of all humanity. From a theological perspective, Short advances the idea that ultimately religious faith provides a hope that enables humanity to see beyond the vicissitudes of daily life and anticipate a wholeness that comes with salvation.

318 Simpson, Lewis P. "Southern Spiritual Nationalism: Notes on the Background of Modern Southern Fiction." In *The Cry of Home: Cultural Nationalism and the Modern Writer*, ed. by H. Ernest Lewald, 189-210. Knoxville: University of Tennessee Press, 1972.

Simpson argues that much of the fiction written by twentieth century authors
from the South has an implicit religious cast to it. Simpson finds the earliest
roots of that religious dimension in Thomas Jefferson's *Notes on the State of
Virginia*, published in 1787, but argues that it was the Civil War that pushed the
religious element to the forefront. The war experience, according to Simpson,
left Southerners as a people in need of redemption, of an identity that would
enable them to transform defeat into victory, loss into triumph, so that they
would regain a sense of control over their corporate experience. Among the
writers that he discusses are John Pendleton Kennedy, Thomas Nelson Page,
William Faulkner, Eudora Welty, and the agrarians.

319 Spencer, Jon Michael. *Black Hymnody: A Hymnological History of the
African-American Church*. Knoxville: University of Tennessee Press, 1992.

Spencer, the foremost writer treating African-American religious music,
organizes this book into three sections, one dealing with Methodists and
Baptists, one with Holiness and Pentecostal groups, and one with Black
Episcopalians and Catholics. He demonstrates how traditional hymns were
modified to reflect the African-American experience, often through the addition
of a refrain and how themes relating to eschatology and salvation have been
particularly powerful in articulating currents of African-American popular
religiosity.

320   Spencer, Jon Michael. *Blues and Evil*. Knoxville: University of
Tennessee Press, 1993.

In this book Spencer argues that the genre of the blues has enabled those who
are victimized, primarily African Americans, to gain a clear perspective of God
and a power that can grant a more viable self-identity. He sees the blues has
reflecting the rural roots of African-American religion that could not be totally
forgotten in the movement of blues from the rural South to the urban North.
Spencer also shows how the blues offer multiple mythologies, theologies, and
theodicies that empower an oppressed people.

321 Spencer, Jon Michael. "God in Secular Music Culture: The Theodicy of
the Blues as the Paradigm of Truth." *Journal of Black Sacred Music* 3 (Fall
1989): 17-49.

This essay sets out some of the interpretation that Spencer developed more fully
in *Blues and Evil*. Here he is particularly concerned to show how blues
addresses unwarranted suffering and evil while still retaining hope in an ultimate

resolution of evil. Even though blues has become a mainstay of secular music, according to Spencer it has retained its essential religious dimension in seeking to reconcile the existence of suffering and evil with an affirmation of the fundamental goodness of life.

322 Spencer, Jon Michael. "A Theology for the Blues." *Journal of Black Sacred Music* 2 (Spring 1988): 1-20.

Spencer focuses on the development of blues prior to World War II, building on the work of African-American theologian James Cone who was among the first to offer serious religious analysis of the blues. For Spencer, pre-war blues musicians create what is basically autobiography; their works portray the "invisible religion" of ordinary black Americans who lived on the periphery of social institutions, including religious institutions. In telling and singing the truth, whether it concerned racism or sex, blues musicians were experiencing justification in a religious sense and affirming the possibility of conversion, understood as a hope for redirection in life.

323   Suderman, Elmer F.   "Elizabeth Stuart Phelps and The Gates Ajar Novels." *Journal of Popular Culture* 3 (1969): 91-106.

Suderman builds his analysis of Phelps's work around the claim that her humanized heaven had extraordinary popular appeal. By demystifying eternity, Phelps made it familiar and therefore more directly a part of everyday life. In other words, Phelps brought heaven and the afterlife from the realm of abstract theology into the popular consciousness. Suderman also notes that there were many other novels of a similar cast by different authors, although none had the immense popularity that Phelps's enjoyed.

324 Thiesen, Lee Scott. "'My God, Did I Set All of This in Motion?' General Lew Wallace and *Ben Hur*." *Journal of Popular Culture* 18, 2 (1984): 33-41.

The title of this article calls attention to the surprise that Lew Wallace professed at the wild success of *Ben Hur* as well as its transformation into a piece for the stage and later into a feature-length film. Although *Ben Hur*, as many popular novels, received mixed critical reviews when it was published, it sold thousands of copies a month in the first five years after it was published. Its success propelled Wallace onto the lecture circuit, one of the popular entertainment media of the day. Thiesen is less interested in looking at how Wallace's fictional portrayal meshes with what Christian scripture says (the approach taken in much commentary stemming from a religious perspective). Rather, he sees

Ben Hur as a means of entering into the popular mind of the late nineteenth century, for he believes the novel first and foremost reflects its own time and place in American society. This approach makes the essay helpful for students of popular religiosity.

325 Tucker, Stephen R. "Pentecostalism and Popular Culture in the South: A Study of Four Musicians." *Journal of Popular Culture* 16 (Winter 1982): 68-80.

The four musicians at the heart of this article are James Blackwood, Tammy Wynette, Jerry Lee Lewis, and Johnny Cash, although the bulk of attention is given to Lewis and his early religious background in the Assemblies of God. Tucker's point is that none of these musicians could jettison the core beliefs of Pentecostal Christianity and that a careful look at their work will reveal a Pentecostal foundation at their base.

326   Ueda, Reed T.   "Economic and Technological Evil in the Modern Apocalypse: Donnelly's *Caesar's Column* and *The Golden Bottle.*" *Journal of Popular Culture* 14 (Summer 1980): 1-9.

Analysts of modern American popular religion are frequently drawn to examination of apocalyptic themes in material targeted for a mass market that was written in the later twentieth century, most likely because the century's end is also the end of a millennium. This article demonstrates that there was a popular apocalypticism in some best-selling works of the later nineteenth century. The two novels by Ignatius Donnelly that form the focus for this essay both appeared in the 1890s, although they are actually set in 1988. What prompts them both is the concern for the moral decay that many thought an inevitable accompaniment of the late nineteenth century industrialization of American society. The dehumanization of laborers could well lead to an impending cataclysm, one that Donnelly sees pushing to an apocalyptic, but optimistic future by the late twentieth century.

327 VanAllen, Rodger. *The Commonweal and American Catholicism: The Magazine, the Movement, the Meaning.* Philadelphia: Fortress, 1974.

Appearing in the year that the *Commonweal* celebrated fifty years of publication history, VanAllen's study of this Catholic journal of opinion is itself intended primarily for a lay audience. Van Allen demonstrates that although the *Commonweal* was founded to provide a Catholic alternative to cognate Protestant magazines, it quickly became more than that. When the *Commonweal* began publication in 1924, American Catholicism still retained an identity predicated on an ambivalence toward American culture, especially the pluralism that had come to mark the American religious scene. Over the years, however, editorials and stories in the *Commonweal* reflected a greater acceptance of many aspects of that pluralism, including the tendency if not the right of American Catholics as individuals to formulate for themselves what was an appropriate Catholic response to prevailing social conditions and issues. This elevation of the authority of the individual on religious matters is one of the characteristics of popular religiosity. Hence in its own way the *Commonweal* became an agency sustaining a popular religiosity informed by Catholic sensibilities.

328 VanBenschoten, Virginia. "Changes in Best Sellers Since World War I." *Journal of Popular Culture* 1 (1967): 379-88.

The focus of this article extends well beyond religious best sellers, but its commentary on such books and on the religious content of other best sellers touches directly on matters of popular religiosity. VanBenschoten demonstrates, for example, that a more pronounced class consciousness evident in best sellers in general is also present in religious novels, particularly those of Harold Bell Wright. More important, she concludes that fiction best sellers tend to locate real or authentic religion outside the structures and strictures of organized religious institutions. In other words, the arena of popular religiosity is seen as more vital than what religious organizations offer.

329 Walker, Wyatt Tee. *"Somebody's Calling My Name": Black Sacred Music and Social Change.* Valley Forge, Pa.: Judson Press, 1979.

A revision of Walker's doctoral dissertation, this study shows how central recurring themes of popular religiosity have been to black sacred music. The major message that Walker discerns is the possibility of victory over suffering and oppression in this life or the hope of gaining power through faith that will give those who are powerless in an empirical sense real control over their own destinies. When these themes are transferred from the individual to the corporate level, they become supports in the movement for social change.

330 Wolfe, Charles. "Bible Country: The Good Book in Country Music." In *The Bible in American Popular Culture*, ed. by Allene Phy, 85-101. *The Bible in American Culture* 2. Philadelphia: Fortress, 1985.

Although Wolfe traces religious dimensions in country music to the 1840s, he concentrates on the period from the 1890s on. A constant theme is identifying the Bible and authentic religiosity with the domestic sphere. Wolfe calls particular attention to the role of the religious mother in country music. He also suggests that country music portrays the Bible in a literal fashion; it is a sacred text that offers a practical guide for daily living. In this sense, country music advances ideas that are central to popular religiosity.

331   Wolfe, Charles M.   "Presley and the Gospel Tradition."   *Southern Quarterly* 18 (Fall 1979): 135-50.

Wolfe insists that in addition to country and bluegrass, white gospel music was a primary source for the music of Elvis Presley. He bases his claim in part on Presley's strong connections to Memphis, itself a center for white gospel. In particular, he argues that the Blackwood Brothers, a quartet, exerted considerable influence on Presley, who also claimed to have a personal fondness for white gospel.

332   Wolniewicz, Richard.   "In Whose Image?   Church Symbols and World Views."   *Journal of Popular Culture* 11 (1978): 877-94.

Contemporary religious architecture forms the focus for this article. Wolniewicz claims that the Eastern and Southern European roots of much immigrant Catholic experience are reflected in architecture and the material culture that accompanies it. For example, he suggests that the prevalence of the crucifix stems in part from the way Catholic immigrants saw themselves as being on a cross in that they were powerless to control or even influence their lives. In contrast, the Protestant emphasis on the resurrection comes through in the greater use of space and light in religious architecture. That, according to Wolniewicz, echoes their position of power in the larger culture. Hence he concludes that the ideas of God communicated in architecture are based primarily on the images that humans have of their own situation in the social order.

333 Wright, H. Elliott.   "Jesus on Stage: A Reappraisal."   *Christian Century* 89 (19 July 1972): 785-86.

Wright looks at two Broadway shows popular at the time of writing that had Jesus as a central character: "Jesus Christ Super Star" and "Godspell." He then argues that putting Jesus on stage was a sign of how religious institutions had smothered the real Jesus in dogma. At the same time, Wright finds fault with images of Jesus projected by both. The Jesus of "Godspell" is too comical to be an accurate reflection of the biblical Jesus, while the anxious Jesus of "Jesus

Christ Super Star" is so human as to lose the dimension of divinity.

334 Wright, Jeremiah A., Jr. "Music as Cultural Expression in Black Church Theology and Worship." *Journal of Black Sacred Music* 3 (Summer 1989): 1-5.

This piece argues that only the spiritual, hymns by black hymnists, and black gospel authentically reflect the black religious experience, even though they constitute only part of the music used in African-American Christian worship. Much of the rest, including common meter hymns, arranged spirituals, and anthems of European origin, does not, even if it is prominent in formal worship. Wright notes that among the more affluent black churches there has been greater opposition to using indigenous black sacred music. In this context, he notes some of the reluctance to incorporate the music of Thomas A. Dorsey into the worship life of the churches because its chord progressions and rhythmic syncopation were deemed too much like those of the blues, and the blues were thought too secular.

335 Zophy, Angela Marie. "For the Improvement of My Sex: Sarah Josepha Hale's Editorship of *Godey's Lady's Book*, 1837-1877." Ph.D. diss., Ohio State University, 1978.

Hale's tenure as editor of the popular magazine for women, *Godey's Lady's Book*, ended early in the period covered by this bibliography. Yet some of the principles that guided Hale's editorship had more longstanding influence. Although as an editor, Hale had herself moved beyond the Victorian gender strictures that determined women's roles, she nevertheless implicitly and explicitly reinforced popular assumptions about women and religion. *Godey's Lady's Book* with Hale at the helm presented religion as primarily a matter of the domestic sphere where the proper Victorian woman reigned. Yet in viewing religion as a private concern, Hale was in essence elevating the individual as the arbiter of authentic religiosity and thereby helping sustain currents of popular religiosity.

7

Self-Help and Recovery Movements

336 Anker, Roy M. "Popular Religion and Theories of Self-Help." In *Handbook of American Popular Culture* 2, ed. by M. Thomas Inge, 287-316. Westport, Conn.: Greenwood, 1980.

Anker offers an historical introduction to religious ideas of self-help in American culture from the popularity of John Bunyan's *Pilgrim's Progress* in the colonial epoch to Norman Vincent Peale's "positive thinking" and Robert Schuller's parallel "possibility thinking" in the twentieth century. The latter half of the essay is a bibliographical discussion of major primary and secondary works appearing up to the time of publication. The historical section is very informative; Elise Chase's *Healing Faith* is more comprehensive for works appearing after 1970.

337 Beckford, James, ed. *New Religious Movements and Rapid Social Change*. Paris: UNESCO, 1986.

Among the essays in this volume germane to understanding American popular religion is Robert Wuthnow's "Religious Movements and Counter-Movements in North America." Wuthnow shows how those groups that were regarded as fringe movements in the 1950s gained greater social acceptability. At the same time, he argues that the roots of later movements such as the fascination with Transcendental Meditation and Yoga, the human potential (self-help) movement, and others are also to be found in the 1950s, since in that decade some of the currents of social change that made these later movements plausible were underway. Among those currents, Wuthnow here identifies the increase in the average educational level of the American population, the growth in the youth cohort of the population, and the nearly uncritical acceptance of science and technology as pointing the way to the future.

338   Bednarowski, Mary Farrell.   *New Religions and the Theological Imagination*. Bloomington: Indiana University Press, 1989.

This book focuses on nineteenth century Mormonism, Christian Science, and theosophy and on the Unification Church (Moonies), Scientology, and the New Age movement in the twentieth century. Bednarowski assumes that all these have a fundamental theological integrity as she looks at their respective ideas of the universe, deity, human nature, the good life, and human destiny after death. All of them, she asserts, emerged from among the people rather than from among the religious elite; hence all are manifestations, at least in their early days, of strands of popular religiosity. Bednarowski rightly warns against judging these and similar religious manifestations by norms identified with institutionalized Protestant traditions.

339 Braus, Patricia. "Selling Self Help." *American Demographics* 14 (March 1992): 48-53.

This article documents the surge of interest of Americans in the phenomenon of self help as a means to achieving happiness and inner peace. Braus particularly notes the tremendous increase in the publication of self-help books targeted to a mass audience primarily composed of baby boom generation men and women who have reached middle age, but who feel that they have somehow not attained personal happiness. Braus notes that most who buy self-help literature are not actually those who need its presumed benefits. She also points out the appeal of self-help approaches to employers who are looking to cut health care costs. Self-help, she claims, is an effective, low cost supplement to expensive mental health programs.

340 Cosgrove, Mark P., and James D. Mallory. *Mental Health: A Christian Approach*. Grand Rapids, Mich.: Zondervan, 1977.

This short book, with a brief bibliography at the end, claims that there are three distinctive ingredients to a Christian understanding of mental health in contrast to psychiatric methods that lack a Christian foundation. Counselling that proceeds from a Christian base, they maintain, is more oriented to the whole person, taking into account the spiritual dimension that they regard as fundamental to human nature. A Christian approach also presumes that through divine help, the mind can actually be restructured and refocused. Finally, they assert that genuine mental health is intricately connected to moral behavior which, they believe, must have a religious center.

341 Cunningham, Raymond. "From Holiness to Healing: The Faith Cure in America, 1872-1892." *Church History* 43 (1974): 499-513.

Cunningham's essay serves as a valuable reminder that the contemporary concern for emphasizing the connections between faith and recovery from illness has a long heritage in American religious life. He demonstrates that the faith cure movement popular in the later nineteenth century had roots in the perfectionism identified with the Holiness Movement and gained currency largely because of reports in the popular press of miraculous cures. Then as now critics were skeptical of the authenticity of cures and eager to emphasize the number of failures (that advocates attributed to lack of faith or the wisdom of divine providence). Cunningham looks particularly at the work of Charles Cullis, William E. Boardman, and Albert B. Simpson, but understands that the interest in the faith cure had as its context a larger concern to maintain a place for the miraculous in human life in an age when the higher criticism of scripture and other intellectual currents seemed to minimize the miraculous and stress the rational.

342 Dillow, Joseph C. *Solomon on Sex*. New York: Thomas Nelson, 1977.

Dillow wrote this book in part to counter the prevailing popular perception that evangelical Christians had a negative view of sex and all sexual activity. While affirming the morality only of sexual relations between husband and wife in a monogamous relationship, Dillow provides an erotic manual for Christians based on the Song of Songs (popularly called the Song of Solomon) in the Old Testament.

343 Dresser, Horatio W. *A History of the New Thought Movement*. New York: Thomas Y. Crowell, 1919.

Although now somewhat dated, Dresser's work remains a standard study of the early years of New Thought. It is valuable for understanding how later nineteenth New Thought advocates looked at the mind as a point of contact between the empirical world and a realm of supernatural power and how proper use of the mind could enable individuals to gain a sense of control over their own destinies by tapping into a reservoir of supernatural power. Dresser's work is also helpful to those interested in understanding the antecedents of the later twentieth century self-help movement and such phenomena as Norman Vincent Peale's "positive thinking" and Robert Schuller's "possibility thinking."

344 Fish, Melinda. *When Addiction Comes to Church*. Old Tappan, N.J.:

Fleming H. Revell, 1991.

Writing from a distinct evangelical perspective, Fish offers an alternative to the view that addictions of many sorts result from a moral lapse. To that extent, her approach is marked by realism, for she recognizes that addiction is a much more complex issue than those who insist it is a behavioral matter based on free choice usually admit.   She is also aware that addiction and addictive personalities are prevalent within the evangelical ranks and therefore must addressed from a religious perspective. In this vein, she sees value in having churches provide a range of groups that might combine traditional religious activity with self-help therapy, especially that based on the twelve step format, if they are to engage in effective ministry in today's society.

345 Fuller, Robert C. *Alternative Medicine and American Religious Life*. New York: Oxford University Press, 1989.

Fuller gives a sensitive historical overview of connections between popular (rather than professional, scientific) medical theories and practices and American religion. His scrutiny extends to such diverse phenomena as Thomsonian herbal medicine, the Grahamist diet, chiropractic, Christian Science, and the contemporary interest in holistic medicine.   Fuller argues that alternative medicine has a distinct religious base, whether or not it is articulated. That base is a belief in the correspondence between the natural and supernatural realms and the conviction that treatment of disease and other disorders has a spiritual as well as a physical dimension. Hence alternative medicine represents an ongoing means by which ordinary Americans participate in a sacred realm.

346   Gottschalk, Stephen.   "Christian Science and Harmonialism."   In *Encyclopedia of the American Religious Experience*, ed. by Charles H. Lippy and Peter W. Williams, 2:901-916. New York: Scribners, 1988.

Gottschalk provides a solid historical sketch of the development of Christian Science and cognate religious currents that scholars have often called "harmonial religion." All of them presume that ordinary men and women can achieve both physical and mental health and well-being if they acknowledge the power of the mind and seek to live in harmony with spiritual forces that ultimately control the universe. To this extent, they exhibit some of the fundamental qualities that mark most strands of popular religiosity, namely a desire to secure a personal identity through bringing daily life into some kind of balance with a transcendent realm. Where many of these movements go further is in their seeing disease and other physical problems as resulting primarily from a lack of such balance.

347 Gottschalk, Stephen. *The Emergence of Christian Science in American Religious Life*. Berkeley and Los Angeles: University of California Press, 1973.

Gottschalk's study remains the standard for exploring the work of Mary Baker Eddy and the early Christian Science movement. It looks at the connections between Eddy and other currents in the nineteenth century, such as mind cure and the teachings of Phineas Quimby, that also stressed mental control over the physical as a means to personal wholeness, health, and happiness. Readers will readily note parallels between several of these currents and their later manifestations in the New Age movement. Gottschalk, however, also notes that Eddy and the embryonic Christian Science movement did not simply absorb ideas and techniques from mind cure or Quimby. He ultimately locates Christian Science in the developing tradition of American pragmatism, both because it is result-oriented and because it shared some concerns with the philosophy of pragmatism that was being advanced at the same time Eddy was at her peak by thinkers such as William James and Charles Peirce.

348 Judah, J. Stillson. *The History and Philosophy of the Metaphysical Movements in America*. Philadelphia: Westminster, 1967.

The primary value of Judah's work is its encyclopedic character; it remains a valuable reference tool for those who wish a solid overview of many of the metaphysical religious movements that have flourished in American society. Judah, as others, gives the label "metaphysical" to those religious expressions that posit a reality beyond the empirical level, usually accessible through the mind, that is superior to everyday reality and usually regarded as what is "really real." All metaphysical movements, according to Judah, promise experiential knowledge that will give meaning to life through both the mind and feelings. He also notes that virtually all have as a primary concern a focus on health, both physical and mental.   Among the movements that Judah scrutinizes are Spiritualism, Theosophy, the work of Phineas Quimby and Warren Felt Evans, New Thought, Divine Science, the Church of Religious Science, Christian Science, and Unity.

349 Kaminer, Wendy. *I'm Dysfunctional, You're Dysfunctional: The Recovery Movement and Other Self-Help Fashions*. Reading, Mass.: Addison-Wesley, 1992.

A scathing critique of popular self-help therapies, Kaminer's work argues that the American people have been duped into believing they are all psychologically dysfunctional to a greater or lesser degree by counselors, writers, publishers, and others who stand to gain from the success of the burgeoning self-help movement. Although often somewhat shrill in tone, Kaminer does point out how all approaches to self-help presume that there is a normative model for happiness or self-fulfillment that differs from the ordinary reality of most people's lives. She also suggests that by identifying some abuse or addition from which it is necessary to recover in order to become a whole person may be a way for persons to deny taking responsibility for their own actions and behavior. Kaminer's purview is not limited to the religious sphere, but spans a wide gamut of self-help and recovery movements.

350 Kaminer, Wendy. "Saving Therapy: Exploring the Religious Self-Help Literature." *Theology Today* 48 (Fall 1991): 301-325.

Appearing shortly before the publication of her *I'm Dysfunctional, You're Dysfunctional*, Kaminer's article is a bibliographic essay looking at the burgeoning array of materials that approach popular self-help therapy from a religious (often Christian) perspective. An attorney by training, Kaminer highlights the work of M. Scott Peck, James Dobson, Charles Swindoll, Fulton Sheen, Charles Stanley, and others. In all the literature, she finds recurring themes: a view that the universe is just and moral, but cannot be navigated without divine help; an understanding that individualism, competitiveness, and achievement are essentially evil because they isolate people from God and from each other; a conviction that self-love is as important as love of neighbor, leading to the conclusion that low self-esteem is also evil; a belief that much of the evil humans encounter is really a manifestation of a personality disorder; and a theology that sees God as a good and loving parent.

351 Kurtz, Ernest. "Alcoholics Anonymous: A Phenomenon in American Religious History." In *Religion and Philosophy in the United States of America* 2, ed. by Peter Freese, 447-62. Essen, Germany: Verlag Die Blaue Eule, 1987.

Kurtz's essay, although published in Germany, was among the first to look at the twelve-step program developed by Alcoholics Anonymous as a religious phenomenon and Alcoholics Anonymous, along with its cognate groups, as representing a popular religious movement. Kurtz goes beyond the obvious religious element in the twelve-step emphasis on reliance on a higher power to see the religious dimensions in the understanding of human nature as weak and in need of divine assistance to become whole, in the sense of community that emerges when members of an Alcoholics Anonymous group bond together, and in the emphasis placed on moral responsibility and ethical behavior that is basic to the approach. In other words, Alcoholics Anonymous is able to provide guidance in the development of personal spirituality for its participants.

352 LaHaye, Tim, and Beverly LaHaye. *The Act of Marriage: The Beauty of Sexual Love.* Grand Rapids, Mich.: Zondervan, 1976.

In its 31st printing by 1981, this book claims to have sold more than one million copies. Its fundamental self-help premise is that religious people enjoy sex more than other persons. The LaHayes use basic evangelical doctrinal emphases as tools to enrich the sex lives of believers. For example, they claim that because forgiveness of sin frees the conscience, those who confess their sins to the Almighty will remove one cause of orgasmic malfunction. But the authors operate on the basis of a narrow evangelical understanding of gender roles. Women who surrender their wills to their husbands, they assert, will have more frequent and better orgasms; yet they also suggest that it is appropriate for the Christian wife to be assertive in the bedroom, provided that she is not assertive in other areas of domestic life.

353 Lippy, Charles H. "Sympathy Cards and Death." *Theology Today* 34 (1977): 167-77.

In this article, Lippy explores the popular custom of sending sympathy cards to friends and acquaintances when they experience the death of a loved one. He demonstrates that the custom grew as dealing with the reality of death became a matter for professionals, thus depriving ordinary folk of a vocabulary and means of accepting the reality of death. The messages of cards tend to focus on seeing death as a passage to another realm, thus playing down the harshness of death itself, and draw on ambiguous religious images as a way of reinforcing the popular perception that trust in divine power is the most effective means of coping with death.

354 Lippy, Charles H. "Sympathy Cards and the Grief Process." *Journal of Popular Culture* 17 (Winter 1983): 98-108.

Lippy here extends the theses advanced in his "Sympathy Cards and Death" to look at how the practice of sending such cards aids ordinary men and women in dealing with the grief process. As card recipients read and reread cards during the grief process, they begin to accept the reality of death. At the same time, cards reinforce a vaguely defined network of association with others that helps those who grieve sustain their sense of identity and redefine that identity after experiencing the death of a loved one.

355 Mallory, James D. *The Kink and I: A Psychiatrist's Guide to Untwisted Living.* Wheaton, Ill.: Victor Books, 1981.

First published in 1973 when the self-help movement was experiencing great growth in popularity, Mallory presents a decidedly evangelical Christian understanding of the personal wholeness that is the intended outcome of self-help. Writing for a mass audience, Mallory insists that such wholeness is impossible apart from authentic religious faith. His essential thesis is that any approach to self-fulfillment must begin with the recognition that human beings are fundamentally spiritual entities. Hence Mallory believes that many, perhaps most, psychological issues are at base spiritual matters that cannot be resolved by any therapy not predicated on the awareness that the relationship between human beings and God is the starting point for all healthy living.

356 Maudlin, Michael G. "Addicts in the Pew." *Christianity Today* 35, 8 (22 July 1991): 19-21.

This article is essentially a transcription of an interview Maudlin had with professional counselor Dale Ryan of the National Association for Christian Recovery. Ryan is a firm believer in the benefit of self-help recovery programs in part because he insists that every congregation has individuals who could benefit from any one of a number of such programs (addiction recovery, surviving child abuse, and so on). However, Ryan also emphasizes that such recovery programs should not be seen as alternatives to the church as an evangelical worshipping community.

357 Meyer, Donald. *The Positive Thinkers: Popular Religious Psychology from Mary Baker Eddy to Norman Vincent Peale and Ronald Reagan.* Middletown, Conn.: Wesleyan University Press, 1988.

Meyer's work, updated in 1988, is now a classic historical study of the ties between religious faith and popular psychology. The recurring theme that Meyer emphasizes is how positive thinking, regardless of how it is named or described, promises believers power in times of psychological ill-being. That sense of power is fundamental to popular religiosity. Meyer also analyzes the strong links between the Victorian image of the ideal woman, which defined female identify almost exclusively in terms of motherhood, and the attractiveness of positive thinking movements to women; when a woman's children were grown, she was left without a viable identity and, to counter the depression that followed, turned to mind cure, New Thought, or one of the other positive thinking fads of the day. Meyer, however, claims that by the 1970s and 1980s, positive thinking was losing its appeal because persons no longer saw all problems as internal to the self but as societal issues beyond the self. He can make this claim only because he does not include the self-help movement within the orbit of positive thinking, although the two are related intimately.

358 Miller, J. Keith. *Hunger for Healing: The Twelve Steps as a Classic Model for Christian Spiritual Growth.* San Francisco: Harper Collins, 1991.

While numerous writers have noted the religious aspects of the twelve step approach to self-help, their increasing use by support groups connected to religious institutions, and both the problems and possibilities in seeing the twelve steps as a religious phenomenon, Miller goes in a different direction. Influenced by the psychological understanding that correlates religious style to stages in the life process and by the recent increased interest in spiritual formation, he sees in the twelve-step approach not only a method for inner healing but also a discipline that can be fruitfully used for enriching what an earlier age would have called a life of piety and devotion. Mastery of each step draws the individual closer to God. Historians of Christianity will note parallels between what Miller advocates and devotional exercises promoted by the medieval mystics.

359 Osborne, Cecil. *The Art of Understanding Yourself.* Grand Rapids, Mich.: Zondervan, 1968.

Osborne is an early advocate of the religious use of the small group as a spiritual force. Responding to the quest for a viable identity that many have seen as a mark of the post-modern age, he argues that group therapy is a viable antidote for the perceived loneliness that he believes challenges contemporary men and women. In the small group, individuals learn to listen, first to others, then to themselves, and finally to God. For Osborne, it is this last step that grants the therapy based on the small group its religious quality. As participants in group therapy come to accept themselves through the support of others in the group, they also come to accept the love of God by extension.

360 Parker, Gail Thain. *Mind Cure in New England: From the Civil War to World War I.* Hanover, N.H.: University Press of New England, 1973.

Parker's book is one of the standard scholarly studies of popular healing movements that flourished in post-bellum United States, especially in New England. Most of them had overt religious dimensions; among the most well-known is Christian Science, founded by Mark Baker Eddy and ultimately centered in Boston. But Parker tells the story of many movements, including the one that gives her the title, all of which drew on the fashionable sentimentalization of sickness in the Victorian era and the growing popular belief that the mind was the only true reality. More narrowly focused in terms of one time period than Donald Meyer's *The Positive Thinkers*, Parker's study joins that one in showing how mind cure consistently emphasizes the immanence of God (usually as Mind) at the expense of divine transcendence. But an immanent God is one whose power can be appropriated directly by ordinary women and men, a basic premise of much popular religiosity.

361   Riesman, Frank.   "The New Self-Help Backlash."   *Social Policy* 21 (Summer 1990): 42-48.

Among analysts of the popular self-help movement, Riesman was among the first to note that there was an ironic twist to the entire phenomenon. While therapists and religious writers churned out books initially intended to help persons with real problems and disorders, they unwittingly created a culture in which it was assumed that everyone had psychological problems and disorders from which it was imperative to be in recovery. What began to fill a need in turn both created and sustained the need. Hence the number of those who have real needs for therapy is grossly exaggerated. As well, Riesman argues that some persons actually become addicted to self-help groups themselves. He also questions the therapeutic wisdom in regarding recovery as a lifetime process. As well, Riesman notes that many recover on their own without benefit of small group therapy and that the now classic twelve-step approach has no higher rates of success than alternative understandings. Finally, he challenges the wisdom of predicating recovery exclusively on a sense of personal powerlessness and criticizes the self-help movement for diverting attention from the societal ethos that breeds addiction.

362 Schuller, Robert A. *Just Because You're on a Roll . . . Doesn't Mean You're Going Downhill.* Old Tappan, N.J.: Fleming H. Revell, 1990.

This book, by the son of popular religious television personality Robert H. Schuller, is rooted in sociological deprivation theory that asserts that persons may feel themselves deprived (of happiness, health, or some other presumed benefit) even if no empirical deprivation may be documented. Such perceived deprivation is indeed very real to the person who experiences it and may be one cause of depression or other psychological problems. Schuller argues that when anyone wants more from life than they already have (whether it be the ability to stick to a diet, manage personal moods, develop a larger network of friends, or build a happy home life), they can attain what they wish if they put God first and then formulate a vision of precisely what they need to achieve happiness. Schuller's approach is in keeping with the positive thinking strand of popular religiosity in looking at faith in strictly practical terms.

363 Shedd, Charlie W., and Martha Shedd. *Celebration in the Bedroom.*

Waco, Tex.: Word Books, 1979.

Written as American culture was nearing the end of a presumed "sexual revolution," this book by a popular evangelical husband and wife team exhorts married couples who would seek to add some spice to their sex lives to turn to the Bible for guidelines. They suggest, for example, that persons would do well to read the Song of Songs (Song of Solomon) for clues to erotica arousal.

364 Smedes, Lewis B. *Sex for Christians*. Grand Rapids, Mich.: Eerdmans, 1976.

Smedes joins the ranks of evangelical writers who offered self-help guidebooks for Christians in an effort to end the popular connection between sex and pornography and promiscuity. Smedes argues that sexual activity is a natural and intended part of God's creation designed to bring both pleasure and fulfillment. His personal religious perspective leads him to assert that this pleasure and fulfillment come only in heterosexual activity between a husband and wife who are totally faithful to each other.

365 Stafford, Tim. "The Hidden Gospel of the Twelve Steps." *Christianity Today* 35, 8 (22 July 1991): 14-19.

Stafford proposes that twelve-step approach to recovery from addiction that has been adapted in a variety of formats for many self-help programs has an implicit religious message that both complements the traditional evangelical Protestant gospel and is inimical to it. Stafford is reluctant to give blanket endorsement to twelve-step therapy because, despite its emphasis on relying on a Higher Power however defined, its fundamental premise assumes that humans possess the free will and personal power to turn their lives around. Rather, the Higher Power in his mind must be identified with Jesus Christ as understood by evangelical Protestants. As well, he is wary of the virtual guarantee of success that the twelve-step approach seems to offer so long as individuals adhere to the program. That, he believes, is a false gospel (good news), for he insists that abiding personal transformation results only from individuals' placing their total trust in divine power. The danger is that the recovery group itself becomes seen as the Higher Power.

366 Stapleton, Ruth Carter. *The Gift of Inner Healing*. Waco, Texas: Word Books, 1976.

The sister of former President Jimmy Carter, Stapleton presents in this short book one of the earlier attempts to give a religious twist to the popular psychological theories that stressed the need to recognize and release the "inner child" that lurks within all persons; many others have echoed her themes. Written in a breezy, conversational style, the book claims that most persons suppress hurtful experiences to the detriment of their emotional and psychological health. Through prayer, Stapleton claims, the Holy Spirit can bring these damaging experiences to conscious attention and at the same time resolve or cure them, freeing the individual for a healthy life.

367 Starker, Steven. *Oracle at the Supermarket: The American Preoccupation with Self-Help Books*. New Brunswick, N.J.: Transaction Books, 1989.

Starker takes his title from the popular practice of having book racks filled with self-help books written for a mass audience located near checkout counters in supermarkets. Starker suggests that the recent surge of interest in self-help has deep roots in the American psyche. It is a manifestation of the tendency to fashion an image of the "ideal" typical American that is not only larger than life, but more a construct than a reality. The preoccupation with self-help draws on the heritage of rugged individualism, the myth of the frontier hero, the myth of the self-made American, and a host of other images that lift the image of what an American should be to such a plane that virtually no one can attain it.

368 "Taking the Twelve Steps to Church." *Christianity Today* 32, 18 (9 December 1988): 31.

This very brief article outlines the adaptation of the well-known Twelve Steps of Alcoholics Anonymous by Vernon Bittner, the founder of the Institute for Christian Living. Bittner's aim is to use the model to produce a cognate to develop an evangelical spirituality. Hence, for example, instead of having the individual admit powerlessness over alcohol or some other addiction, Bittner's approach has the individual admitting the need of God's gift of salvation. The ambiguous Higher Power of the Twelve Steps becomes Jesus Christ, while the self-examination becomes an ongoing moral inventory that acknowledges one's need for divine help to eliminate shortcomings.

369 Wagner, Melinda Bollar. *Metaphysics in Midwestern America*. Columbus: Ohio State University Press, 1983.

This book is a study of the Spiritual Frontiers Fellowship, founded in Evanston, Illinois, in 1956, based on field work done by Wagner in 1975 and 1976. She demonstrates that the appeal of this loosely-knit movement lies in its offering adherents a way to break out of a pervasive sense of individual meaningless that has resulted from the increasing social fragmentation of contemporary American society. By regarding the individual as the ultimate religious authority, the Spiritual Frontiers Fellowship urges participants to find a truth that makes sense to themselves, not necessarily to a community of believers. In this way, the Spiritual Frontiers Fellowship epitomizes what popular religiosity is all about. At the same time, even before the fascination with self-help and support groups became major forces in American religious life, the Spiritual Frontiers Fellowship used the small study and small group exercises as its basic tools to promote self-realization.

370 Wagner, Melinda Bollar. "Metaphysics in Midwestern America." *Journal of Popular Culture* 17 (Winter 1983): 131-48.

This article, that carries the same name as Wagner's monograph on the same subject, briefly summarizes how the Spiritual Frontiers Fellowship promotes individual spiritual growth through exercises, conducted in small groups, that are designed to increase awareness of one's divine inner self. The result is the development of idiosyncratic, syncretistic belief systems that are the hallmark of popular religiosity. Wagner notes, however, that the approach advocated by the Spiritual Frontiers Fellowship appeals primarily to middle-class persons of an intellectual bent.

371 Weiss, Richard. *The American Myth of Success: From Horatio Alger to Norman Vincent Peale.* New York: Basic Books, 1969.

Weiss's intent is not to describe a religious phenomenon, but to trace the importance of success to the American character. However, virtually all the material that he examines has either implicit or explicit religious qualities, for it is all a part of what Weiss calls the "religion of optimism" that sustains the popular American notion that everyone can be a success. Weiss gives particular attention to popular novels of the later nineteenth and early twentieth centuries along with the contributions of persons such as Ralph Waldo Trine and movements such as New Thought in making an emphasis on individual initiative fundamental to the American understanding of what it means to achieve happiness. At the same time, Weiss makes it clear that to be a success is also to have power to control one's destiny, a feature recurring in many strands of popular religiosity.

372 Wuthnow, Robert, ed. *"I Come Away Stronger": How Small Groups Are Shaping American Religion.* Grand Rapids, Mich.: Eerdmans, 1994.

Sociologist Wuthnow edited this collection of essays that in one way or another all look at how small groups, group therapy, support groups, and groups based on the twelve-step approach have had an impact on American religious life. As the title suggests, the recurring motif is that in the later twentieth century it is in the small group that individuals feel they find the personal strength to gain control over their lives, whether that group be one organized by the Salvation Army or operating under the auspices of Alcoholics Anonymous. Many special interest groups, such as those oriented to women or to businessmen, are part of the same larger movement. By drawing on a particular constituency, groups help members develop a secure identity that in turn will presumably bring enduring happiness. Larger groups, such as traditional religious congregations, have lost much of their effectiveness to provide this identity, although presumably they once did so, because they are too diffuse in membership.

373 Wyatt, Michael. "What Must I Believe to Recover? The Spirituality of Twelve Step Programs." *Quarterly Review* 10, 4 (Winter 1989): 28-47.

Wyatt, an Episcopal priest and substance abuse counselor, argues that the Twelve Step approach is based on a profound understanding of spirituality that involves surrender to the Power that restores and gives new life. He also notes that for many who are involved in Twelve Step programs, traditional religion is itself a source of abuse and a means of perpetuating abusive behavior. Hence religious groups need to be aware of how they can draw on the spirituality inherent in the Twelve Steps in their own efforts to empower individuals.

8

Biographical Studies

374 Bahr, Robert. *Least of All Saints: The Story of Aimee Semple McPherson.* Englewood Cliffs, N.J.: Prentice-Hall, 1979.

Bahr provides a decidedly non-scholarly biography of evangelist Aimee Semple McPherson that he admits is speculative. Bahr takes frequent liberties with facts and often creates dialogue so that his work resembles fiction more than biography. Yet given the veil of secrecy with which McPherson shrouded her own life, Bahr manages to capture some of the spirit that catapulted McPherson into prominence and made her message of faith in a Christ who was savior, baptizer, healer, and coming king plausible to Americans of the Depression era who were desperately looking for a transcendent truth.

375 Bjorn, Daniel W. *Victorian Flight: Russell H. Conwell and the Crisis of American Individualism.* Washington: University Press of America, 1979.

Bjorn argues that Conwell and his version of the "gospel of success" must be understood in the context of an American society undergoing a painful transition from Victorian-rural simplicity to urban-industrial complexity. Bjorn sees Conwell as a microcosm of the tension that marked that transition, one whose personal identity crises paralleled those of the culture at large. Combining psychological constructs with those drawn from intellectual and social history, Bjorn offers a highly interpretive analysis of one of the most popular preachers and public speakers at the turn of the century.

376 Blumhofer, Edith L. *Aimee Semple McPherson: Everybody's Sister.* Library of Religious Biography, ed. by Mark A. Noll and Nathan O. Hatch. Grand Rapids, Mich.: Eerdmans, 1994.

McPherson, who billed herself as "your sister in the King's glad service," was one of the premier female evangelists of the early twentieth century. Finally centering her ministry around the Angelus Temple in Los Angeles, McPherson organized followers into the Foursquare Gospel movement. Blumhofer provides a sensitive, but analytic brief biography as part of a series that Eerdmans is publishing. Informed by scholarly research and understanding, this biography is written for non-specialists. Blumhofer offers a solid, yet brief introduction to the life and career of one of the leading female shapers of popular religiosity in the period leading up to World War II.

377 Connelly, James T. "William J. Seymour." In *Twentieth-Century Shapers of American Popular Religion*, ed. by Charles H. Lippy, 381-87. Westport, Conn.: Greenwood, 1989.

Seymour was pastor of the holiness-based Azusa Mission in Los Angeles in 1906. Most historians credit a revival that erupted there in April 1906 as launching the modern Pentecostal movement with its emphasis on glossolalia and other gifts of the Spirit. The movement spread quickly throughout Holiness groups, spawned new denominations, and has remained a force within American Christianity on the popular level since. The direct access to supernatural power that marks the Pentecostal experience of speaking in tongues is one of several ecstatic expressions of popular religiosity. Connelly's brief essay includes not only biographical information about Seymour, but also commentary on secondary works treating Seymour and the Pentecostalism of the early twentieth century. It concludes with a helpful bibliography of works by and about Seymour.

378 Cranston, Sylvia. *H.P.B.: The Extraordinary Life and Influence of Helena Blavatsky, Founder of the Modern Theosophical Movement*. New York: Jeremy P. Tarcher, 1993.

The presence of Theosophy began to be manifest in American culture in the late nineteenth and early twentieth centuries. Combining elements of Eastern mysticism and popular understandings of reincarnation with belief in the power of the mind to transcend the limits of empirical reality, Theosophy offered adherents access to sacred power and a heritage of life within a realm of power that stretched across boundaries of time and place. At the center of that movement was Helena Petrovna Blavatsky, who popularized her ideas in writings that while esoteric to some were intended for a mass audience. Many remain in print today. Several elements of the religious philosophy that Blavatsky advocated, including living in harmony with cosmic Consciousness through use of aids such as astrology, have made their way into New Age thinking that is an important current in late twentieth century popular religiosity.

379 Dorsett, Lyle W. *Billy Sunday and the Redemption of Urban America*. Library of Religious Biography, ed. by Mark A. Noll and Nathan O. Hatch. Grand Rapids, Mich.: Eerdmans, 1991.

Billy Sunday was the premier popular Protestant evangelist in the United States in the late nineteenth and early twentieth centuries. Known and criticized by the religious establishment for his exaggerated pulpit style and use of slang and for creating in his revival tents an ethos akin to that of vaudeville, Sunday had a brief career as a professional baseball player before becoming an itinerant evangelist. Dorsett's biography, part of a series treating key figures in American religious history, is informed by scholarly research, but in an effort to appeal to a non-academic audience appears without notes. Dorsett is aware that Sunday was the subject of heavy criticism and that Sunday's popularity faded rapidly in the wake of scandals over a ghostwritten book and questions about Sunday's having reaped great financial gain. However, Dorsett is so appreciative of the way Sunday popularized Christian teaching that he steps back from serious analysis. Nonetheless, Sunday is a central figure in the history of American popular religion.

380 D'Souza, Dinesh. *Falwell: Before the Millennium. A Critical Biography*. Chicago: Regnery Gateway, 1984.

Jerry Falwell became a national figure in the 1970s and 1980s through his television program, "The Old Time Gospel Hour," and his political arm, the Moral Majority. An evangelical independent Baptist, Falwell claimed to speak for millions in his defense of fundamentalism and his equation of patriotism with conservative political positions on issues such as abortion, women's rights, gay rights, and the like. Consequently he reaped much criticism, more for his vitriolic attacks on those whose views differed from his than for the posture he adopted. D'Souza's biography, while claiming to be critical, is really a defense of Falwell. D'Souza is a conservative journalist by profession; consequently he seeks to provide support for Falwell in the face of presumed liberal opposition.

381   Epstein, Daniel Mark.   *Sister Aimee: The Life of Aimee Semple McPherson*. New York: Harcourt Brace Jovanovich, 1993.

Written in a journalistic, breezy style that will appeal to a non-academic audience, Epstein's biography of the flamboyant evangelist and founder of the International Church of the Foursquare Gospel offers little direct analysis of the forces that shaped McPherson and her work. Although McPherson started the first religious radio station in the United States, she reached millions more with her popular magazine, the *Bridal Call*. Divorced for most of her career, McPherson hardly fit the mold of the evangelist. But her attribution of her call to ministry to a direct experience of God resonated with countless Americans who themselves inhabited a world where supernatural power was real.

382 "Father Coughlin (pronounced Kawglin)." *Fortune* 9, 2 (February 1934): 34-39, 110, 112.

That this brief article appeared in a popular magazine suggests the extent of Charles Coughlin's influence on the popular mind of the Depression era. Coughlin, a Roman Catholic priest headquartered in Michigan, was among the first religious figures to take to the airwaves with his message that in time reeked of political and economic radicalism and brought him into disfavor with church authorities. In many ways, Coughlin is a forerunner of the televangelists of the later twentieth century.

383 Findlay, James F., Jr. *Dwight L. Moody: American Evangelist, 1837-1899*. Chicago: University of Chicago Press, 1969.

Findlay's biography remains the best scholarly analysis of America's premier evangelist of the later nineteenth century. Findlay shows how Moody was able to develop and maintain an appeal to the average Protestant American and how the simple supernaturalism and millennialism of Moody's message was not only plausible to millions in the Gilded Age but became basic to many strands of popular Protestant religiosity for decades after Moody's death.

384 Fishwick, Marshall W. "Father Coughlin: The Radio and Redemption." *Journal of Popular Culture* 22, 2 (Fall 1985): 33-47.

Fishwick, who has written extensively on modern American popular culture, emphasizes how Coughlin had an instinctive feeling for the radio public that enabled him to reach an audience that some estimates place as high as thirty million. But Fishwick also notes that Coughlin predicated his message on hatred while claiming to speak for the "little man." It was Coughlin's genius to be able to articulate the inchoate feelings that were an undercurrent of many strains of popular world views in the 1930s.

385 Frady, Marshall. *Billy Graham: A Parable of American Righteousness*.

Boston: Little, Brown, 1979.

A newspaper journalist by profession, Frady has written a highly interpretive biography of the premier popular evangelist from the middle of the twentieth century on. Frady stridently argues, sometimes in an exaggerated fashion, that Billy Graham has epitomized the values of middle-class America and has been as much a voice for the fears and hopes of the middle-class at mid-century as a spokesman for Christianity. Frady believes that Graham too readily fused a naive patriotism with his evangelical message and too uncritically sought identification with political figures to give added legitimacy to his stance.

386   Frank, Thomas E.   "Norman Vincent Peale."   In *Twentieth-Century Shapers of American Popular Religion*, ed. by Charles H. Lippy, 326-34. Westport, Conn.: Greenwood, 1989.

This brief sketch of Peale's life and works about Peale emphasizes Peale's fascination with personal power, his conviction that mastery of principles would enable individuals to gain power over their lives, his insistence that authentic religion was practical in that it made such principles accessible, and his belief that religious faith should serve the needs of ordinary people. Frank concludes his essay with a selected bibliography of works by and about Peale.

387 Fuller, Daniel P. *Give the Winds a Mighty Voice: The Story of Charles E. Fuller.* Waco, Tex.: Word Books, 1972.

Charles E. Fuller was one of the first twentieth-century evangelists to master the use of radio for religious purposes, regularly broadcasting "The Old Fashioned Revival Hour" from Long Beach, California. Fuller was more than a popular evangelist, however, and his views deeper than the simple fundamentalism that echoed through his messages. Fuller's ministry extended to establishing the Fuller Theological Seminary, intended to provide a solid academic training rooted in what has become known as the "new evangelicalism" of the twentieth century, an evangelicalism rooted in orthodox Protestant theology, but more intellectually sophisticated and centrist than fundamentalism. Fuller clearly deserves serious scholarly scrutiny. This book is the only full-length biography to date. Written by Fuller's son, it is not uncritical, but lacks scholarly distance from its subject.

388   Gehring, Mary Louise.   "Russell H. Conwell: American Orator." *Southern Speech Journal* 20 (Winter 1954): 117-24.

The driving force behind the establishment of Temple University in Philadelphia, Conwell was known primarily for his popular lecture, "Acres of Diamonds" that he delivered to rapt audiences for decades and that has been reprinted in numerous popular anthologies. Its essence was that those who seek success ("diamonds") have all the materials for its attainment ("acres") already at their fingertips. This essay is not concerned with the religious content of Conwell's simple message, but with his rhetorical style and the power he exuded as a speaker in the last decades of the popularity of the public lecture as a form of mass entertainment.

389 George, Carol V. R. *God's Salesman: Norman Vincent Peale and the Power of Positive Thinking*. New York: Oxford University Press, 1993.

George, a historian by profession, has penned the first critical biography of Peale that draws on Peale's personal manuscripts as well as interviews with Peale and his associates. George capably shows how Peale's enormously popular "positive thinking" was rooted in ideas long present on the margins of American religious life, including Swedenborgianism, Mesmerism, New Thought, and kindred metaphysical movements. George is not content to see Peale simply as a voice for a twentieth-century version of "mind over matter." Rather, she takes pains to show that Peale was also a product of a more traditional conservatism in both religion and politics as well as being a force forging what later became a more pronounced religious-political right in the closing years of Peale's life.

390 Gordon, Arthur. *Norman Vincent Peale: Minister to Millions*. Englewood Cliffs, N.J.: Prentice-Hall, 1958.

This study appeared at the crest of Peale's early popularity when Peale was a virtual fixture on best-seller lists. Not intended to be a critical analysis, the book offers more an expository biography, placing particular emphasis on Peale's upbringing and the impact of Charles Clifford Peale on his son. The elder Peale was a physician who entered the Methodist ministry after he experienced what he regarded as a miracle in recovering from illness. Gordon suggests that the interplay between prayer and health that were the hallmarks of Peale's message were had their roots here. Those roots were nourished by associations with physicians and the process of healing that came to Peale as a Methodist pastor in Syracuse, New York, in the late 1920s and then by Sidney Blanton, a psychiatrist who became a close associate after Peale assumed the pastorate of New York City's Marble Collegiate Church in 1932.

391 Harrell, David E., Jr. *Oral Roberts: An American Life*. Bloomington: Indiana University Press, 1985.

Harrell, a distinguished historian who has written extensively about healing and charismatic movements in American religious life, provides here the most even-handed analysis of one of twentieth-century America's most well-known faith healers and evangelists. Harrell locates Roberts in the matrix of Pentecostalism and its emphasis on the Holy Spirit. At the same time, Harrell argues that Roberts is distinctively American in his exploitation of popular media to carry his message to millions. Oral Roberts, in Harrell's view, reluctantly assumed the mantle of the public religious figure. Those who wish to pursue further study of Roberts will find Harrell's bibliographical essay especially helpful.

392 Harrell, David E., Jr. *Pat Robertson: A Personal, Political, and Religious Portrait*. San Francisco: Harper and Row, 1987.

Harrell brings to his study of Robertson the same fair spirit that he had in his appraisal of Oral Roberts. Rather than dismissing Robertson as a conservative fanatic or self-aggrandizing preacher-politician, Harrell suggests that Robertson is a complex individual. Within Robertson's life, in Harrell's recounting, there is a constant interplay of ideological forces. As a historian of religion, Harrell gives primary attention to the Southern Baptist, charismatic, and broad evangelical dimensions of Robertson's identity. But Harrell also notes that in Robertson's background there is a long heritage of political activity and of seeking to find appropriate expressions in the public realm of the ethical and religious beliefs that form the basis of personal values.

393 Jervey, Edward D. "Henry L. Mencken and American Methodism." *Journal of Popular Culture* 12 (1978): 75-87.

Mencken was an acerbic critic of much organized religion in the 1920s. A Baltimore Episcopalian, Mencken brought biting satire to his essays on religion in the South, his comments on a fundamentalism that he abhorred, and his assault on Methodism, then America's numerically largest Protestant denomination. In other words, Mencken attacked much of what formed the nexus of popular religiosity in his day. Jervey demonstrates that part of Mencken's hostility stemmed from his conviction that organized religion too often attempted to force its conception of life on the whole of society. In the case of American Methodism, that imposition derived from the denomination's passionate support for Prohibition, a movement that Mencken also thought misdirected.

394   Lagerquist, L. DeAne.   "Aimee Semple McPherson."   In *Twentieth-Century Shapers of American Popular Religion*, ed. by Charles H. Lippy, 263-70. Westport, Conn.: Greenwood, 1989.

Lagerquist's brief essay highlights McPherson's willingness to sample untried techniques to advance her healing and evangelistic ministry. Theatrical in style, McPherson achieved much in a time when women's roles in American society were changing. Lagerquist points out, however, that McPherson was hardly a forerunner of late twentieth-century feminism. A helpful bibliography of works by and about McPherson conclude the essay.

395 Legget, Carol. *Amy Grant*. New York: Pocket Books, 1987.

Amy Grant has emerged as one of the major figures in the field of "contemporary Christian music," a phenomenon that denotes the evangelical appropriation of musical styles and formats rooted in popular rock music. Designed especially to appeal to adolescents and young adults, Grant and her music have won numerous awards. Legget's appreciative biography is likewise designed for a popular audience and portrays Grant as an evangelical Christian woman whose deep personal faith and religious experience inform her lyrics. Since this book appeared, Grant has become more controversial for her more recent music has a decidedly secular bent, according to critics, and addresses issues of moral behavior that some of her early evangelical supporters question.

396 Lewis, L. David. "Charles E. Fuller." In *Twentieth-Century Shapers of American Popular Religion*, ed. by Charles H. Lippy, 148-55. Westport, Conn.: Greenwood, 1989.

Lewis comments that Fuller was "the most popular American revivalist between Billy Sunday and Billy Graham" (p. 153). He also stresses how Fuller's willingness to experiment with what was then the latest communications technology, radio, to gain a national reputation and wide hearing for his message. Lewis also notes that much of Fuller's popularity revolved around his wife, Grace, who read on the weekly broadcasts excerpts from letters received from listeners that offered testimony to how their lives had been transformed by the supernatural power that Fuller saw as fundamental to religious faith. Lewis provides a helpful survey of the literature about Fuller as well as a selected bibliography of other secondary treatments.

397 Lippy, Charles H., ed. *Twentieth-Century Shapers of American Popular Religion*. Westport, Conn.: Greenwood, 1989.

Lippy opens this collection with an essay on the importance of studying popular religion if one hopes to understand the dynamics of religious life in America in the twentieth century. There follow sixty-two essays by different scholars that give a brief biography of their subjects, an appraisal of their significance, and a survey of critical writing about them. Each concludes with a selected bibliography of works by and about the subject. The book includes several persons whose primary influence has been in Canada. As well, women, African Americans, and Native Americans are also represented. A few of the individual essays are annotated separately in this book.

398 McCarthy, Colman. "Sunday Morning with the Rev. Dr. Peale." *New Republic* 160 (25 January 1969): 14-15.

Having officiated at the wedding of the daughter of President-elect Richard Nixon in late 1968, Peale was once again in the limelight when this critical essay appeared. McCarthy takes Peale to task for the excessive individualism of his message. McCarthy argues that Peale's stress on providing persons with ready formulas to achieve happiness in spite of the vagaries wrought by a hostile society meant that Peale virtually ignored social problems. For McCarthy, Peale was the quintessential pessimist who thought the larger society could not be transformed, but would always represent the specter of doom and destruction for individuals.

399 McCauley, Deborah Vansau. "Kathryn Kuhlman." In *Twentieth-Century Shapers of American Popular Religion*, ed. by Charles H. Lippy, 225-33. Westport, Conn.: Greenwood, 1989.

Although Kuhlman was noted as a popular faith healer, McCauley reminds us that Kuhlman herself rejected that label and claimed that she preached only the Holy Spirit and by the power of the Holy Spirit. Nevertheless, Kuhlman is a major figure in the popular deliverance revivals of the mid-twentieth century. McCauley demonstrates that Kuhlman gave fresh plausibility to the experience of being "slain in the Spirit" to middle-class neo-Pentecostals during the charismatic renewal of the 1960s and 1970s, making such an intensive, personal experience a legitimate part of worship. As with other essays in this volume, this one concludes with a selected bibliography of works by Kuhlman and studies about Kuhlman and her evangelistic career.

400 McLoughlin, William G. "Aimee Semple McPherson: 'Your Sister in the King's Glad Service.'" *Journal of Popular Culture* 1 (1967): 193-217.

Prior to the appearance of biographies by Edith Blumhofer and Daniel Mark Epstein, this essay by historian William McLoughlin was the best secondary treatment of evangelist Aimee Semple McPherson. He claims that despite the bizarre elements in her personal life, especially her claim to having been kidnapped when she disappeared from public view for several weeks, McPherson was essentially a simple, sincere pietist who was an authentic product of American civilization.

401 McLoughlin, William G. *Billy Graham: Revivalist in a Secular Age*. New York: Ronald Press, 1960.

Until the appearance of William Martin's biography more than thirty years later, this was the standard scholarly treatment of Graham. It now appears dated, but remains valuable in its analysis of Graham's early message that was marked by a strident anticommunism and a fear that national destruction loomed imminent unless Americans returned to a simple, evangelical faith. Critics indeed found Graham's message in the 1950s as overly simplistic, but none can challenge the way Graham's themes resonated with the lived fears and hopes of millions of Americans and provoked a response nationally and internationally that elevated Graham to a position of tremendous influence in popular religious life.

402 McLoughlin, William G. *Billy Sunday Was His Real Name*. Chicago: University of Chicago Press, 1955.

For many years McLoughlin was among the leading interpreters of modern American revivalism, and this analytic study of Sunday was among the earliest of his important works in that area. McLoughlin shows how the professional baseball player who became an evangelist was adept at working the crowds who flocked to hear him. His coarse and often vulgar language, offensive to the elite, was not only natural to Sunday, but a technique Sunday employed to reach ordinary folk. Although other studies of Sunday have appeared, this one remains the most astute appraisal of the most popular revivalist of early twentieth-century America.

403 Marcus, Sheldon. *Father Coughlin: The Tumultuous Life of the Priest of the Little Flower*. Boston: Little, Brown, 1973.

Marcus's biography is no doubt the best to date of the popular, but controversial radio priest. Marcus portrays Coughlin as one who was simultaneously savior and destroyer, patriot and demagogue. He notes that Coughlin's popular appeal was such that his listeners and supporters came from a variety of religious backgrounds. But Marcus also shows how Coughlin's ability to articulate the inchoate fears of millions spurred hatred and discord.

404 Martin, William. *A Prophet with Honor: The Billy Graham Story*. New York: William Morrow, 1991.

Martin's study of America's most well-known evangelist of the later twentieth century is the most sophisticated and sensitive to date. Martin had access to unpublished papers and letters in preparing his work; he also was able to interview Graham, his family, and many of those associated with Graham's ministry over the decades. The result is a highly readable, richly nuanced biography. Martin calls attention to the ways Graham's understanding of human concerns became more complex with time as a result of his international travels and his relationships to political leaders. Yet Graham remained convinced that his essential proclamation of trust in the power of God offered the only hope for lasting happiness for individuals and the resolution of social problems.

405 Meyer, Donald. "The Confidence Man." *New Republic* 133 (11 July 1955): 8-10.

Meyer takes a look at Norman Vincent Peale in this brief article that appeared while Peale was basking in the popularity that resulted from the publication of *The Power of Positive Thinking* in 1952. According to Meyer, Peale so mourned the passage of American society from a culture oriented to the small town to one based in the complexities of urban life that be believed the inner self was the only aspect of existence over which the individual could still gain control. Hence while positive thinking on the surface appeared to be optimistic in holding out hope for human happiness, it was essentially nostalgic in holding up the ideal of a culture that had vanished. Meyer expands on his interpretation of Peale in *The Positive Thinkers*.

406 Millard, Bob. *Amy Grant: A Biography*. New York: Doubleday, 1986.

Millard's biography appeared as Amy Grant emerged as a leading singer and composer in the now burgeoning "contemporary Christian music" industry. Highly laudatory, Millard's work is as much a promotional piece as an analytical portrait. Since this book appeared, Grant's career has moved in new directions. While not abandoning the religious element entirely, Grant's more recent music has a more decidedly secular quality. Critics have therefore questioned whether a religious intent is as central a motivating factor in her work as Millard suggests.

407   Miller, Robert Moats.   *Harry Emerson Fosdick: Preacher, Pastor, Prophet.* New York: Oxford University Press, 1985.

Fosdick has often been seen as a popularizer of liberal theology and a common-sense approach to religious faith through his radio preaching that reached a weekly audience of two to three million listeners for nearly two decades. Scholars recall him as a major figure in the fundamentalist-modernist controversy of the 1920s.   Miller's definitive study adds to that picture by calling attention as well to the depth of Fosdick's theological learning and his personal work in promoting civil liberties, world peace, and family planning. Although based on impeccable research, Miller avoids conventional documentation.   But the bibliographic essays that conclude the book are extraordinarily valuable for those wishing to pursue further study of Fosdick.

408   Miller, Timothy.   *Following In His Steps: A Biography of Charles M. Sheldon.* Knoxville: University of Tennessee Press, 1987.

Sheldon's best-selling novel of a group of Christians who sought to apply their faith to everyday decision making remains in print in 1995, a century after its initial appearance. Miller's uncritical biography of Sheldon presents the pastor-author as one who consciously saw himself as a popularizer of a simple Christian faith, who sincerely believed that religion was at base a practical matter.   To this extent, Miller suggests it was appropriate that the novel appeared in comic book form in 1977, albeit with the characters and situations changed to fit the times.

409   Miller, William L.   "The Gospel of Norman Vincent Peale."   *Union Seminary Quarterly Review* 10 (January 1955): 15-22.

This highly critical appraisal of Peale's theology was reprinted in numerous other periodicals in the mid-1950s.   Miller argues that the positive thinking advocated by Peale represents a distortion of Christianity. For Miller, positive thinking is simply a rehash of the gospel of success or gospel of wealth that was prominent in some Protestant circles in the late nineteenth century.   It also suffers from the same fatal weakness in substituting reliance on the self for trust in a providential God. If sin were merely a sign of mental weakness, as Miller argued that Peale proclaimed, then there was no place for the Christian story of redemption.   Miller's attack became the basis for much of the criticism of Peale's approach, and Peale himself was reportedly painfully stung by it for he was convinced that the criticism was unfounded and unjust. Miller's perspective represents an elitist assault; Peale's defenders would claim that Peale had indeed tapped into the popular religiosity of the masses and given them a means to access divine power for their own well being.

410 Molson, Francis J. "Francis J. Finn, S.J.: Pioneering Author of Juveniles for Catholic Americans." *Journal of Popular Culture* 11 (1977): 28-41.

Francis Finn was among the first American writers to produce literature target for Roman Catholic youth, especially boys. His *Tom Playfair* (1891), *Harry Dee* (1892), and *Claude Lightfoot* (1893) are among the better known. As other juvenile literature with a religious bent, Finn's work had a didactic focus. But writing for Catholic youth had an additional burden. Since Catholicism was a minority religion and since many Catholics were recent immigrants at the time Finn wrote, his young readers faced an alien environment where their motives were often suspect. Molson demonstrates that Finn intended his work to show that Catholic religious devotion was compatible with both good citizenship and prevailing cultural notions of masculinity. The novels also provide insight into the popular religiosity shaped by Catholic sensibilities.

411 Montgomery, Edrene Stephens. "Bruce Barton and the Twentieth Century Menace of Unreality." Ph.D. diss., University of Arkansas, 1984.

Montgomery's dissertation is the most comprehensive study of Barton, author of the best-selling *The Man Nobody Knows*. Montgomery argues that Barton believed religious faith could provide ordinary men and women with a sense of power, a conviction that they did have some control over their lives. At the same time, she shows that Barton's career in advertising worked almost at cross purposes in creating an unreal fantasy world to which few actually had access. Montgomery dismisses the common criticism that Barton's fictional biography of Jesus was an effort to give a religious justification for capitalism. Rather, she insists that the appeal of Barton's work stemmed from its presenting an interpretation of Jesus that resonated with the lives of ordinary men and women. If Barton's advertising created a world that was unreal, his Jesus reflected a world that was very real to the average American.

412 Morken, Hubert. *Pat Robertson: Religion and Politics in Simple Terms*. Old Tappan, N.J.: Fleming H. Revell, 1987.

Morken's book appeared as Pat Robertson was emerging as a major player in Republican Party politics leading up to the 1988 presidential election. Using Robertson's unpublished speeches and interviews as well as more accessible materials, Morken seeks to demonstrate how Robertson's essentially conservative political views emerge directly from his religious ideas. Morken admits, however, that in the process of working on the book, his personal antipathy to Robertson as a preacher turned politician evaporated and he became a Robertson supporter. While this change of orientation on Morken's part makes the book overly sympathetic in several places, it does not take away its value in unpacking the direct and indirect connections between Robertson's politics and his personal religious faith.

413 Murphy, Mary. "The Next Billy Graham." *Esquire* 90 (10 October 1978): 25-30.

In this illustrated essay, Murphy predicted that Jerry Falwell would emerge as the unofficial successor to Billy Graham in the popular mind. She also speculated that Falwell would eventually seek a career in politics in which Falwell would bring together his "harsh Puritanism" and fierce competitiveness. While the intervening years may have proved Murphy wrong, her article is a valuable introduction to the early public career of Falwell. Murphy, as others, highlights the influence of evangelist Charles E. Fuller and his radio program on shaping Falwell's media ministry.

414 Nelson, Clyde K. "Russell H. Conwell and the 'Gospel of Wealth'." *Foundations* 5 (1962): 39-51.

Nelson provides a distillation of his doctoral dissertation in this article. He argues that Conwell was a more complex figure when it came articulating social thought than many commentators have assumed. Nelson refutes the once-standard interpretation that Conwell was merely a voice for the Gospel of Wealth, although Conwell's well-known *Acres of Diamonds* certainly popularized many ideas associated with it. Rather, Nelson insists that Conwell's social and economic thinking increasingly moved away from the simplistic ideas of wealth and progress and that Conwell became more aware of social and economic disparities in American society.

415 Neuchterlein, James A. "Bruce Barton and the Business Ethos of the 1920's." *South Atlantic Quarterly* 76 (1977): 293-308.

Neuchterlein advances that hypothesis that Barton's idealistic understanding of business not only reflected the economic climate of the 1920s, but was actually a conservative response to the liberal thinking associated with the Social Gospel. Like Social Gospel thinkers, Barton was drawn to the ethical teaching of Jesus. However, Barton was inclined to seek ways that this ethic could be applied within the structures of capitalism; he did not wish to bring to capitalism the more radical alterations that were popularly identified with the Social Gospel movement.

416 Parsons, Wilfred, S.J.. "Father Coughlin and Social Justice," *America* 53, 6 (18 May 1935): 129-31; "Father Coughlin and the Banks," ibid. 53, 7 (25 May 1935): 150-52; "Father Coughlin's Ideas on Money," ibid. 53, 8 (1 June 1935): 174-76.

In this three-part series, Parsons summarizes popular radio demagogue Charles Coughlin's thinking on social issues, noting that Coughlin at the time was more controversial than any public figure besides Hitler. He concludes that Coughlin's ideas are not in keeping with the developing Roman Catholic position, especially as articulated by John A. Ryan, and that many of Coughlin's theories, if implemented, would lead to the creation of a totalitarian state. Hence Parsons reminds readers that Coughlin's views are his as an individual, not as a representative of the Roman Catholic tradition.

417 Paz, D. G. "Lloyd Cassell Douglas." In *Twentieth-Century Shapers of American Popular Religion*, ed. by Charles H. Lippy, 118-25. Westport, Conn.: Greenwood, 1989.

As the other essays in this volume, this one offers a brief overview of Douglas's life, his early career as a pastor, and his success as a popular novelist whose work centered on religious themes. Paz also looks at Douglas's writing that was targeted more directly to clergy and the kind of skills clergy should develop. He suggests that there is a common thread that runs through Douglas's work, namely that religion should have practical benefits for ordinary people. Hence he encouraged pastors to learn from marketing and psychology how to package their message even as he sought to should how ordinary human life could be enriched through religious faith in his novels. Paz provides a helpful summary of literature about Douglas as well as a selected bibliography of material by and about Douglas.

418 Quebedeaux, Richard. *I Found It! The Story of Bill Bright and Campus Crusade.* San Francisco: Harper and Row, 1979.

Although Bill Bright has been a key player in the neo-evangelical movement since the late 1940s when he founded Campus Crusade, with its aggressive evangelistic program targeted to college and university students, there is a dearth of secondary literature about him. Quebedeaux's study is the only biography to appear to date. It portrays Bright on a grand scale as one who recognized the dangers of secularism on campuses to traditional evangelical faith and who responded by using sophisticated marketing techniques and appropriating dimensions of popular culture to make his "four spiritual laws" attractive to the student generation.   Quebedeaux also highlights the patriarchal, virtually absolute control that Bright has exerted over Campus Crusade, despite its expansion, and the way Bright and his organization have consciously advocated traditional gender roles for men and women.

419   Sittser, Gerald.   "Bruce Barton."   In *Twentieth-Century Shapers of American Popular Religion*, ed. by Charles H. Lippy, 20-29. Westport, Conn.: Greenwood, 1989.

Sittser's overview of Barton argues that most interpretation has been too simplistic.   In his view, Barton was not out to provide a religious justification for capitalism or an easy accommodation of religious belief with popular cultural currents.   Sittser suggests that there is an irony in Barton's life.   As an advertising executive he promoted ideals that stood in stark contrast to those emerging from his popular portrayal of Jesus as one who was both successful and humble.   In other words, Sittser sees Barton as caught in a constant struggle to balance his religious instincts with his understanding of business and his inherent idealism.   Sittser also provides a survey of the literature about Barton as well as useful bibliographies.

420   Smith, Albert Hatcher.   *The Life of Russell H. Conwell*.   Boston: Silver, Burdett, 1899.

Written while Conwell was at the peak of his fame as pastor of Philadelphia's Baptist Temple, founder of what became Temple University, and orator on the lecture circuit, Smith's biography is representative of hagiography.   Yet although it offers no critical appraisal of Conwell but applauds his advocacy of a simple gospel of success, Smith's study does provide a catalogue of details about Conwell that are useful to those who wish to pursue more scholarly appraisals.

421   Spivak, John L.   *Shrine of the Silver Dollar*.   New York: Modern Age Books, 1940.

Although this book purports to be a study of popular radio demagogue Charles Coughlin, it is more in the genre of the expose and lacks such apparatus as notes, bibliography, and index that would make it more valuable to others. Spivak is especially critical of the way Coughlin raked in vast sums of money from his supporters and channeled it into private investments, particularly in property, without either the knowledge or approval of his superiors in the Roman Catholic Church. The Coughlin who emerges here is a schemer who is out to dupe the public with his fanatic attacks and propaganda.

422 Stoppe, Richard Leon. "Lloyd C. Douglas." Ph.D. diss., Wayne State University, 1966.

This dissertation concerns itself primarily with Douglas's preaching style during his tenure as pastor of Lutheran churches in North Manchester and Lancaster, Indiana, the Luther Place Memorial Church in Washington, D.C., and Congregationalist parishes in Ann Arbor, Michigan, Akron, Ohio, Los Angeles, and Montreal. Stoppe examines Douglas's work from the perspective of rhetoric, showing how Douglas was unusually adept at using rhetorical techniques to advance his belief that Christianity provided ordinary women and men with a kind of psychological power.

423 Teahan, John F. "Warren Felt Evans and Mental Healing: Romantic Idealism and Practical Mysticism in Nineteenth-Century America." *Church History* 48 (1979): 63-80.

Evans, whose thought had a direct impact on Christian Science founder Mary Baker Eddy, was a precursor of contemporary self-help thinking and in many ways the ideological antecedent of persons such as Norman Vincent Peale and Robert Schuller. The subtitle of Teahan's essay reveals his basic thesis: Evans's emphasis on the power of the mind had roots in both romanticism and mysticism. Yet like those who followed him, Evans believed that the value of both lay in their practical use by individuals who sought to gain a sense of control over their own destinies.

424 Tull, Charles J. *Father Coughlin and the New Deal*. Syracuse, N.Y.: Syracuse University Press, 1965.

For a time, Fr. Coughlin used his immensely popular radio program to support the causes championed by President Franklin D. Roosevelt in the New Deal. This support made Coughlin appear to be something of a populist. But there was another side to Coughlin, and bitter attacks on Roosevelt and everything that the New Deal represented gradually replaced that early enthusiastic endorsement. Tull traces the changes in Coughlin's public position as hatred and venom came to dominate Coughlin's message.

425 Ward, Louis B. *Father Charles E. Coughlin: An Authorized Biography.*
Detroit: Tower Publications, 1933.

Because this early biography was prepared with Coughlin's open support, there
is little in it by way of critical analysis. Ward's book appeared when Coughlin
was nearing the zenith of his popularity thanks to his radio programs. Coughlin
comes across almost as a savior figure whose idiosyncratic fusion of political
and religious ideas offer the masses their only hope for the future. Most critical
studies present a very different portrait of Coughlin as a man who became
consumed with hatred and whose demagoguery did little to hide his political
fanaticism.

426 Williams, Peter W. "Fulton J. Sheen." In *Twentieth-Century Shapers of
American Popular Religion*, ed. by Charles H. Lippy, 387-93. Westport,
Conn.: Greenwood, 1989.

Although successful as a professor of philosophy and scholarly writer, Sheen
became the first person to win an Emmy award for a religious television
program. His broadcast career began with a radio program that debuted in 1930
and ran for more than two decades when Sheen launched the first of several
television series. Williams's brief essays is one of the few scholarly endeavors
to look at Sheen not only as a media personality, but as one who was able to
popularize the application of Catholic tenets to daily life and public issues of the
1950s, especially anti-communism and Freudian psychology. Williams provides
a helpful appraisal of the scant secondary literature about Sheen as well as
bibliographies of works by and about the one-time bishop of Rochester, New
York.

427 Wilson, Thane. "Russell H. Conwell: Who Has Helped 3,000 Young Men
to Succeed." *American Magazine* 81 (April 1916): 15.

This article, laudatory in the extreme, appeared in a popular magazine when
Conwell himself was one of the most well-known preachers and public speakers
in the United States. It picks up on both the practical focus of Conwell's "Acres
of Diamonds" speech that spurred individuals to help themselves to success and
on the educational work Conwell began under the auspices of his Philadelphia
congregation. Originating as a program that offered free classes in the evenings
to ordinary workingmen, Conwell's educational enterprise became what is now
Temple University. This sketch praises Conwell for bringing financial and
personal success to thousands of ordinary folk.

428 Wimmer, John R. "Russell H. Conwell." In *Twentieth-Century Shapers of American Popular Religion*, ed. by Charles H. Lippy, 80-88. Westport, Conn.: Greenwood, 1989.

Wimmer's combines biography and analysis in this short essay. He notes that Conwell is usually portrayed as a popularizer of the gospel of success. Wimmer claims, however, that Conwell did much more than give religious validation to the pursuit of wealth. He was a major voice in giving an identity to the emerging urban middle class by accommodating "popular religious culture to both the new accumulation of capital and the democratic right of anyone to pursue it" (p. 84). Wimmer also provides a helpful survey of scholarly criticism of Conwell as well as bibliographies of works by Conwell and secondary studies about him.

9

Traditional and Unconventional Approaches to Personal Spirituality

429 Adler, Margot. *Drawing Down the Moon: Witches, Druids, Goddess-Worshippers, and Other Pagans in America Today.* Rev. ed. Boston: Beacon, 1986.

Adler's massive study probes the entire range of phenomena associated with the popular neo-pagan revival in contemporary America. She identifies as pagan whatever has at its base a polytheistic nature religion and argues that the value of neo-pagan religiosity is its elimination of a distinction between the sacred and the secular, the spiritual and the mundane. Adler examines in detail why such neo-pagan expressions have been particularly attractive to women in quest of a spirituality that reflects feminine experience. She offers an especially perceptive chapter on the sources of the Wiccan revival and provides an extraordinarily helpful bibliography for further study, as well as an annotated listing of popular periodicals and similar resources.

430 Albanese, Catherine L. "Fisher Kings and Public Places: The Old New Age in the 1990s." In *Religion in the Nineties,* ed. by Wade Clark Roof, 131-43. *Annals of the American Academy of Political and Social Science,* 527. Newbury Park, Calif.: Sage Periodicals, 1993.

Albanese challenges the traditional scholarly interpretation that emphasizes the links between the contemporary New Age movement and the theosophical thrust of the later nineteenth century. She argues instead that New Age phenomena should be seen as expressions of an ongoing nature religion that underlies much of American religiosity. Albanese also makes a case that the New Age nature religion has a lively moral and ethical dimension that is often overlooked. It is this social ethic that propels New Age adherents to develop concerns for environmentalism and related ecological issues.

431 Baer, Hans. "Towards a Systematic Theology of Black Folk Healers."
Phylon 43 (Winter 1982): 327-43.

Baer rightly understands that there is a profound difference between the faith
healing associated with Pentecostalism and the tradition of folk healers among
African-Americans. The latter draws as much on the African heritage, with its
appreciation of those who were endowed with spiritual power to conjure, as it
does the adopted and adapted Christian theological tradition. What may bring
them together and form the base for constructing a systematic theology of black
folk healing is the sense of supernatural power and of the way such power
operates in human life that underlies them both.

432 Bigsby, C. W. E., ed. *Superculture: American Popular Culture and
Europe*. Bowling Green, Ohio: Bowling Green University Popular Press, 1975.

An essay by British sociologist of religion Bryan Wilson, "American Religious
Sects in Europe" (pp. 107-122), is pertinent to the study of modern American
popular religion. Although some of the groups to which Wilson directs
attention (the Mormons, Christian Science, Jehovah's Witnesses, and Seventh-
Day Adventists) have lost some of their sectarian characteristics and have
become so institutionalized as to be no longer reflective of a popular religiosity
in the American context, the opposite holds true in Europe, where all these
groups are relatively new. In the European setting, they still demonstrate a
popular religious protest against contemporary cultural lifestyles.

433   Budapest, Z[suzsana].   *Grandmother Moon.*   San Francisco:
HarperSanFrancisco, 1991.

Budapest is a witch living in Los Angeles who was born in Hungary. She has
been at the forefront of efforts to reclaim ancient mysteries and rituals that speak
to women's experience. In this book, she examines many of the stories that
hearken back to a primal female deity, shows the relevance of those stories for
women's spirituality today, and thus contributes to the sustenance of a female-
based popular religiosity that is highly eclectic, but ever sensitive to supernatural
power.

434 Budapest, Z[suzsana]. *The Grandmother of Time: A Women's Book of
Celebrations, Spells, and Sacred Objects for Every Month of the Year*. San
Francisco: HarperSanFrancisco, 1989.

Drawing on a keen sense of the reality of supernatural power, Budapest develops a series of contemporary rituals that build on the long heritage of feminine-oriented religious practices that stretch back millennia.   Some deal with experiences unique to women such as menstruation, menopause, and childbirth. The thrust of Budapest's work is to suggest that matters of fertility and the sacrality of the feminine remain central to strands of popular religiosity that enable women to have a sense of power over their own lives and destinies.

435 Budapest, Z[suzsana]. *The Holy Book of Women's Mysteries*. Oakland, Calif.: Wingbow, 1989.

This work is a good introduction to occult-related spirituality that is centered on the goddess and the unique experiences of women. The mysteries speak of a realm of supernatural power that only women can access through rituals and kindred activities. In tapping these mysteries, women are able to assume control over their own lives in a way superior to any manifestation of power in the empirical world.

436 Bush, Trudy. "On the Tide of the Angels." *Christian Century* 112, 7 (1 March 1995): 236-38.

Bush gives a brief theological critique of the surge of interest in angels, which she traces to the appearance of Billy Graham's *Angels: God's Secret Agents* that was published in 1975. She notes that contrary to much of the theological traditions of both Judaism and Christianity, contemporary understanding of angels assumes that these supernatural beings always work for the good of humanity. Hence although she attributes intrigue with angels to the constant desire of humans for the spiritual and for signs of certainty that there is more to life than just the material, she argues that recent books on angels present these beings as ones who simply give people what they want, whether it be inner peace, enjoyment, or release from potentially hazardous situations. The article contains helpful references to several of the recent popular titles dealing with angels, including some written for children.

437 Cross, Tom Peete. "Witchcraft in North Carolina." *Studies in Philology* 16 (1919): 217-87.

Cross traces accounts of witchcraft in North Carolina into the early years of the twentieth century.   On the one hand, he notes the links to conjure among purported manifestations of witchcraft among African Americans. On the other, he recognizes that much presumed witchcraft reflects a form of sympathetic magic thought particularly powerful in curing illness. However, rather than seeing such power as connected to a pervasive understanding of the supernatural, Cross attributes its survival to the tenacity of ancient superstitions.

438 Ellwood, Robert S. "Occult Movements in America." In *Encyclopedia of the American Religious Experience*, ed. by Charles H. Lippy and Peter W. Williams, 2:711-22. New York: Scribners, 1988.

Ellwood's historical survey is among the best brief introductions to occult phenomena in American life. He traces fascination with the occult from the colonial period to the present, noting that the appeal of the occult is not in its system of thought per se, but in how occult belief, when translated into ritual practice and the like, endow individuals with "a sense of significance, power, and harmony with the universe at all levels" (p. 722). A helpful bibliography concludes the essay.

439 Ellwood, Robert. "Polytheism: Establishment or Liberation Religion?" *Journal of the American Academy of Religion* 42, 2 (1974): 344-49.

Ellwood examines the revival of interest in polytheism that transpired in American culture in the late 1960s and early 1970s. He argues that polytheism carries its own set of problems. In his view, polytheism skirts issues relating to perceived human alienation. Ellwood also believes that the practice of polytheism is so relegated to the private sphere that it can not serve as a force for social cohesion, a factor that he sees as essential to religion.

440 Friedman, Jean E. *The Enclosed Garden: Women and Community in the Evangelical South, 1830-1900*. Chapel Hill: University of North Carolina Press, 1985.

The latter sections of this book focus on dimensions of female spirituality in the Southern United States in the decades following the Civil War. Friedman shows how evangelical spirituality enabled white women to form networks or communities of feeling that only gradually supplanted kinship as a primary aspect of women's identity. Indeed, kinship often undergirded evangelical community, in part because emphasizing ties of kinship did not threaten the racist structure of Southern society. Slowly, however, a spiritual kinship nurtured by evangelicalism drew white women into more political activism. Racism also meant that evangelicalism and kinship fostered a parallel, but separate spiritual community among black women. By the close of the century, Friedman argues, the antilynching movement finally began to draw black and white evangelical women together.

441 Gifford, Carolyn DeSwarte, ed. *The American Deaconess Movement in the Early Twentieth Century*. New York: Garland, 1987.

This book reprints several works published in the first decade of the twentieth century that deal with the deaconess movement in the Methodist Episcopal Church. Together they reveal how becoming a deaconess was one way women could extend their traditional functions and develop their own spirituality. While the deaconess still represented one who was a nurturer, care giver, teacher, and the like, by working in urban areas and responding to the needs wrought by immigration and industrialization, the deaconess could foster a rich personal religiosity that broke away from established norms.

442 Gifford, Carolyn DeSwarte, ed. *The Ideal of "The New Woman" According to the Women's Christian Temperance Union*. New York: Garland, 1987.

The "new woman" of which the title speaks comes from images portrayed in three works by Frances Willard that are here reprinted. Willard's essential argument, woven throughout all three, is that a private religiosity is integral to women's self-definition, and that women could maintain direct contact with the Divine more readily than men. This religiosity and the power that accompanied it allowed women to be independent even in a cultural ethos that emphasized the submission of women to men.

443 Goodman, Felicitas D. *How About Demons? Possession and Exorcism in the Modern World*. Bloomington: Indiana University Press, 1988.

Goodman wants to take seriously the experience of both demon possession and exorcism. She brings considerable anthropological and psychological erudition to this analysis, linking both possession and exorcism to the phenomenon of ecstatic religious experience that transcends or lies outside the realm of rationality. Goodman connects possession and exorcism to a profound belief in the reality of supernatural power and the conviction that supernatural forces are active in the empirical world. Cross-cultural analysis is another strength of Goodman's work.

444 Goodman, Felicitas D. *Speaking in Tongues: A Cross-Cultural Study of Glossolalia*. Chicago: University of Chicago Press, 1972.

Goodman's study demonstrates that the prevalence of glossolalia is by no means limited to its expressions in Pentecostal forms of religiosity. As with her work on possession and exorcism, she scrutinizes glossolalia with keen anthropological and psychological awareness. She links speaking in tongues to an altered state of consciousness, particularly to hyperarousal dissociation. Goodman charts patterns of pulse, rhythm, and intonation of the ordinary speech of a subject and then for the same person when speaking in tongues. She notes that data are incomplete and inconsistent in determining whether the glossolalia utterance actually constitutes a language. Goodman prefers to see glossolalia as a particular type of behavior.

445 Greeley, Andrew. "Superstition, Ecstasy, and Tribal Consciousness." *Social Research* 37, 2 (1970): 203-211.

Sociologist Greeley argues that contemporary intrigue with superstition, ecstasy, and tribal consciousness refutes the conventional interpretation that secularization has eroded religiosity. All three in his view are attempts to resacralize human life since all three represent forms of protest against hyper-rationality. The three also share several common assumptions: the essential goodness of human nature, a desire for salvation, and belief in the possibility of an ideal or millennial reality that can be brought into being.

446 Kildahl, John P. *The Psychology of Speaking in Tongues*. New York: Harper and Row, 1972.

Kildahl gives a brief history of glossolalia in Christianity and in western culture before summarizing seven different psychological theories to account for it. He moves on to examine whether persons who speak in tongues are of a particular psychological personality type or could be classified in any traditional category of mental health. His empirical studies require a negative response to both. However, Kildahl does show that there may be psychological factors in the glossolalia experience (anxiety, maturity, crisis) and that there may be some correlation to group behavior that is a catalyst to glossolalia. He concludes that there remain many unanswered questions (connections to hypnotism, the role of group dynamics, persons who cease to speak in tongues, explaining cases of glossolalia among children). Kildahl includes a helpful bibliography of books and articles on glossolalia that appeared prior to 1970, some going back to the eighteenth and nineteenth centuries.

447 Kloos, John. "The Upper Room." In *Popular Religious Magazines of the United States*, ed. by P. Mark Fackler and Charles H. Lippy, 478-82. Westport, Conn.: Greenwood, 1995.

The *Upper Room* has become one of the most popular Christian daily devotional magazines in the years since it first appeared in 1935. Although the magazine now appears in numerous international editions and is printed in different locations around the globe, its headquarters are in Nashville, Tennessee. Kloos's essay is one of the few scholarly pieces to look at both its content and its import in sustaining popular religiosity. Kloos notes that the daily features are drawn from ordinary life and reflect a simple, but abiding belief in the reality of divine presence and power. They also assume that through prayer and devotional exercises, individuals can have access to that power.

448   Lawless, Elaine J.   *Handmaidens of the Lord: Pentecostal Women Preachers and Traditional Religion.*   Philadelphia: University of Pennsylvania Press, 1988.

Lawless describes the tension that has prevailed among women who have been called as preachers in Pentecostal churches. While they have a sense of being different, they have struggles with their own abilities and their own spirituality. The reason for this struggle stems largely from the expectation that these women preachers will also not break with traditional gender roles. Lawless also shows how the sermons preached by these Pentecostal women reflect female concerns for connectedness and community and the keen sense of reliance on divine power that is basic to strands of popular religiosity.

449   Leonard, Bill.   "Getting Saved in America: Conversion Event in a Pluralistic Culture."   *Review and Expositor* 82 (Winter 1985): 111-27.

Leonard shows that having the event of a distinct and conscious has become a uniquely American form of personal religiosity. He traces its development in American life from the age of the Puritans to the present, noting the importance of distinguishing between the conversion event (which may be a corporate phenomenon as in revivals) and the conversion experience (which is a private and personal matter). As American religious life became more pluralistic even in its Christian manifestations, Leonard claims that it became impossible to program a single conversion event or to insist on one style of personal conversion experience that would have relevance for everyone.

450 Lewis, James R., and J. Gordon Melton, eds. *Perspectives on the New Age*. Albany: State University of New York Press, 1992.

This collection of essays provides one of the best introductions to New Age phenomena that have mushroomed in American religious life in recent years.

The opening section focuses on the historical roots of the contemporary New Age movement, while the second scrutinizes particular themes or topics The opening section   focuses on   the historical roots   of the contemporary New(channeling, the evangelical response, and the like). A third section offers comparative studies, while the final section examines New Age manifestations in countries other than the United States. The volume includes a bibliography for just four of the nineteen chapters, but footnotes for all contain valuable references.

451 Marty, Martin E.   "The Occult Establishment." *Social Research* 37, 2 (1970): 212-30.

As other commentators, Marty begins by noting that the recent fascination with occult phenomena represents nothing new; the occult has a long history in American life. He uses astrology as a major example to make his case. Marty demonstrates that serious practitioners of astrology do not fit the popular stereotypes; that is, astrology does not attract primarily those who are amoral, part of the youth culture, or advocates of illicit drugs. Rather, astrology is predicated on the assumption that life is guided by cosmic forces whose power can be discerned through signs and constellations.

452 Melton, J. Gordon. "Another Look at New Religions." In *Religion in the Nineties*, ed. by Wade Clark Roof, 97-112. *Annals of the American Academy of Political and Social Science*, 527. Newbury Park, Calif.: Sage Periodicals, 1993.

Melton rightly wishes to abandon use of the label "cult" when discussing new or unconventional religious movements. Basing his analysis on a study of more than 800 new religions that have taken root in the United States in the twentieth century, he argues instead that they should be seen as part of the global diffusion of religions. Melton claims that the revised immigration laws of 1965 and 1990 paved the way for a much greater infusion of Asian and Middle Eastern immigrants to the United States who brought with them their own forms of religion. They practiced these religions, adapted them to different cultural conditions, and found others drawn to them. In turn, they became new or unconventional religions in the eyes of others, but not cults.

453 Melton, J. Gordon. "The Revival of Astrology in the United States." In *Religious Movements: Genesis, Exodus, and Numbers*, ed. by Rodney Stark, 279-99. New York: Paragon House, 1985.

Melton demonstrates that the rise of interest in astrology among Americans since the 1960s represents that transmission of an old occult tradition, not a new religious consciousness or a faddish fascination with Eastern religiosity. He shows that in the United States, there has been a steady intrigue with astrology at least since the 1880s and that many of the popular periodicals that promote astrological thinking have been part of the mass market since the 1920s.

454 Miles, Judith M. *The Feminine Principle: A Woman's Discovery of the Key to Total Fulfillment.* St. Louis: Bethany Fellowship, 1975.

In contrast to those women who have fostered a personal spirituality based on the unique experience of females that has often involved an eclecticism in its appropriation of traditional concepts as well those associated with the occult, Miles offers a very traditional approach. She argues that women can find meaning in life only through submission, obedience, and total surrender of themselves to God, Christ, and their husbands.

455 Miller, David. *The New Polytheism: Rebirth of the Gods and Goddesses.* 2nd ed. Dallas: Spring Publications, 1981.

Operating from a Jungian base, Miller argues that the apparent recent rebirth of interest in polytheism stems from the need of women and men to incarnate or be aware of the presence of supernatural powers so that they can live out myths in their daily lives. Gods and goddesses then are much more than the value centers that non-Jungian interpretation claims. Miller then proceeds to use Greek mythology to explain modern society in a highly speculative section of the monograph.

456 Morgan, Marabel. *The Total Woman.* Old Tappan, N.J.: Fleming H. Revell, 1973.

This book, a best seller of 1974 by a former beauty queen who was a housewife in Miami when she wrote, is an effort to bring the sexual revolution in to the Protestant evangelical household. Morgan argues for a different kind of female submissiveness, one that lures by sex, through acceptance of the husband as he is, admiration of his qualities and his body, adaptation to his wishes, and appreciation of his role. Critics argued that Morgan had made women into slaves of their husbands; her thesis is that true liberation for women and inner peace come through the choice of the right man to whom to be enslaved.

457 Needleman, Jacob. *A Sense of the Cosmos: The Encounter of Modern Science and Ancient Truth.* New York: Doubleday, 1975.

Needleman suggests that the contemporary concern for wholeness can learn much from the ancient traditions of magic where a profound sense of the inter-relatedness of all things prevailed. As modern science has reshaped some of the perennial questions about meaning in life that have haunted humanity, it can also benefit from the resolutions that a primeval, more blatantly religious consciousness advanced about the unity of the self and the power and force of the universe. In other words, Needleman calls for a renewed appreciation for what he calls the "spiritual sensation" that lies deep within the self. That sense, of course, is also where much popular religiosity is nurtured.

458 Ostling, Richard N. "When God Was a Woman: Worshipers of Mother Earth Are Part of a Goddess Resurgence." *Time* 137 (6 May 1991): 73.

In this brief piece intended for a mass audience, Ostling tried to describe the resent intrigue with feminine spirituality oriented to the occult and the goddess among American women. He claims that more than 100,000 are devoted to the goddess, although he also notes that many combine this spirituality with more traditional forms. In fashioning this idiosyncratic spirituality, women are thus keeping alive strains of a popular religiosity that has an abiding sense of the supernatural and looks for practical ways to access the power of the supernatural.

459 Ruether, Rosemary Radford. "Women-Church: Emerging Feminist Liturgical Communities." In *Popular Religion,* ed. by Norbert Greinacher and Norbert Mett, 52-59e. Edinburgh: T. and T. Clark, 1986.

While focusing on recent (post-1975) developments among feminist liturgical communities in modifying traditional Christian rituals and developing new ones geared to women's experience, Ruether argues that they are linked historically to the spontaneous expressions of religiosity characteristic of folk and peasant cultures. More specifically, she believes that those that seek to recover the goddess or the feminine dimension of the sacred represent a rebirth from patriarchy and a rejection of the male dominance that has marked both the Jewish and Christian traditions.

460 Scanzoni, Letha Dawson, and Nancy A. Hardesty. *All We're Meant to Be: Biblical Feminism for Today.* 3rd rev. ed. Grand Rapids, Mich.: Eerdmans, 1992.

This carefully annotated study explores the ways biblical resources may be used to help create a spirituality that speaks directly to the experiences of women. The authors look at women in the Bible, the creation stories, early Christianity, and other theological currents and relate them to matters of marriage, reproduction, abortion, singleness, lesbianism, and the role of women in the church today. Each chapter contains questions to promote further reflection and study, and there are a very helpful bibliography and separate indexes for names and subjects and also biblical references at the end of the book.

461 Schmitt, Peter. "The Church in the Wildwood: The Nature Cult in Urban America, 1830-1930." *Journal of Popular Culture* 2 (1968): 113-18.

Schmitt takes a critical look at the way in which Americans developed an idealized view of the rural and bucolic as urbanization became central to the larger culture. Not only was the realm of nature more idyllic, it was also somehow more pure and therefore a kind of sacred space. Schmitt shows how these ideas were transmitted through popular song and hymnody, using examples such as "America the Beautiful" with its paean to the majesty of the landscape and "This Is My Father's World," a rhapsody on the divine presence in nature. Schmitt suggests that this view of nature served as a counter to perceptions of the city as potentially corrupt and dangerous and therefore devoid of the supernatural presence basic to popular religiosity.

462 Setta, Susan M. "Healing in Suburbia: The Women's Aglow Fellowship." *Journal of Religious Studies* 12, 2 (1986): 46-56.

Setta's article is one of the few secondary treatments of a growing parachurch movement composed primarily of Protestant evangelical women. The Women's Aglow Fellowship began in 1967 as an offshoot of the Full Gospel Businessmen's Fellowship International. According to Setta, at its base is a doctrine of supernatural healing and the conviction that physical and spiritual healing go together to produce the whole woman. Illness, however, is seen to result from the work of supernatural demonic forces. Meetings often combine religious activities with those thought to appeal to traditional women, such as presentations on fashions and cosmetics.

463 Sevre, Leif. *The Story of the Upper Room.* Nashville, Tenn.: Parthenon, 1965.

An uncritical history of one of the most popular American devotional magazines, Sevre's work appeared to mark the thirtieth anniversary of the publication of the

Upper Room. Sevre offers some valuable statistics that buttress the claim of popularity. From a first printing of 100,000 copies, by its thirtieth year this devotional magazine had a circulation in excess of 3 million copies and a readership of more than 10 million. Sevre also notes the range of auxiliary publications prepared by the staff that are designed to promote personal and family worship and individual spirituality.

464 Starhawk. *The Spiral Dance: A Rebirth of the Ancient Religion of the Great Goddess.* San Francisco: Harper and Row, 1979.

Starhawk offers one of the more comprehensive treatments of modern Wicca, placing its renewed appeal in broad social and cultural context. She discusses not only the theory of the supernatural and occult that informs Wicca and much of the attraction to the goddess, but also provides rituals and related exercises that demonstrate how women may enter a realm of supernatural power and harness its energy for their own happiness and self-fulfillment.

465 Titon, Jeff Todd. *Powerhouse for God: Speech, Chant, and Song in an Appalachian Baptist Church.* Austin: University of Texas Press, 1988.

Titon brings expertise in ethnomusicology to this superb example of a local study. He is particularly adept at showing how theological content and formal belief are less important to personal spirituality in the Appalachian setting than the affective response generated by distinctive speech patterns and rhythm as well as their use in chant utterance and song. What is important is the kind of feeling generated and the way that feeling communicates a sense of power and contact with supernatural power for ordinary men and women. In these emphases, Titon unravels several strands of popular religiosity.

466 Tucker, Ruth A. *Another Gospel: Alternative Religions and the New Age Movement.* Grand Rapids, Mich.: Academie Books, 1989.

Writing from a decidedly conservative Christian perspective, Tucker nonetheless does not ridicule the groups she seeks to expose for she recognizes that common practice is to label as a cult any group that espouses beliefs and practices different from one's own. Her historical comments are generally sound, although it is clear that Tucker does not see the groups she studies as legitimate religious alternatives. Among her subjects are the Mormons, Seventh-Day Adventists, Jehovah's Witnesses, Christian Science, New Thought, Unity, the Worldwide Church of God, the Way International, the Children of God, the Unification Church (Moonies), Hare Krisha, Baha'i, Scientology, and the New

Age movement.

467 Weimann, Gabriel. "Mass-Mediated Occultism: The Role of the Media in the Occult Revival." *Journal of Popular Culture* 18, 4 (Spring 1985): 81-88.

Weimann claims that the contemporary occult revival peaked in the 1970s and that it relied on coverage in the popular media as the primary means to propagate its beliefs and practices. To this extent, he describes adherents of occult religiosity as an "audience cult" created by the media. Weimann also argues that perhaps unwittingly the media created the leadership of the occult movement; giving publicity to selected figures identified with the occult actually granted them a popular status that they would not have attained otherwise.

468 Willard, Frances. *Women in the Pulpit*. Chicago: Women's Temperance Publishing Association, 1889.

Something of a radical voice for her time, Willard was among the first to protest the domination of the ranks of the clergy by men and call for the ordination of women to the professional ministry. She bases part of her argument on the unique spirituality of women, although here she betrays some of the cultural assumptions of her day (for example, that women by nature were less prone to evil influences than men). But she argues forcefully that the nurturing qualities fostered by women's religiosity would bring a much needed dimension to professional ministry were women to be admitted to its ranks.

469 Wilson, Elizabeth. *Fifty Years of Association Work among Young Women, 1866-1916*. New York: National Board of the Young Women's Christian Association of the United States, 1916. Reprint, New York: Garland, 1987.

This history of the first half century of the Y.W.C.A. is helpful in providing understanding of some of the transformations that were coming to the religiosity of women during in the later nineteenth century. With its program oriented to single women who were working in the burgeoning urban centers of the nation, the Y.W.C.A. was already addressing issues that marked a change in the traditional role of women. Many of the specific programs that Wilson discusses were designed to reinforce women's commitment to the evangelical style of Protestant Christianity. But because these activities were open only to women and conducted in what was then a new environment for single women especially, they also helped nurture a spirituality that helped sustain currents of popular religiosity emerging from women's experience.

470 Wimberly, Robert C., et al. "Conversion in a Billy Graham Crusade: Spontaneous Event or Ritual Performance." *Sociological Quarterly* 16 (1975): 162-70.

Writing from a sociological perspective, Wimberly and his associates demonstrate that the kind of intensive personal religious experience associated with conversion at a Billy Graham crusade is really a carefully orchestrated and structured ritual event. Although the individuals who claim to experience such conversion appear to be acting spontaneously, the components of the revival service, the content of the revival message, and the format of coming forward to receive counselling and blessing take on the character of a ritual performance. This article does not discount the reality or legitimacy of such conversions, but suggests simply that they are less spontaneous than they appear at first glance to the casual observer.

471 Wittenmeyer, Annie Turner. *Women's Work for Jesus*. New York: Nelson and Phillips, 1873. Reprint, New York: Garland, 1987.

Wittenmeyer accepts some of the cultural assumptions of her day regarding the superior spirituality of women because of their traditional domestic role, but draws different conclusions from them than did most of her contemporaries. She argues, for example, that womanhood itself is a divine calling and that women, because precisely because they were endowed with a superior spirituality, were uniquely equipped to combat the supernatural forces of evil that plagued the nation's cities. In other words, the religiosity of women offered a more effective access to supernatural powers of good than did that of men.

472 Wuthnow, Robert. *Experimentation in American Religion: The New Mysticisms and Their Implications for the Churches*. Berkeley: University of California Press, 1978.

Two chapters of this sociological treatise are especially relevant for understanding the dynamics of popular religiosity: "The Appeal of Astrology" (pp. 44-60) and "The Coming of Religious Populism" (pp. 189-201). Wuthnow demonstrates that although astrology has a widespread appeal on a casual basis, it prompts little sustained commitment as a religious movement. Astrology, he claims, takes on a religious dimension primarily for the socially marginalized and culturally disenchanted because it offers a source of comfort. In understanding astrological signs and movement, one finds the world less capriciously fatalistic. Wuthnow finds the new religious populism or a new individualism in religiosity nourished by popular education and the mass media as well as by the cultural pluralism that prevails in the United States. He characterizes this religious populism as placing primary belief in the validity of personal or popular will, having fluid standards often subject to popular fads, manifesting tremendous diversity in ideas and organization, reaping the scorn of religious elites and intellectuals, and developing organizations that treat individuals as a mass market or mass audience.

10

The Ethnic Dimension of Popular Religion

NATIVE AMERICANS

473 Aberle, David F. *The Peyote Religion among the Navaho.* Chicago: Aldine, 1956.

Aberle's study is among the earliest to look at the emergence of ritual use of peyote among Native Americans. When ingestion of peyote became more common in the later nineteenth century, it represented a popular religious response to the extensive cultural dislocation that had come to the Navaho (and other tribal groups) as Euro-Americans took over tribal lands and either urged cultural accommodation or dismissed tribal life as uncivilized. Peyote, with its hallucinogenic qualities, became a new means of accessing a realm of power superior to that of those perceived to be bent on the destruction and annihilation of tribal culture. Aberle shows how use of peyote became fused with both established tribal religious patterns and aspects of Christianity brought by missionaries to create a genuine popular religiosity marked by syncretism.

474 Bailey, Paul. *Wovoka: The Indian Messiah.* Los Angeles: Westernlore Press, 1957.

Wovoka, also known as Jack Wilson, was a Paiute who gave renewed vigor to the Ghost Dance following personal religious visions in the winter of 1888-89. Although Wovoka's message essentially a peaceful one looking forward to a millennial paradise, it became transformed as the Ghost Dance spread into a call for militant resistance to the encroachment on Native American lands of Euro-Americans and to U.S. Indian policy. Bailey's study, more exposition than critical analysis, looks at Wovoka as a messianic figure whose call to action was cut short by the tragic massacre at Wounded Knee that effectively brought to an end Ghost Dance practices among the Sioux.

475 Dobyns, Henry F., and Robert C. Euler.   *The Ghost Dance of 1889 among the Pai Indians of Northwestern Arizona. Prescott College Studies in Anthropology No. 1.* [Prescott, Ariz.]: Prescott College Press, 1967.

Based on field interviews with several Pai Indians who had seen the Ghost Dance performed, this study reinforces the standard interpretation of the phenomenon by casting the Dance as a millennialist movement that emerged as a response to conquest and oppression. Dobyns and Euler also call attention to the intended redistribution of power that was expected to follow and thereby connect the Dance to strains of popular religiosity.

476 Dorsey, George A. *The Arapaho Sun Dance.* Chicago: Field Museum of Natural History, 1903.

Akin to the Ghost Dance, the Sun Dance emerged as a popular movement to revitalize tribal consciousness and traditional religious practice among the Arapaho in the latter half of the nineteenth century. Dorsey's work is primarily an ethnographic study, but valuable for the factual information it provides about one strand of popular religiosity among Native Americans.

477 DuBois, Cora. "The 1870 Ghost Dance." *Anthropological Records* 3, 1. Berkeley: University of California Press, 1939. 1-131.

Although the Ghost Dance phenomenon of 1889-90 is better known, Ghost Dance practice first surfaced among tribal cultures in Nevada and California around 1870. As the later manifestation, the Ghost Dance of 1870 had distinct millennialist overtones, combining elements of traditional tribal religiosity with ideas absorbed from the Christianity of Euro-Americans. This syncretism is characteristic of popular religiosity. DuBois provides the most complete exposition of this earlier ritual dance, which offered to those seized by ecstatic frenzy immediate access to a supernatural realm, and the central figure, Wodziwub, around whom the dance developed among the Paviotso of western Nevada.

478 Hittman, Michael. "Ghost Dances, Disillusionment and Opiate Addiction: An Ethnohistory of Smith and Mason Valley Paiutes." Ph.D. diss., University of New Mexico, 1973.

Hittman looks first at the two most prominent manifestations of the Ghost Dance, that of 1870 and that of 1890. The former he classifies as a transformative movement; the latter he calls a redemptive movement. Part of this concern is to see if the apparent collapse of both brought such disillusionment with the prophecy itself, the belief system inherent in the dance, and any organizational structures that emerged from the Ghost Dance that would account for the rapid increase in opiate addiction after 1890. He does not find that level of disillusionment, but attributes the addiction in part to the desire to escape from the loss of traditional culture and its trappings that followed on the destruction of Paiute society.

479 LaBarre, Weston. *The Ghost Dance: The Origins of Religion*. New York: Dell, 1972.

LaBarre's work is one of the standard expositions of the Ghost Dance as it took hold among many tribes of Plains Indians and made inroads in tribal cultures from Nevada to the Dakotas.   LaBarre goes beyond much standard interpretation in using the Ghost Dance as a model to explore the origins of religion in human culture. LaBarre shows how the dance rekindled a sense of tribal pride and renewed belief in the supernatural at a time when the increasingly restrictive Indian policies of the U.S. government were undermining the integrity of tribal cultures, if not destroying them. LaBarre thus connects the Dance to cultural crises, problems of cultural accommodation, the continuing prominence of the shaman in tribal religious expression, and the sense of power (mana) that pervades tribal religiosity.

480 LaBarre, Weston. *The Peyote Cult*. New York: Schocken, 1969.

Near the end of the nineteenth century, religious practice centered around the ingestion of peyote in a ritual context gained currency among numerous tribal groups.   LaBarre's study is among the first to examine this phenomenon seriously, appearing first in 1938. It demonstrates how the hallucinogenic experience that accompanied peyote use was an expression of ecstatic religiosity that allowed participants to communicate with a supernatural realm and in turn gain strength for coping with daily life and giving meaning to human experience. LaBarre also calls attention to the ways peyote practice incorporated some Christian symbols into its ritual forms. Additions to the 1938 text are primarily bibliographical essays that discuss studies of peyotism appearing through 1964.

481 Lanternari, Vittorio. *The Religions of the Oppressed*. New York: New American Library, 1963.

Lanternari provides valuable interpretive information about several strands of popular religiosity among Native Americans in the later nineteenth and early twentieth centuries.   For example, he devotes one chapter primarily to an examination of Smohalla, whose syncretistic blending of tribal hopes and Christian millennialist expectation in the mid-nineteenth century paved the way for the development of both manifestations of the Ghost Dance. Lanternari also gives considerable insight into the development of the Peyote religion. As the title of the book suggests, Lanternari argues that ecstatic religious expression offering access to supernatural power carries great plausibility among oppressed peoples who are devoid of power in an empirical sense. The supernatural power, of course, is perceived to be superior to the powers fostering oppression and will ultimately triumph.

482 Lockett, Hattie Greene. *The Unwritten Literature of the Hopi. University of Arizona Social Science Bulletin No. 2.* Tucson: University of Arizona Press, 1933.

Lockett devotes a few pages to material that is explicitly religious. There is, for example, valuable information about the role of the kachina and how the Hopi, in infusing all of life with a religious dimension, seek ways to ally the tribe with the supernatural forces of good. Lockett provides helpful notes, but the lack of an index makes the volume somewhat difficult to use for the person interested only in how the religious and the social are intertwined in Hopi life.

483 Loftin, John D. *Religion and Hopi Life in the Twentieth Century.* Bloomington: Indiana University Press, 1991.

Loftin's work reinforces the awareness that among Native American tribal societies, religion and culture are indissolubly linked. Society itself takes on a sacred quality, protected and preserved through ritual practice. Loftin calls particular attention to the importance attached to prayer, even as there has been erosion of many traditional rituals in the twentieth century given the devastation that has marked much tribal life. The reason, he suggests, is that prayer has a very practical dimension; it offers immediate access to a realm of superior, supernatural power.   Such practicality is a standard feature of popular religiosity.

484 Marriott, Alice, and Carol K. Rachlin. *Peyote.* New York: New American Library, 1971.

Anthropologists Marriott and Rachlin link the origins of Peyotism to the apparent failure of the Ghost Dance; in the wake of defeat, Native American cultures were ripe for a new religion that had more direct roots in the tribal heritage. Much of this books describes various tribal variants of peyote rituals leading up to the formation of the Native American Church in 1918. Marriott and Rachlin claim that peyotism began as the private practice of individuals, but gradually became tribal and nearly pan-tribal as the religion developed. Although they raise the question of whether long-term use of peyote will have deleterious effects, they defend the legitimacy of the Native American Church on constitutional grounds.

485 Miller, David H. *Ghost Dance*. Reprinted, Lincoln: University of Nebraska Press, 1975.

Miller's work is one of the more academic examinations of the Ghost Dance phenomenon. First published in 1959, it was reissued in 1975 at a time when a resurgence of ethnic pride was a prominent theme in the larger culture. Miller makes some connections between Ghost Dance personnel like Wovoka and the shaman figure fundamental to most North American tribal societies. Miller's study represents a standard historical approach that is supplemented by the more anthropological analysis of Vittorio Lanternari and others.

486 Mooney, James. *The Ghost-Dance Religion and the Sioux Outbreak of 1890*. Ed. by Anthony F. C. Wallace. Chicago: University of Chicago Press, 1965.

Mooney's early ethnographic account has for years been among the most important materials for examining the Ghost Dance. Primarily descriptive rather than analytic, Mooney's work is based on material gathered in 1896 and is particularly helpful in understanding why United States government officials found the Ghost Dance so threatening and therefore moved to quash it at Wounded Knee. The belief that divine intervention would bring an end to white oppression and the accompanying conviction that the supernatural power released in the dance ritual would render the Sioux immune to harm were both sources of fear for those seeking to implement government policy. Mooney's material provides much evidence of the dynamics of popular religiosity and how popular practice links the empirical and the supernatural for he emphasizes how the Dance was an ecstatic religious movement, a response to cultural stress, and a revitalization effort.

487 Slotkin, J. S. *The Peyote Religion: A Study in Indian-White Relations*. Reprint, New York: Octagon Books, 1975.

The bulk of this work, which first appeared in 1956, is devoted to notes and bibliography that are most helpful to those wishing to pursue further inquiry. In the brief narrative section, Slotkin attributes much of the plausibility of the peyote religion to the devastation of tribal life that came with the westward expansion of the United States. Throughout the work, it is clear that peyote religion is about power, especially about bringing a superior power to those who are powerless. At the same time, Slotkin shows that whites often misunderstood the practice of peyote, particularly in its ritual fusion of tribal practice with overt Christian symbols (for example, in identifying the power revealed in the peyote with Jesus Christ). Much of Slotkin's understanding comes from his personal involvement with the Native American Church, although he also brings his training as an anthropologist to bear in his descriptive history.

488 Stewart, Omer C. *Peyote Religion*. Norman: University of Oklahoma Press, 1987.   Idem., *Peyotism in the West: A Historical and Cultural Perspective*. Salt Lake City: University of Utah Press, 1984.

Stewart has offered some of the more recent appraisals of peyote religion in these complementary studies. As peyote practice became something approaching a pan-Indian popular religiosity, it took institutional form in Oklahoma with the chartering of the Native American Church in 1918.   Stewart links peyote religion to some traditional features of tribal religious life, such as the sense of the supernatural that penetrates the natural realm, as well as explaining its relevance as an alternative to the Christianity brought to reservations by well-intentioned missionaries who nevertheless lacked an appreciation for the dynamics of tribal culture. Stewart also explores the roots of peyote religion in Mexican tribal cultures before examining its rapid growth among United States tribes, especially the Kiowa and Comanche in Oklahoma, between 1885 and 1918. Finally, Stewart discusses the early efforts to suppress the ritual use of peyote.

489 Utley, Robert M. *The Last Days of the Sioux Nation*. New Haven: Yale University Press, 1963.

Utley is primarily interested in tracing the events that led to the disruption of the Sioux nation with the massacre at Wounded Knee in 1890. In that context, he gives careful attention to the role of the Ghost Dance in revitalizing Sioux life in the year or so prior to the "rebellion" at Wounded Knee. On a larger scale, Utley's study is helpful in understanding how religious currents influence what seems fundamentally political; in this sense, the book is a valuable case study for looking at larger issues of how popular religiosity has implications for social and political behavior.

ROMAN CATHOLICS

490   Barton, Josef L.   "Religion and Cultural Change in Czech Immigrant Communities, 1859-1920." In *Immigrants and Religion in Urban Culture*, ed. by Randall M. Miller and Thomas D. Marzik, 3-24. Philadelphia: Temple University Press, 1977.

Barton explores the transplantation of folk religious ways from peasant Czech villages to urban America. He notes that in the European context, religion was locally and family oriented, with the celebration of religious feast days and devotion to patron saints reinforcing extended family kinship ties. Many of the ritual occasions and voluntary associations that served to maintain this communal identity were brought to the cities of the United States where Czech immigrants settled. For the immigrants, they became major mechanisms of social control and helped build a network of relationships that not only linked people to the church and parochial school, but also affirmed a sense of identity. In this way, this fusion of religious and cultural customs formed a significant stratum of Catholic popular religiosity.

491 Brown, Alden V. *The Grail Movement and American Catholicism, 1940-1975*. Notre Dame, Ind.: Notre Dame University Press, 1989.

This revision of a 1982 doctoral dissertation examines the evolution of a community of Catholic laywomen known as the Grail Movement. Brown provides important insights not only into the way such a movement strengthened commitment to the church, but also into the subtle ways the Grail Movement nurtured a distinctive female spirituality. Students of popular religiosity will find the book helpful in probing the ways an organization with structural ties to institutional religion can at the same time foster strands of popular devotion and piety that supplement and are complementary to the formal doctrines of a tradition.

492 Bukowczyk, John. "'Mary the Messiah': Polish Immigrants, Heresy, and the Malleable Ideology of the Roman Catholic Church in America, 1869-1930." In *Disciplines of Faith: Studies in Religion, Politics, and Patriarchy*, ed. by Jim Obelkevich, Lyndal Roper, and Raphael Samuel, 371-89. New York: Routledge, 1977.

Bukoczyk's essay looks at the ethnic (national) parishes and parochial schools that served the Polish immigrant communities and how dimensions of Polish nationalism that became fused with immigrant spirituality brought separation from institutional Catholicism in some areas of eastern Pennsylvania. Here the

Mariavite movement, with its claim to special revelation, became suspect as the immigrant working class used it to feed their anticlericalism and prolabor sentiments. Other concern centered around the popular understanding of Mary who was viewed as nurturing and protective, but also as a coredemptor with Christ. The understanding of redemption had political nuances that challenged the were more troublesome in the European than in the American context for it sustained a political messianism. The most obvious example is the cult of sorrows that developed around the Polish Resurrectionist Fathers in Chicago.

493 Bullard, F. Lauriston. "Malden--In Retrospect and Prospect." *Atlantic Monthly* 145 (1930): 537-45.

This article offers a brief account of one shrine, the grave of Fr. Patrick J. Power (1844-1869) in the Holy Cross Cemetery near Boston. In 1929, pilgrims to the grave site claimed to have experienced miraculous healing. This conviction that the devout could draw on supernatural power for such a practical end as physical healing brought crowds to the cemetery in November 1929 that were estimated to have reached nearly 850,000. Bullard describes the scenes of those praying at the grave and their accounts of healing, especially when rain turned the dirt around the grave into mud which was then rubbed onto the body of those seeking healing. The episode powerfully reinforced popular belief in supernatural power, although institutional Catholicism maintained an "official agnosticism" about the authenticity of the cures because of a presumed lack of evidence.

494 Click, Patricia C. "High Technology Meets the Spiritual: Objectivity, Popular Opinion, and The Shroud of Turin." *Journal of Popular Culture* 21, 4 (1988): 13-23.

In the late 1970s and early 1980s there was renewed interest in the Shroud of Turin in part because of the hope that contemporary technological methods could not only accurately date the shroud, but also authenticate the shroud as that in which the body of Jesus was wrapped after the crucifixion, if the shroud proved to date from the first century of the common era. Click provides a brief history of the shroud and the popular devotionalism that developed around it. She also discusses the Shroud of Turin Research Project (STURP) that began in 1978 and drew on the expertise of 32 American scientists and engineers in the endeavor to date and authenticate the shroud. Click rightly notes that even if the shroud could be dated to the first century, the project could never definitively demonstrate that it was indeed the shroud used in the burial of Christ.

495 Curtis, James R. "Miami's Little Havana: Yard Shrines, Cultural

Religion, and Landscape." *Journal of Cultural Geography* 1 (Fall 1980): 1-16. Reprint, *Rituals and Ceremonies in Popular Culture*, ed. by Ray B. Browne, 105-119. Bowling Green, Oh.: Bowling Green University Popular Press, 1980.

Curtis has studied shrines erected in the yards of homes belonging to Cuban immigrants who live in Miami, particularly those dedicated to Santa Barbara, Our Lady of Charity, and St. Lazarus. He shows that the style of the shrines reflects a popular Cuban religiosity and tradition more than official Roman Catholicism, noting that many have been built by Cuban immigrants who are also followers of Santeria. The religiosity they sustain thus represents a fusion of Catholic, Cuban, and African (especially Yoruba) stands of popular belief and practice.

496 Dolan, Jay P. *Catholic Revivalism: The American Experience, 1830-1900*. Notre Dame, Ind.: University of Notre Dame Press, 1978.

Dolan's classic study examines the parish missions movement that was in some ways a Catholic response to the revivalism that flourished among evangelical Protestants. From the perspective of popular religiosity, what is important about the parish missions is the way they promoted participation in the sacraments of Penance and the Eucharist. Eucharistic participation especially nurtured a popular religiosity based on a profound sense of the sacred and the mystery of the Mass, with its offering of access to supernatural power.

497 Dolan, Jay P. "A Catholic Romance with Modernity." *Wilson Quarterly* 5 (Autumn 1981): 120-33.

Dolan makes the case that the American experience produced a unique form of Catholicism. Its roots go back to the era of the American Revolution when there were calls to abandon use of Latin in favor of English in the celebration of the Mass. More important in giving an idiosyncratic flavor to American Catholicism, according to Dolan, was the way popular ethno-religious practices of immigrants provided identity and cohesion in the midst of the strident opposition of nativists and other expressions of anti-Catholicism. One result was that the fears of Americanization that troubled the institutional hierarchy of the Catholic church were of little concern to immigrants who simply went about the business of developing their own forms of popular religiosity sustained by Catholic sensibilities.

498 Ede, Alfred J. *The Lay Crusade for a Christian America: A Study of the American Federation of Catholic Societies, 1900-1919*. New York: Garland,

1988.

Historians have devoted considerable attention to Protestant efforts, especially in the nineteenth century, to create a "Christian America" that reflected evangelical beliefs and values. Ede shows that there was a Catholic counterpart that came as immigration swelled the Catholic ranks. At the center of that endeavor were numerous voluntary societies organized and initially controlled by the Catholic laity. Their ultimate intent was to gain cultural dominance or at least acceptance of Catholic mores in an environment marked by Protestant hostility to things Catholic. However, as the institutional hierarchy moved to gain control over the societies during the years of the First World War, they lost the dimension of being vehicles to sustain a popular Catholic religiosity.

499   Fenner, Kay T.   *American Catholic Etiquette.*   Westminster, Md.: Newman Press, 1961.

Fenner's work is illustrative of one genre of popular Catholic writing, namely practical guides to appropriate Catholic behavior in a wide range of circumstances. Fenner notes that not all Roman Catholic etiquette is unique, but it is distinctive because it is rooted in a particular sacramental understanding. The sacraments of the church serve as mechanisms to structure personal life and behavior. Hence there is discussion not only of Catholic sacraments, but also of education of Catholic children, correct modes of address, how to make weddings more Catholic in style, how to organize home life to nurture Catholic spirituality, and the like. What is important about this book and its cognates is the way they provide a lens through which to view the inculcation in individuals of a religiosity informed by Catholic doctrine.

500 Galush, William. "Faith and Fatherland: Dimensions of Polish-American Ethnoreligion, 1875-1975." In *Immigrants and Religion in Urban Culture*, ed. by Randall M. Miller and Thomas D. Marzik, 84-102. Philadelphia: Temple University Press, 1977.

Galush's title derives from that of a Polish newspaper first published in Chicago in 1887 to serve the Polish Catholic immigrant community there. Galush demonstrates that for a generation or more there was a fusion of Polish nationalism with Catholic identity among this immigrant community that led to frequent controversy with the church hierarchy, particularly because of the Polish opposition to the Irish dominance of the schools that served Polish parishes. Galush also calls attention to the prominence attached to celebration of feasts in Polish national parishes. Whereas in the European context the parish was an integral part of the popular cultural life of a village, the situation

was different in American cities. The feasts thus became a vital means of
sustaining the folk or popular religiosity of the Polish immigrants in an
environment where the larger culture offered little support and the Irish-
dominated hierarchy within the church sometimes offered direct opposition. In
time, however, as later generations became more removed from the specific
ethnic dimension of this strain of popular religiosity, they became more loyal
to Catholicism as a tradition than to Polish Catholicism as a popular ethnic
variant.

501 Greeley, Andrew M. *The Catholic Myth: The Behavior and Beliefs of
American Catholics*. New York: Scribners, 1990.

Sociologist and popular novelist Andrew Greeley has written many studies that
seek to unpack the popular mind of American Catholics. Conventional wisdom
has looked to the Second Vatican Council (1962-1965) as a watershed in
generating a crisis of authority within institutional Catholicism because it has
long been argued that Council-endorsed reforms led individual Catholics to
formulate personal religious world views that were often at odds with the
official teaching of the church. In this book, Greeley traces the challenge to
authority within American Catholicism to the 1960s, but sees it as a trend
already in place by the time the impact of Vatican II began to be felt. Greeley
notes that the challenge to traditional authority comes from both the conservative
and liberal ends of the spectrum if one measures that challenge in the
diminishing financial support of Catholics for the church as an institution.
Conservatives believe that the church has drifted too far from its moorings;
liberals are more inclined to question church teaching and practice because they
have forged their own Catholic identities that often betray an eclecticism in
matters of belief.

502 Jonas, Thomas J. *The Divided Mind: American Catholic Evangelists in the
1890s*. The Heritage of American Catholicism, 17, ed. by Timothy Walch.
New York: Garland, 1988.

Jonas in this study examines Catholic efforts, especially those inspired by Walter
Elliott and the Paulist Fathers, to convert American Protestants. Avoiding
polemic, these evangelists sought to show how Catholic values were compatible
with those fostered by American democracy and how the religious liberty touted
by Americans would ultimately lead to espousal of Catholic truth.   The
movement reported no major numerical successes in part because there was
considerable indifference to the movement among American priests and among
an immigrant constituency who were more intent on maintaining their own
religiosity with its blend of ethnic and Catholic elements.   Jonas provides

students of popular religion with insight into the ways those who hoped to proselytize for a particular tradition packaged their beliefs and values for a popular audience.

503 Kselman, Thomas, and Steven Avella. "Marian Piety and the Cold War in the United States." *Catholic Historical Review* 72 (July 1986): 403-424.

From the mid-nineteenth century on, devotion to the Virgin Mary shaped a vital stratum of popular Catholic religiosity in the United States. While for many years, that popular devotionalism looked to appearances of Mary at Lourdes for sustenance, after World War II it became based more on Fatima. In 1936, the only surviving woman of those who had first received visions of the Virgin at Fatima published a diary in which she claimed that Mary was anti-Communist. In 1950, that devotionalism with its strain of anti-communism received a boost when a woman in Necedah, Wisconsin, claimed she would receive a direct message from the Virgin. Some 100,000 pilgrims came to Necedah, some for healing, but most to hear a message that bolstered the anti-Communist climate of the Cold War years. Never endorsed by the Catholic hierarchy, this extreme devotionalism reflects a popular Catholic religiosity that fused personal religious belief with a particular political stance.

504 MacDonald, Fergus. *The Catholic Church and the Secret Societies in the United States*. Ed. by Thomas J. McMahon. United States Catholic Historical Society Monograph Series, 22. New York: United States Catholic Historical Society, 1946.

While many of the fraternal organizations for men such as Freemasonry at one time limited their membership to Protestants, there was also a keen interest in such societies among Catholics. The church as an institution had strong reservations about such societies because of fears of competing commitments and the way the secret dimension might undermine the authority of the church. One response that sought to capitalize on Catholic response was the formation of the Knights of Columbus for Catholic men. MacDonald claims that in the early twentieth century, lodges might well have outnumbered churches in the larger cities of the United States. Their appeal can be traced in part to the way they allowed for the expression of a popular male religiosity, Catholic or Protestant.

505 Mitchell, Brian, ed. *Building the American Catholic City: Parishes and Institutions*. New York: Garland, 1988.

This solid collection of reprints of articles includes Jay Dolan's important essay,

"Immigrants in the City: New York's Irish and German Catholics" (pp. 43-57), Ralph Janis's "Ethnic Mixture and the Persistence of Cultural Pluralism in the Church Communities of Detroit, 1880-1940" (pp. 134-50), and Susan S. Walton's "To Preserve the Faith: Catholic Charities in Boston, 1870-1930" (pp. 251-303). Dolan's article emphasizes the intertwining of religion and ethnicity in popular Catholic practice, more so among German than among Irish immigrants. For the German Americans, the parish was the center of both social and religious life and hence reflected strains of popular spirituality rooted in German folkways. Janis shows how resistance to intermarriage across ethnic lines actually increased after 1880 with the massive immigration from southern, central, and eastern Europe. One result was that cultural pluralism persisted and thereby helped reinforce the popular fusion of ethnic and religious practice among immigrant groups. Janis notes that similar patterns prevailed at other times for Lutheran and even Anglo-Protestant immigrants. Susan Walton's piece shows how societies formed among Irish Catholics in Boston to help destitute and orphaned children in time came to express Irish Catholic middle-class sensibilities and a consequent blend of middle-class and Catholic strands in popular religious identity.

506   Orsi, Robert Anthony.   *The Madonna of 115th Street: Faith and Community in Italian Harlem, 1880-1950.* New Haven, Conn.: Yale University Press, 1985.

Orsi's book is one of the best studies of immigrant popular religiosity. He scrutinizes the annual *festa* of the Madonna of Mount Carmel on New York City's E. 115th St. The procession, held on 16 July, launches a street festival that continues for several days and reflects the popular religiosity of Southern Italian immigrants whose religion was based on devotionalism, pilgrimages, shrines, icons, and an abiding belief in the presence of supernatural powers of both good and evil (especially the "evil eye"). Because the Italian immigrants did not see religion as tied to the Catholic church as an institution, many of the rituals that were part of the festival had no official sanction or precedent. Long after the Italian immigrant community in East Harlem had declined in numbers with the movement of the people elsewhere, thousands would return for the festival each year to give voice to this "theology of the streets" that revolved around a popular Mariology and an understanding of devotion as discipline and a near fatalism when it came to understanding human experience. Orsi's work is a model for other studies of the same genre.

507 Perko, Michael J., S.J., ed. *Enlightening the Next Generation: Catholics and Their Schools, 1830-1980.* New York: Garland, 1988.

This collection of article reprints offers a good historical of Roman Catholic parochial education in the United States, concentrating on the nineteenth century. Several place great emphasis on the role of ethnicity in shaping parochial education and the way that national groups sought to control the style and content of education in the schools that served their parishes. In this way, parochial education would help sustain strains of popular religious belief and practice that were rooted in the pre-immigrant experience in European towns and villages where Catholicism often had a folk character.

508 Thomasi, Silvano M. *Piety and Power: The Role of the Italian American Parishes in the New York Metropolitan Area, 1880-1930.* Staten Island, N.Y.: Center for Migration Studies, 1975.

The early sections of Thomasi's book show the vital role that Italian parishes played in keeping alive the religious sensibilities of Italian peasant Catholicism and thereby helped encourage a popular religiosity that was frequently anticlerical if not anti-church. But Thomasi also documents the slow, but for him inexorable movement of Italian Americans into the mainstream of American Catholicism and then into American society.   One consequence is the diminishing importance of the sense of the supernatural that pervaded the popular religiosity of the immigrant generations.

509 Vecoli, Rudolph J. "Cult and Occult in Italian-American Culture: The Persistence of a Religious Heritage." In *Immigrants and Religion in Urban America*, ed. by Randall M. Miller and Thomas D. Marzik, 25-47. Philadelphia: Temple University Press, 1977.

Vecoli focuses on the folk religion/popular religion of the Italian immigrants. Of fundamental importance was the family orientation and kinship ties that had been fostered by the village culture of Italy. He argues convincingly that feast days, celebrations honoring patron saints, and practices of magic of the *contadini* (Southern Italian peasants) helped sustain kinship ties of the extended family in the American urban context. Of particular interest to students of popular religion is Vecoli's discussion of the religious style of the *contadini* for whom "every moment and every event was infused with religious and magical significance" (p. 26) and how patron saints became substitutes for the individual gods that had flourished in villages in pre-Christian days. The folk religion of the immigrants, an authentic popular religion, had an entire sacred world of its own that was much more highly-charged than the religion of the Catholic tradition institutionalized in the church.

510 Vecoli, Rudolph J. "Prelates and Peasants: Italian Immigrants and the Catholic Church." *Journal of Social History* 2 (Spring 1969): 217-68.

This essay highlights the fierce anti-clericalism of Italian immigrants who were often hostile to the church. The counter was an abiding suspicion of the "Americanization" of Italian immigrants on the part of church leaders who recognized in the continued practice of European folkways, the persistence of popular belief that bordered on magic, and the willingness of Italian immigrants to follow political figures often deemed radical as challenges to the authority of the church.

511 Veverka, Fayette Breaux. *"For God and Country": Catholic Schooling in the 1920s.* The Heritage of American Catholicism Series, ed. by Timothy Walch. New York: Garland, 1988.

Veverka zeroes in on the time of cultural transition that came to American Catholicism in the 1920s with the change from the pre-World War I immigrant church. Twin themes dominated: the need for accommodation to American ways and an ambiguity about American society that was often hostile to Catholic ways. Veverka shows how compromise in these areas helped create a "ghetto mentality" as Catholic schools attempted to nurture individual spirituality while at the same time preparing students for professional careers in an alien environment.

512 Weigle, Marta. *Brothers of Light, Brothers of Blood: The Penitentes of the Southwest.* Albuquerque: University of New Mexico Press, 1976.

Weigle provides a good description of the rituals practiced by the Penitentes, clusters of Catholic laymen concentrated in the Southwest who have developed a unique strand of popular religiosity. Practices of mortification such as self-flagellation become ways of symbolizing total surrender to the supernatural and thereby help sacralize the whole community. By the later twentieth century, church officials frowned on the Penitentes, but their persistence indicates the prevalence of popular religiosity. Weigle includes a very helpful bibliographical essay that is essential for those wishing to pursue further inquiry into this strain of Catholic religiosity.

513 Wills, Garry. *Bare, Ruined Choirs: Doubt, Prophecy, and Radical Religion.* Garden City, N.Y.: Doubleday, 1971.

This work, now virtually a classic, was among the first studies written for a general audience on the impact of those changes in Catholic practice authorized by the Second Vatican Council.   Wills laments the loss of a distinctively Catholic ethos and regards such phenomena as the celebration of the Mass in the vernacular and the end of the prohibition against eating meat on Fridays (except during Lent) as undermining the Catholic sense of the supernatural and sacred that sustained Catholic identity and popular belief for centuries.

514   Woods, Ralph L., and Henry Woods.   *Pilgrim Places in North America.* New York: Longman, Green, 1939.

This older study is a guide to some eleven Catholic shrines in the United States that were established before 1880.   Five developed because they housed imported relics or were built as replicas of European shrines.   But six emerged because they were places where supernatural events were thought to have occurred.   All were vital in encouraging a popular religious belief   in supernatural power since almost all of the shrines had stories of miraculous cures attached to them.   Only one, the Chapel Shrine of the Immaculate Conception in Robinsville, Wisconsin, was directly opposed by church authorities because local clergy claimed that the purported visions of Adele Brice at the site of the shrine were fabricated.   This study reinforces the understanding of popular religiosity that sees ordinary men and women engaging in practices that will support their personal religious world views apart from the formal liturgies of the church.

AFRICAN-AMERICANS

515   Burkett, Randall M.   *Garveyism as a Religious Movement.*   Metuchen, N.J.: Scarecrow, 1978.

Burkett examines the movement led by Marcus Garvey after his arrival in the United States from Jamaica in 1916 that was formally called the United Negro Improvement Association.   While the goal of the movement was to foster pride in the African heritage of American blacks and to return them to Africa, it had a distinct religious dimension that Burkett scrutinizes.   Garvey, for example, talked about planting the Temple of God in individual human hearts and the inner peace persons would experience as a result.   Such notions are in keeping with the postulates of popular religiosity.   Although Burkett does not use the term parachurch to describe Garveyism, he portrays the movement as one akin to the parachurch movements of the later twentieth century, for it drew people from many religious backgrounds into an association that existed alongside of the churches and developed much of the apparatus of a religious organization.

516 Drake, St. Clair, and Horace R. Cayton. *Black Metropolis: A Study of Negro Life in a Northern City*. Rev. ed. 2 vols. New York: Harper and Row, 1962.

This classic study contains several chapters that deal with religion. Drake and Cayton look especially at the transplantation of Southern rural religious styles to Chicago, the city that is the focus of the book, along with the phenomenon of store front churches and a number of indigenous movements that often centered around charismatic preachers. They do not discuss popular religion by that designation, but they do explore the function of religion in terms that students of popular religiosity will appreciate, for they recognize that religion served as a means by which persons drew on a variety of beliefs and practices in an ongoing effort to give meaning and coherence to their experience in an urban environment.

517 Hamilton, Virginia. *The People Could Fly: American Black Folktales*. New York: Knopf, 1985.

Many of the folktales that form the focus of Hamilton's study have a distinct religious flavor to them. They reveal the persistence and pervasiveness of a sense of supernatural power in the African American experience, power that individuals could muster for themselves in their endeavors to control their own destinies. Indeed the tale that forms the basis for the title provides a good example of this appropriation of popular religiosity for the belief that people could fly, albeit told in the form of a folk tale, is a symbolic way of talking about the supernatural that could give individuals a power superior to anything that was part of empirical reality.

518 Jackson, Bruce. "The Other Kind of Doctor: Conjure and Magic in Black American Folk Medicine." In *American Folk Medicine: A Symposium*, ed. by Wayland D. Hand, 259-72. Berkeley: University of California Press, 1976.

Jackson looks at the notion of conjure in African American culture, arguing that conjure and magic represent a way to give sense to the world. Belief that persons could conjure, that they could be possessed of supernatural power, was a means of understanding causation. Nothing, including illness, occurred at random; hence belief in conjure was also a rejection of fatalism. As conjure became connected to medicine in Haiti and Africa and took root in Louisiana as a concomitant of voodoo, it abolished the traditional boundaries between medicinal practice and religious manipulation. Although outsiders saw conjure as superstition based on ignorance, believers connected it to their ongoing appreciation of supernatural power based in forces of both good and evil.

Jackson also notes that conjure could readily be fused with features of orthodox Christian belief, such as when the conjurer used supernatural power in the name of Christ. Hence conjure becomes part of one substratum of African American popular religiosity.

519 Jones-Jackson, Patricia. "Oral Tradition of Prayer in Gullah." *Journal of Religious Thought* 39 (Spring-Summer 1982): 21-33.

Jones-Jackson looks at the form and content of prayer among practitioners of Christianity in coastal areas where Gullah is spoken. She notes that there is an eclectic dimension to such prayer that makes it a good example of one strain of African-American popular religiosity. West African speech patterns still endure both in the use of the call-response format and in the rhythms of speech. As well, the content of prayer reveals a powerful belief in the presence of supernatural power, often expressed in the way those praying refer to God, Jesus, and the Spirit. The kind of power they are thought to possess and use on behalf of those beseeching them is also reminiscent of African popular belief in the supernatural.

520 "Kwanzaa: Celebrate in Holiday Style." *Essence* 20 (1989): 50.

There are few studies to date that give careful consideration to Kwanzaa, a holiday introduced to the United States in 1966 by M. Ron Karenga that is based on the African festival of the harvest of the first crops. The seven-day festival, in some respects an African-American alternative to Christmas since it begins on 26 December, celebrates qualities of African-American culture such as unity, self-determination, collective work and responsibility, cooperative economics, purpose, creativity, and faith. This article, appearing in a popular magazine geared to an African-American audience, offers tips for celebration of Kwanzaa in the home.

521 Levine, Lawrence. *Black Culture and Black Consciousness: Afro-American Folk Thought from Slavery to Freedom.* New York: Oxford University Press, 1977.

Levine's study provides historical background for understanding the persistence of belief in conjure and trickster figures in African-American popular religiosity. He looks at the world view that slaves brought with them from Africa, in which supernatural power was a constant presence in every day reality and the universe was replete with signs of supernatural presence to those who could discern them. Levine also notes that as African Americans appropriated Christianity, they combined its tenets with their own popular world views so that, for example, Christian preachers were often conjurers as well.

522 Lincoln, C. Eric. *The Black Muslims in America.* Rev. ed. Boston: Beacon, 1973.

Lincoln's study is the classic exposition and analysis of the Nation of Islam in the United States, although it is now somewhat dated. Although as the Nation of Islam developed organization and structure, it become more of an institution than an expression of popular religiosity, Lincoln's work is helpful in understanding how Elijah Muhammad and the Black Muslims were able to draw on popular beliefs that flourished among African Americans in gaining adherents to a religion and way of life that in theory stood in sharp contrast to Christianity. Students of popular religiosity will recognize in the promise of personal empowerment the Nation of Islam offered to adherents one of the key elements of popular religion.

523 Lincoln, C. Eric, and Lawrence H. Mamiya. *The Black Church in the African American Experience.* Durham, N.C.: Duke University Press, 1990.

This monumental study explores the changing role of Christian denominations among African Americans in the later twentieth century. Curiously, Lincoln and Mamiya claim that popular religion has had little impact on African Americans, but they understand popular religion to refer only to televangelism. As well, their denominational focus and assumption that religious institutions represent the normative aspect of religion means that they do not give adequate attention to the eclecticism that prevails in the personal belief systems of many African Americans who would claim affiliation with a Christian denomination. For example, they do not discuss the persistent presence of belief in conjure or in the pervasiveness of supernatural powers, especially of evil, that one must learn how to contain in order to be able to control one's own destiny.

524 Murphy, Joseph M. *Santeria: African Spirits in America.* 2nd ed. Boston: Beacon, 1992.

Although the media have highlighted ritual practices such as animal sacrifice among adherents of Santeria and some communities have sought to restrict if not outlaw some practices associated with it (generally unsuccessfully), few studies treat Santeria seriously from a religious perspective. Murphy's book is one of them. The very name, santeria, suggests the eclecticism associated with popular religiosity for it means "the way of the saints." Santeria emerged in Cuba and other Caribbean areas in a fusion of Catholic and African (primarily Yoruba) religious sensibilities. Yoruba belief in a realm of spirits blended with the spiritual power of Catholic saints to fashion a supernatural realm whose force could be tapped not only through the church, but even more efficaciously through popular rituals and practices grounded in the African heritage. Those who had knowledge of such rituals could call on spiritual forces to work actively in the empirical realm for their benefit.

525 Nelsen, Hart M. "Unchurched Black Americans: Patterns of Religiosity and Affiliation." *Review of Religious Research* 29, 4 (June 1988): 398-412.

Nelsen found that there are more unchurched African Americans in urban areas outside the South than elsewhere. His research revealed that the most important predictor of whether black Americans would remain formally affiliated with an organized religious institution was the religiosity of their mothers. In urban areas outside the South, Nelsen found the same forces working to bring the increasing privatization of religion, a concomitant of popular religiosity, to African Americans. But he also noted that the most frequent criticism of that unchurched black Americans have of organized religion is rooted in the perception that traditional religious institutions are too restrictive in matters of personal morality.

526 Simpson, Janice C. "Tidings of Black Pride and Joy." *Time* 138 (23 December 1991): 81.

This brief piece introduces the mass readership of *Time* to the celebration of Kwanzaa. It notes the way Kwanzaa is patterned after African agricultural practice and in some areas includes the presence of an African Santa Claus to attract children. Simpson also calls attention to the way African American Christians have adapted Kwanzaa to fit in with the celebration of Christmas and make it a festival that does not compete with Christmas, but transforms both Christmas and Kwanzaa into an affirmation of a black popular religiosity that fuses things Christian and things African into a cohesive whole.

527 Smith, Theophus H. *Conjuring Culture: Biblical Formations of Black America.* New York: Oxford University Press, 1994.

Smith uses conjure as a lens to focus on African American use of the Bible. He understands conjure as a magical means of transformation so that to view the Bible as a "conjure book" is to see scripture as offering access to a realm of power that will transform empirical reality. In the case of African Americans, that meant seeing supernatural power as accessible in generating social change such as that brought by the civil rights movement. Smith suggests that there is a larger theological significance to this enterprise, for the African American world view has had a significant impact on the formation and transformation of American culture as a whole.

528 Southgate, Martha. "Merry Kwanzaa to All." *Glamour* 89 (December 1991): 120.

This is a very short description of suggested ways for families to celebrate Kwanzaa, along with a sketch of how Kwanzaa originated. It overemphasizes the connections between Kwanzaa and Christmas that result because the first ritual in the seven-day Kwanzaa festival comes on 26 December, the day after Christmas.

529 Turner, William C., Jr. "Black Evangelicalism: Theology, Politics, and Race." *Journal of Religious Thought* 45 (Winter-Spring 1989): 40-56.

Turner is aware that many African Americans regard themselves as evangelicals and/or belong to religious groups that could be classified as evangelical. However, he points out that there are some clear distinctions between black evangelicalism and the style that has become associated with the resurgence of the religious Right. The most obvious ones have to do with the long heritage of black evangelical involvement in social issues and politics in a very different way from recent white evangelical forays into the political realm. Turner notes that matters pertaining to race and civil rights have long been central to black evangelicalism and are as central to black evangelicalism as calls for a personal experience of conversion.

530 Turner, William C., Jr. "The Musicality of Black Preaching: A Phenomenology." *Journal of Black Sacred Music* 2 (Spring 1988): 21-34.

In this essay, Turner examines the oratorical style long associated with black preaching. He highlights what he calls its musicality--its cadence and sense of rhythm--that distinguish it from other pulpit styles. These give a heightened sense of drama to sermon presentation. More important from the perspective of popular religion, they also hearken back to the African experience and therefore represent one way there has been an amalgamation of elements from different traditions, African and Christian, in shaping black preaching. Turner argues that the rhythm and cadence reflect both the power of God and the force of life and thus transform the sermon into a kratophany or manifestation of power.

531 Washington, James M. "Origins of Black Evangelicalism and the Ethical Function of Evangelical Cosmology." *Union Seminary Quarterly Review* 32 (Winter 1977): 104-116.

Washington regards a sense of the supernatural as basic to black evangelicalism. The power of the supernatural is not limited to the transcendent, but potentially very much present in every day life. Hence black evangelical cosmology is one where the entire world is a realm of power. Washington also insists that this understanding of the world has ethical implications. Because African Americans are keenly aware of the presence of social injustice, they look to this pervasive power as ultimately reversing injustice and transforming the whole of society.

JEWS

532 Friedman, Norman. "Jewish Popular Culture in Contemporary America." *Judaism* 24 (Summer 1975): 263-77.

Friedman distinguishes between Jewish elite culture (that of the synagogues and organizations) and Jewish popular culture. The latter he defines as consisting of the "ordinary consumption/leisure products and activities of a non-elite Jewish or Jewish-related character" (p. 265). Friedman discusses three elements of this Jewish popular culture: foods mostly of Eastern European origin that are commonly thought to be Jewish foods and generate a nostalgia among Jews; media Jewishness that includes portrayals of Jews in novels and films, some but not all the products of Jewish writers and film makers; and basic Yiddish, or the social importance for Jewish identity of knowing the Yiddish words for certain items. This Jewish popular culture, Friedman argues, may be either a supplement to or substitute for traditional Jewish belief and practice. Always it is highly individualized.

533 Glazer, Nathan. "Jewish Loyalties." *Wilson Quarterly* 5 (Autumn 1981): 134-45.

Glazer discusses the impact of the "new pluralism" on traditional political loyalties of the American Jewish community. He notes that concerns over Affirmative Action have undermined the longstanding Jewish support for civil rights and that controversies over unquestioning support for Israel as a nation state have cause much dissent among Jews. The new pluralism is forcing a rethinking of Jewish identity, and, in keeping with the principles of popular religiosity, more and more Jews are determining what constitutes a viable Jewish identity in relation to political issues on an individual basis.

534 Greenberg, Blu. *How to Run a Traditional Jewish Household.* New York: Simon and Schuster, 1983.

Given the resurgence of interest in aspects of traditional Jewish practice in recent years, Greenberg offers this book to women who are intent on adapting such customs to contemporary life. She includes, for example, discussion of how to make a dishwasher Kosher, along with current issues such as abortion and birth control. While Greenberg views the maintenance of a Jewish household as the province of women, she also adheres to traditional understanding of gender roles. Hence, rather than decide for herself, the contemporary Jewish woman should "ask the rabbi" (who is assumed to be male) when in doubt.

535 Hand, Wayland D. "Jewish Popular Beliefs and Customs in Los Angeles." In *Studies in Biblical and Jewish Folklore*, ed. by Raphael Patai, Francis Lee Utley, and Dov Noy, 309-326. Bloomington: Indiana University Press, 1960.

Working from with a framework of folklore studies, Hand focuses his attention on the Jewish community in Los Angeles. He found that there was an important stratum of popular religiosity that had endured and was distinct from any system of belief identified with Judaism as a religious tradition. Much of the popular belief had to do with a sense of the reality of supernatural forces of evil and how to contain their influence.

536 Harrison, Walter L. "Six-Pointed Diamond: Baseball and American Jews." *Journal of Popular Culture* 15 (Winter 1981): 112-18.

Harrison is intrigued with the Jewish fascination with baseball, particularly in the culture of the immigrant ghetto. On the one hand, playing baseball in the streets was seen as a sign of Americanization and therefore of accommodation to the larger culture. On the other hand, it was also a threat to the Yiddish culture that shaped the popular religiosity of immigrant clusters. Harrison argues that baseball itself became a "secular religion" for many.

537 Karp, Abraham J. "The Emergence of an American Judaism." In *Encyclopedia of the American Religious Experience*, ed. by Charles H. Lippy and Peter W. Williams, 1:273-90. New York: Scribners, 1988.

Karp's splendid essay provides a solid overview of the ways the religious and ethnic dimensions of Judaism underwent transformation in the American context. As a result, a distinctive American Judaism emerged. One example concerns the range of responses among American Jews to adhering to traditional dietary codes. Because what individuals choose to eat is part of the private sphere, the ways American Jews have dealt with traditional dietary practice suggests how popular religiosity has developed within the Jewish heritage.   Some, for example, adhere to traditional practice within their own homes, but do not do so elsewhere. This shift is one indication of the privatization of religiosity.

538 Neusner, Jacob. *American Judaism: Adventure in Modernity.* Englewood Cliffs, N.J.: Prentice-Hall, 1978.

Neusner's controversial appraisal of Judaism in the middle third of the twentieth century is akin to a jeremiad. Neusner charts many ways that American Jews have abandoned traditional belief and practice (for example, the decline in the traditional observance of the Sabbath). Instead, in keeping with the idea that religiosity has become increasingly a matter of the private sphere, American Jews have come more and more to determine for themselves what constitutes a Jewish identity and religiosity. Neusner is particularly critical of what he calls "checkbook Judaism" in which individuals will make financial contributions to Jewish organizations and causes but will not actively participate in them.

539 Neusner, Jacob. "Judaism in Contemporary America." In *Encyclopedia of the American Religious Experience*, ed. by Charles H. Lippy and Peter W. Williams, 1:311-23. New York: Scribners, 1988.

Neusner points out that in classical ways of thinking, to be Jewish meant to live a holy life as an individual, a life shaped by Torah and tradition. In the contemporary United States, he believes that this understanding has given way to one in which organizations, religious professionals, and group activity have become the primary focus of a public Jewish identity. While Neusner regrets this shift, he does not connect it to the forces identified by sociologists that have for decades been segmenting public religion from private religiosity.

540 Trachtenberg, Joshua. *Jewish Magic and Superstition.* New York: Atheneum, 1974.

Trachtenberg's volume is a helpful in understanding the wide range of popular beliefs and practices that have developed alongside the formal religious traditions of Judaism over the centuries. He notes, for example, the use of amulets and charms, especially among many of the central and eastern European immigrant communities, that were thought to provide a practical means of dealing with supernatural powers of evil. Although Trachtenberg betrays a bias in classifying such as magic and superstition, what he describes is in essence a popular religious world view, remnants of which still endure.

541   Weinrich, Beatrice S.   "The Americanization of Passover."   *Studies in Biblical and Jewish Folklore*, ed. by Raphael Patai, Francis Lee Utley, and Dov Noy, 329-66. Bloomington: Indiana University Press, 1960.

Traditionally, Passover is a family-centered celebration of the exodus of the ancient Hebrews from bondage in Egypt. Weinrich shows how in the United States, changes have come not only to the way Passover is actually celebrated, but in the understanding of the festival itself. Keeping Passover has become one mark of a Jewish identity.   But even more it has become a means of strengthening kinship ties.   In other words, Passover has moved from being central to the formal religious tradition to being one dimension of a popular religiosity informed by Judaism.

11

Miscellaneous Titles

542   Boyd, Tom W.   "Clowns, Innocent Outsiders in the Sanctuary: A Phenomenology of Sacred Folly." *Journal of Popular Culture* 22, 3 (Winter 1988): 101-109.

Boyd sees clowns as performing sacred work because they reveal the true self to the self.   By drawing the individual into the depths of one's own being, clowns open up the most sacred dimension of life and thereby allow persons to recover their real selves.   This recovery, according to Boyd, is indeed redemption.   By placing the emphasis on the self and seeing the inner life as sacred, Boyd provides a places for clowns as mediators of popular religiosity.

543   Chernus, Ira.   "Nuclear Images in the Popular Press: The Age of Apocalypse." In *A Shuddering Dawn: Religious Studies and the Nuclear Age*, ed. by Ira Chernus and Edward Linenthal, 3-19.   Albany: State University of New York Press, 1989.

Apocalyptic images have been integral to many strains of popular religiosity in American culture.   In this essay, Chernus calls attention to the need to redeem the bomb and to be redeemed from the bomb to avoid apocalyptic destruction. He regards the nuclear age as reinforcing the popular belief that the United States has infinite power.   He also highlights another apocalyptic dimension to American identity, namely the sense of dualism that prevails with the United States seen as representing the supernatural forces of good and, in this case, the former Soviet Union as epitomizing the supernatural forces of evil.

544 Frost, Stanley. *The Challenge of the Klan*. Indianapolis: Bobbs-Merrill, 1923.

This early study of the twentieth century manifestation of the Ku Klux Klan is among the few that sees the religious dimension in the Klan. For many the Klan was a logical extension of Protestant religious institutions, and the Klan functioned as a parachurch movement (although that term was not in use at the time) that appropriated many Christian symbols (such as the cross) but transformed their meaning. In this way, the Klan became one expression of a particular style of popular religiosity for it represented the idiosyncratic syncretism that adapts traditional symbols but gives them a meaning that goes well beyond that granted by formal religious traditions.

545 Hill, Bob. *The Making of a Super Pro.* Atlanta: Cross Roads Books, 1979.

Many writers have discussed sport as religion or at least highlighted the religious dimensions of sport. This book takes a somewhat different direction in that it consists of interviews with professional athletes who all claim to be born-again evangelical Christians. What is of primary interest to students of popular religion is the way these athletes repeatedly see supernatural power intervening in athletic events and how they attribute their successes (but not their failures) to the power of the Divine. In other words, they have taken an understanding of God and fashioned it into their own personal religious world views.

546 Himrod, David K. "The Syncretism of Technology and Protestantism: An American 'Popular Religion'? *Explor* 7 (Fall 1984): 49-60.

Himrod looks at the changes in American culture that have come as a result of use of the automobile. For Protestant religious institutions especially, the automobile transformed the notion of the parish, for the ease of transportation even to a distant congregation meant that individuals were not tied to a particular church as they once had been. As a result, there came to the parishes a process of redefinition. More significant for understanding the dynamics of popular religion is Himrod's contention that technological progress as epitomized by the automobile, represents a force that will lead American society into the millennial age. In its own way, then, the automobile becomes a buttress to the strands of millennialism that have undergirded much of American popular religiosity.

547 Hoffman, Shirl J., ed. *Sport and Religion.* Champaign, Ill.: Human Kinetics Books, 1992.

The twenty-five essays collected in this book, many published elsewhere originally, are organized into four divisions. The first section looks at sport as religion, examining sports events as religious rituals and ways in which sport functions as a civil or folk religion; one essay by Joan M. Chandler argues that sport is not a religion. Sport as religious experience forms the focus of the second division. Such topics as whether running is a religious experience and how play might be a religious experience are considered. The third section probes the presence of religious elements in sport itself, including the use of magic by professional athletes and ways in which athletes find a sense of the sacred in sport. The final group of essays deal with ethical and moral issues raised by sport.

548   Holloway, Gary.   *Saints, Demons, and Asses: Southern Preacher Anecdotes*. Bloomington: Indiana University Press, 1989.

This relatively short book retells numerous popular stories about preachers that have been passed down among generations of Southerners. While the ostensible purpose of most is a humorous one, Holloway also demonstrates how such stories portray preachers as moral exempla and how they can be used to sketch doctrinal differences. Although Holloway consigns most of them to the realm of folklore, he recognizes that these stories also communicate much truth about the popular perception of clergy, especially those in the evangelical Protestant traditions.

549 Jeane, D. Gregory. "The Upland South Cemetery: An American Type." *Journal of Popular Culture* 11 (1978): 895-903.

Jeane claims that there is a distinctive type of rural graveyard found in the South. Usually small and located on a hilltop, the graveyards are often located amid groves of cedar trees. They are individualistic in their decor, reflecting popular sentiment, although there are few large tombstones. Jeane connects these graveyards to a Southern cult of piety because of the ways rural communities often promote cemetery work days when nearby residents clean up the cemetery. Working together reinforces a communal sense of piety that transcends denominational differences.

550 Johnson, David M. "Disney World as Structure and Symbol: Re-Creating the American Experience." *Journal of Popular Culture* 15 (Summer 1981): 157-65.

At first glance, this essay might seem to address broad cultural issues such as how theme parks such as Disney World can provide cultural cohesion and reflect common values. However, the article is more superficial and does not probe the deeper symbolic issues that its title suggests. There remains a need to examine how such enterprises, while ostensibly designed to promote recreation, speak to more fundamental issues of the American character, common identity, and sense of shared values that are part of the constellation of popular religiosity.

551 Mecklin, John Moffatt. *The Ku Klux Klan: A Study of the American Mind.* New York: Harcourt and Brace, 1924.

While now nearly three-quarters of a century old, Mecklin's study is worth reading for it is sensitive to some of the religious undercurrents that gave the Klan plausibility. Mecklin, for example, is aware of how a people needs to have some commonly-shared understanding of good and evil and how for some the Klan became a means of creating a world view where the supernatural forces of evil were clearly delineated and defined. In Mecklin's view, there is much more to the Klan than fanaticism run amok.

552   Miller, Michael B.   *The Bon Marche: Bourgeois Culture and the Department Store, 1869-1920.*   Princeton, N.J.: Princeton University Press, 1981.

Miller does not set out to look at the religious dimensions of consumerism and how they might help sustain strands of popular religiosity. But there is much in this study that points precisely in that direction.   Because rapid industrialization brought mass production and improvements in transportation made the shipment of manufactured goods to all parts of the country both possible and economically feasible, the department store emerged as the symbol of a common consumer culture. Its merchandise was designed to appeal to the self-identity and values of an emerging middle class. To this extent, as Miller does note, the department store became a middle-class cathedral, functioning to bring cohesion to the constellation of values that gave the urban middle class a sense of who it was.

553 Neville, Gwen Kennedy. *Kinship and Pilgrimage: Rituals of Reunion in American Protestant Culture.* New York: Oxford University Press, 1987.

Neville looks at a rather narrow cut of American culture in this provocative study. She is interested primarily in family reunions that have been sustained among white Southerners of Scotch-Irish ancestry. She sees these reunions as a type of Protestant pilgrimage rooted in a popular religiosity. For her Southern white Protestants, pilgrimage is to return home as a means of reversing the lack of a sense of family and place that prevails in postindustrial Protestantism. In this way, the Protestant pilgrimage differs from that generated within Roman Catholicism. There pilgrimage involved leaving home to go to a shrine. The Southern white Protestant family reunion thus recreates the world in an idealized sense of what it ought to be. Neville's helpful study would be considerably strengthened if it gave attention to the phenomenon of the family reunion among other groups, even within Southern culture. For example, reunions have also been central to African-American culture in the South, but may serve a rather different social-religious function.

554 Novak, Michael. *The Joy of Sports: End Zones, Bases, Baskets, Balls, and the Consecration of the American Spirit.* New York: Basic Books, 1976.

Novak begins with the assumption that sports somehow constitute a religion because either through participation or observation they satisfy certain parts of the human spirit. He is thus able to speak of the "holy trinity" of baseball, football, and basketball when looking at American society. In addition to the aesthetic dimension that he highlights when describing athletic contests and events, Novak also demonstrates how the passion for sports has refashioned popular notions of sacred time and sacred space in the United States and how fans often create fraternal bonds with each other than sustain a shared identity. Although there are no notes to document this work, there is a helpful bibliography at the end.

555 Prebish, Charles S. "Heavenly Father, Divine Goalie: Sport and Religion." *Antioch Review* 42 (Summer 1984): 306-318.

Prebish probes a symbiotic relationship between sport and religion. He notes, for example, how the realm of athletics provides preachers with countless sermon illustrations and how religion has made use of sports to promote its own ends as in the programs operated by groups like the Y.M.C.A., particularly in its early years. Prayers with teams often precede games (indeed, one such prayer provided the title for the article), leading players to assume that there will be supernatural intervention on their behalf. At the same time, sport has assumed a religious function for growing numbers of Americans, not only because of its sacred vocabulary, rituals, and legends, but also because for some it offers a means of ultimate transformation.

556 Price, Joseph L. "The Super Bowl as Religious Festival." *Christian Century* 101 (22 February 1984): 190-91.

Price argues that the Super Bowl has become more than simply an athletic event to determine the professional football national championship each year. Rather, in the Super Bowl and the festivities that surround it, Price finds a congruence of sports, politics, and religious myth. The elaborate pregame productions have in his mind become a ritual of remembrance; its myths promote a common American identity and a recalling of conquest of territory. Even the mechanics of the game take on religious significance. Possessing the football becomes a cosmogonic symbol in which one team seeks to bring order to the territory it controls. Half-time ceremonies, he claims, provoke a myth of innocence.

557 Staubach, Roger. *First Down, Lifetime to Go*. Waco, Tex.: Word, 1974.

Because of the continuing fascination of Americans with sports, there has also been an increasing demand in evangelical circles for literature that discusses the personal religiosity of sports figures rather than looking at sport as a religion that might compete with established religious traditions for the loyalty of individuals. Staubach's work is one of those. Former Dallas Cowboys quarterback, member of the football Hall of Fame, and one of the top passers in American football history, Staubach gives a chatty testimony to his own evangelical faith in this memoir, making clear the sense of the supernatural that pervades popular religiosity informed by evangelical Protestantism.

558   Toynbee, Arnold J.   "The Religious Background of the Present Environmental Crisis." *International Journal of Environmental Studies* 3 (1972). Also published as "The Genesis of Pollution." *Horizon* 15, 3 (Summer 1973): 4-9.

Noted historian Arnold Toynbee argues that there is a religious cause to much of the current environmental crisis that centers on pollution. In western biblical monotheism he finds the basis for much exploitation of nature. The biblical injunctions to subdue the earth and to be fruitful and multiply have in his mind helped fashion w world view that fails to see the divine in the natural order. He thus calls for abandoning a monotheistic world view in favor of a pre-monotheistic pantheistic one. In recovering a pantheistic perspective that regards nature as a goddess and the environment Toynbee sees hope for a renewed environmental consciousness.

559 Trotter, An R.   "Paradise Lost: Religious Theme-parks in the Southern United States." M.A. thesis, New York University, 1991.

Trotter describes a motley group of religious theme parks, ranging from Fields of the Woods in Murphy, North Carolina, to Paradise Gardens in Georgia and Christus Gardens in Gatlinburg, Tennessee. She also describes visits to Graceland, home of Elvis Presley, the Martin Luther King memorial, and various Native American sites. While her materials are pregnant with possibility for probing the religious dimension of these shrines of popular culture, Trotter brings little analysis to her study. She does note that many of them evoke images of a promised land, the purity of the Garden of Eden, or a paradise that is lost. But she does not move beyond descriptive exposition, remaining more captivated by illustrating the eclecticism of many of these tourist attractions than their significance for popular religiosity.

Author Index

Index entries refer to the page numbers in the introductory chapter and citation entry numbers in the annotated bibliography; the two elements are separated by a semicolon, e.g., pp. 8-10, 23; 089, 367, 408.

Center, 104

Quebedeaux, Richard, 176-179, 418

Rachlin, Carol K., 484
Raphael, Marc Lee, 309
Real, Michael R., 105, 310
Redfield, Robert, p. 6; 012
Reichley, A. James, 106, 107
Ribuffo, Leo P., 180, 311
Rice, Milburn, 312
Riesman, Frank, 361
Roebroeck, E.J.M.G., 013
Roof, Wade Clark, 108-111
Roozen, David A., 232
Rosenberg, Ann Elizabeth, 313
Rosenberg, Ellen MacGilvra, 181
Ruether, Rosemary Radford, 459
Russell, Mary Ann Underwood, 324
Ruthven, Malise, 112

Sandeen, Ernest R., 182
Sanjik, Russell, 315
Scanzoni, Letha Dawson, 460
Schelsinger, Arthur M., Sr., 050
Schmitt, Peter, 461
Schneider, Louis, p. 6; 014
Schroeder, W. Widick, 113
Schuller, Robert A., 362
Schwarz, Hans, 233
Seguy, Jean, 015
Setta, Susan M., 462
Sevre, Leif, 463
Shakarian, Demos, 183
Shedd, Charlie W., 363
Shedd, Martha, 363
Sherrill, Rowland A., 051
Shils, Edward, 016
Short, Robert L., 316, 317
Shriver, Peggy L., 184
Shupe, Anson, 136, 185
Siegelman, Jim, 141

Silk, Mark, 186
Simpson, Janice C., 526
Simpson, Lewis P., 318
Sittser, Gerald, 419
Sizer, Sandra. See Frankiel, Sandra Sizer
Slotkin, J. S., 487
Smedes, Lewis B., 364
Smith, Albert Hatcher, 420
Smith, Jean Louise, 295
Smith, Theophus H., 527
Smith, Timothy L., 114
Smythe, Dallas W., 230
Southgate, Martha, 528
Speak, David M., 115
Spencer, Jon Michael, 319-322
Spivak, John L., 421
Stacey, William A., 185
Stafford, Tim, 365
Staples, P., 017
Stapleton, Ruth Carter, 366
Starhawk, 464
Starker, Steven, 367
Starr, Michael E., 234
Staubach, Roger, 557
Steed, Robert P., 131
Stewart, Omer C., 488
Stoppe, Richard Leon, 422
Suderman, Elmer F., 323
Suess, Paulo, 018
Swann, Charles E., 219, 235
Szasz, Ferenc Morton, 116

Tate, Allen, 117
Teahan, John F., 423
Thiesen, Lee Scott, 324
Thomas, Sari, 236
Thomasi, Silvani M., 508
Titon, Jeff Todd, 465
Towler, Robert, p. 6; 019
Toynbee, Arnold J., 558
Trachtenberg, Joshua, 540
Trotter, An R., 559
Tucker, Ruth A., 466

Title Index

Index entries refer to the page numbers in the introductory chapter and citation entry numbers in the annotated bibliography; the two elements are separated by a semicolon, e.g., pp. 8-10, 23; 089, 367, 408.

Subject Index

Index entries refer to the page numbers in the introductory chapter and citation entry numbers in the annotated bibliography; the two elements are separated by a semicolon, e.g., pp. 8-10, 23; 089, 367, 408.

About the Author

CHARLES H. LIPPY is the LeRoy A. Martin Distinguished Professor of Religious Studies at the University of Tennessee at Chattanooga. He specializes in the study of religion and American culture. Among his other works on American popular religion published by Greenwood Press are *Being Religious, American Style: A History of Popular Religiosity in the United States* (1994), and *Popular Religious Magazines of the United States,* edited with Mark Fackler (1995). Lippy is also coeditor of the *Encyclopedia of the American Religious Experience* (1988).